998/1/01072

CH00942419

PROJECT FINANCE

A legal guide

AUSTRALIA
LBC Information Services
Sydney

CANADA and USA
Carswell
Toronto

NEW ZEALAND
Brooker's
Auckland

SINGAPORE and MALAYSIA
Thomson Information (S.E. Asia)
Singapore

PROJECT FINANCE

A legal guide

by Graham Vinter

SECOND EDITION

**London
Sweet & Maxwell
1998**

Published in 1998 by
Sweet & Maxwell Limited of
100 Avenue Road, London NW3 3PF
http://www.smlawpub.co.uk
Typeset by Dataword Services Limited of Chilcompton
Printed and bound in Great Britain by
MPG Books Ltd, Bodmin, Cornwall

No natural forests were destroyed to make this product;
only farmed timber was used and replanted

A C.I.P. Catalogue record
for this book is available
from the British Library

ISBN 0–421–575–301

For Anne, Rebecca and William

Foreword to the First Edition

It is a privilege to provide the foreword to Graham Vinter's legal guide to project finance. The techniques of project finance are being applied to an ever-increasing range of major projects around the globe. This makes Graham's excellent and accessible book on the legal aspects of the discipline both timely and welcome.

Although project (or "limited recourse") finance is enjoying particular prominence in the 1990s, the concept of a lender looking principally to the cash flow generated by a specific project to service debt has a long history. The commercial code of Athens in the fifth century before Christ recognised a form of debt which was repayable only from the proceeds of the sale of a cargo. If the cargo was lost at sea the loan was not repayable. In times when the penalties for unpaid debt included slavery and imprisonment, such limitations of recourse likely seemed even more attractive to borrowers than analogous mechanisms do today to those seeking to preserve an investment grade credit rating.

The concept of a limited company — the structure within which most private sector economic activity is undertaken around the world today — was developed in the nineteenth century. This form of organisation is now so familiar to us that we can be inclined to forget that its basic premise is the limitation of recourse. In retrospect, many of the capital raisings of the industrial revolution can be seen as project financings.

In more recent times, until the 1980s, project finance featured primarily in mine developments, mineral processing plants, oil and gas field developments and pipelines. In the U.K. in the 1970s and 80s the most prominent application of project finance was in the development of offshore petroleum reserves. Another strand in the history of project finance is the application of the limited recourse concept to public sector infrastructure developed in the United States, where states and municipalities can raise debt against revenues derived from a particular source ("revenue debt") as an alternative to borrowing against their full faith and credit ("general obligation debt"). Although we have this example of the limited recourse concept in public sector projects, it is from the advance of privatisation and deregulation around the world over the past 15 years that project finance has received its latest boost.

Privatisation is the voluntary withdrawal of the state from economic activities it used to control and manage itself. Initially, this manifested itself in the sale of state-owned enterprises. But now the concept also embraces both public service contracting and "green-field privatisation" — the construction in the private sector of elements of infrastructure, or social capital, which would have been public sector undertakings 15 years ago. The industries most affected are transport (road, bridges, tunnels, rail links, airports, ports), power and water (both clean and waste water). Through the U.K.s Private Finance Initiative, and similar initiatives elsewhere, project finance is beginning to invade an even broader range of activities, including hospitals, schools, prisons and information technology. To finance the capital costs involved in such construction projects, or the purchase of such assets, private sector participants in the process are looking to the techniques of project finance.

Because the global demand for infrastructure is so great the impetus has been given for new sources of project risk sharing to be brought into play. For example: contractors are increasingly required to take long term project risk as a condition of being awarded major contracts; the World Bank is developing programmes to assist commercial bank lending into emerging market projects; export credit agencies are more willing to take project risk, rather than universally relying on a sovereign guarantee or equivalent; and the bond markets are developing instruments for broadening the placement of project debt beyond its traditional commercial bank market place.

As these and other developments continue to take project finance into new areas, those involved in the discipline require a sound understanding of its principles and legal aspects. This book makes a significant contribution in laying out the legal basis of project finance and reviewing key issues regularly encountered by practitioners.

In keeping with the remarks in Graham's preface: I read his manuscript and drafted this foreword on flight CP007 between Vancouver and Hong Kong on September 10/11, 1994. For those involved in project finance today, life is not sedentary.

Gordon McKechnie
Director of Project Advisory
NatWest Markets
October 7, 1994

Preface to the Second Edition

When I first began specialising in project finance, some of my colleagues queried the wisdom of what I was doing. My chosen field (they alleged) was something that interested only a small number of people and might vanish overnight. Few would make those claims today. Project finance has become a billion-dollar industry and advisory work in the field has itself become a multi-million dollar industry. Project finance is now an established discipline in its own right. Contractors, banks and law firms which do not have project finance teams are hurriedly trying to assemble them.

The speed with which project finance throughout the world has grown has — for the author of a book on the subject — been terrifying. I realised very early on that a revised edition of my book would be required sooner rather than later. In a sense, however, that is how it should be. Project finance is still a new subject and is constantly evolving. Despite the not inconsiderable pressure of my day job, I am happy to try to chronicle developments while I can.

Very few sections of the first edition have escaped revision. Even if the law had stayed the same, it seemed that practice had moved on. The sections on operation and maintenance agreements and export credit agencies have seen significant expansion and the chapter on insurance aspects has been extensively rewritten. The section on environmental liability has had to incorporate the régime for contaminated land introduced by the Environment Act 1995. There are also a number of entirely new sections. The U.K. government's Private Finance Initiative — a mere fledgling when I wrote the first edition — is vitally important and cannot be ignored. It is more than worthy of a section on its own. Other new sections include sections on competitive tendering, force majeure, co-generation and refinancings. The new section on risk allocation in power purchase agreements is a good example of how the market evolves. I doubt that it would have been possible to write such a section — suggesting as it does that there is now more or less a standard allocation of risk that should apply in international power projects — a few years ago. In addition, the section on bankability has now been promoted to a chapter and (in a move laden with portent) the last chapter — dealing mainly with bonds and the capital markets — has seen its name changed from "The Future" to "Current Trends".

There have also been casualties. I saw no point in continuing to include a section on railways in the U.K. The new Labour government has made it clear that it will not privatise any of the remaining railway assets and there was precious little that could be called true project financing in the privatisation process in any event. This is not meant to be a book on regulation and retaining the section would have detracted from the balance I try to maintain between matters of domestic interest and matters of international interest. Perhaps in keeping with the New Age, the section on railways in the U.K. has been replaced with a section on satellites. I have not been the only slayer of subjects: the changes contained in the Finance Act 1996 have severely limited the extent to which finance leases can be used in U.K. projects and there seemed little point in addressing the subject at length.

I would like to express my thanks to Richard Drummond of ECGD for reviewing and commenting on the sections on commercial and political risk and export credit agencies and to Stephen Carruthers and Maria Hallengren for doing likewise in relation to the sections on the EIB and EIF respectively. I am also again indebted to various colleagues at Allen & Overy for help, materials and advice. These include my wife Anne (also a partner at Allen & Overy), Chris Rushton, Robert Strivens, Michael Scargill, Ross Fairley, Charles Lindsay and Gareth Price. Christian Saunders manfully undertook the unenviable job of updating many of the authorities and Sarah Boyle, my secretary, performed a Herculean task in keeping the manuscript not only accurately typed, but also in general good order. Any mistakes remain mine, not theirs.

One part of this book is already destined to be out of date on publication and that is the dedication page. My wife is currently expecting our third child. It is due in October, long past the latest date for changes to the proofs.

I have endeavoured to state the law and practice current as at May 22, 1997.

Graham Vinter

Quinta da Marinha
Cascais
Portugal

May 25, 1997

Note: After the above was written, the Paymaster General announced (on June 23, 1997) the results of the new Labour government's review of the U.K.'s Private Finance Initiative. Appropriate changes were made to section 10.1 at the proof stage.

Preface to the First Edition

Project finance is a very practical subject. It is very much about making real things happen. From a legal point of view, it is similar to a Masters degree: it is not something you really start with but something you graduate onto. It is, within the law, multi-disciplinary. Everything is there: company law, contract, security, competition law — to name but a few. This book is not intended to be a book on each relevant branch of the law, however: it is instead meant to illustrate and explain how specific parts of each branch are brought into play in a typical project financing. Those seeking a comprehensive explanation of E.C. competition law should look elsewhere.

Although this is very deliberately a legal book, I have tried to write it with the interested layman in mind. Lawyers should not be keepers of the secret flame: the law should be accessible to all. As far as lawyers are concerned, I have tried to explain the banking side of transactions for company and commercial lawyers and the company and commercial side of transactions for banking lawyers. A general commercial lawyer may never become a banking law specialist, but, with a little preparation, he should be able to understand and explain to his clients the basic financing issues involved in a project financing. The same, of course, applies in reverse to banking lawyers.

The subject matter of a book on project finance is potentially so vast that I have of necessity been selective. Given more time, I would have written more on leasing and included a section on political risk. If this book ever reaches a second edition, this may yet happen.

I am grateful to various of my colleagues at Allen & Overy who have been kind enough to check certain parts of what I have written in their specialist areas: these are Ross Fairley (environment), Mark Friend (RTPA), Guy Lougher (E.C.) Patrick Mears (tax), Ed Murray (hedging) and Michael Scargill (cable). Notwithstanding their help, any errors in this book are mine and mine alone. I am also grateful to my clients for instructing me on a number of project financings over a period stretching back nearly 12 years. This book would never have been written if it were not for the opportunities they gave me. My secretary, Lorraine Parker, typed the manuscript from beginning to end and deserves an enormous vote of thanks, if not a medal! Similarly, various of the trainees who have sat with me at

Allen & Overy have uncomplainingly tolerated my unreasonable requests for background materials and thanks are due to Rozanna Salmo, Charles Lindsay, Mary Boakye and Tim Scales.

I began this book one wet evening waiting in Frankfurt airport for the last flight to Heathrow. Jotting down a rough outline for Chapter 1 on a legal pad seemed a good way to kill time. Since then, various parts of this book have been written on planes, in hotel rooms and even on a family holiday in Tuscany. Much of the book has been written after 11 o'clock at night (it probably shows!). My wife endured this rather odd and anti-social activity with more good grace than I had a right to expect but I suspect that she is as relieved as I am that what passes in our lives for normality can now return.

I have endeavoured to state the law and practice current as at August 19, 1994.

Graham Vinter

Buckland Court,
Buckland,
Surrey,

August 21, 1994.

Contents

Table of Cases

Table of Statutes

Table of Statutory Instruments

Table of European Legislation

TREATIES AND CONVENTIONS

DIRECTIVES

Glossary and Abbreviations

ACQ	—	Annual contract quantity
ACT	—	Advance Corporation Tax
ADSCR	—	Annual debt service cover ratio
BOT	—	Build, operate, transfer
Capex	—	Capital expenditure
CAR	—	Contractor's all risks (insurance policy)
CCT	—	Compulsory competitive tendering
CfD	—	Contract for differences
COFACE	—	Compagnie Française d'Assurance pour Le Commerce Extérieur, the French ECA
Computer model	—	A financial model of a project developed using a computer spreadsheet program
DBFO	—	Design, build, finance and operate
DCMF	—	Design, construct, maintain and finance
DCQ	—	Daily contract quantity
Dispatch	—	In its strictest sense, "dispatch" means an instruction to a power plant to generate electricity (sent by the relevant grid operator or its dispatching centre). The term has recently been extended to connote a power plant running in accordance with its dispatch instructions, *e.g.* "the power plant is being dispatched"
Drawdown	—	The borrowing of a loan under a credit agreement
EA	—	Environment Act 1995
EBRD	—	European Bank for Reconstruction and Development
ECA	—	Export credit agency
ECGD	—	The Export Credits Guarantee Department, the U.K. ECA

EEIG	—	European Economic Interest Grouping
EIB	—	European Investment Bank
EoT	—	Extension of time (under a construction contract)
EPA	—	Environmental Protection Act 1990
EPC Contract	—	Engineering, procurement and construction contract (*i.e.* a turnkey construction contact)
Featherweight floating charge	—	A floating charge whose purpose is only to defeat the appointment of an administrator in relation to a company
Financial close	—	The date when all of the project contracts become unconditional and all conditions precedent to the project credit agreement are satisfied or waived
Gearing ratio	—	The ratio of a company's (consolidated) borrowings to its net worth (or shareholders' funds)
Grace period	—	(Depending on the context) the period of time before repayment of a loan must start or the period of time (usually only days) before an event becomes an event of default under a credit agreement
Hermes	—	Hermes Kreditversicherungs A.G., the German ECA
ICB	—	International competitive bidding
IDC	—	Interest during construction
IFC	—	International Finance Corporation, part of the World Bank Group
IPC	—	Integrated pollution control
IPP	—	An independent power project, *i.e.* the construction and operation of a power plant in the private sector
IRR	—	Internal rate of return
ISO	—	International Standards Organisation
ITB	—	Invitation to bid
JEXIM	—	The Export-Import Bank of Japan, the Japanese ECA

JOA	—	Joint operating agreement
LIBOR	—	The London Interbank Offered Rate (the rate at which banks borrow money from other banks in the London interbank market)
MVDS	—	Microwave video distribution system
NGC	—	The National Grid Company plc
NPV	—	Net present value (of projected revenues)
Offtaker	—	A purchaser of product produced by a project
OFT	—	Office of Fair Trading
O&M	—	Operation and maintenance
Opex	—	Operating expenditure
PFI	—	The U.K.'s *Private Finance Initiative*
Pool Rules	—	The rules relating to the operation of the elctricity pool in England and Wales as set out in Schedule 9 to the Pooling and Settlement Agreement (originally dated March 30, 1990) between NGC, the various members of the pool and others
PPA	—	Power purchase agreement
PSC	—	Public sector comparator
REC	—	Regional electricity company
RFP	—	Request for proposal (*i.e.* an ITB)
RTPA	—	Restrictive Trade Practices Act 1976
SACE	—	Sezione Speciale per l'Assicurazione del Credito all'Esportazione, the Italian ECA
SE	—	Societas Europea, the European Company
Soft costs	—	The costs that a sponsor incurs in preparing a bid and taking a project up to financial close. They will usually include legal and financial fees and other out-of-pocket expenses. They may include a charge for time spent on the project by the sponsor's own employees
Sponsor	—	A commercial party promoting a project
SPV	—	Special purpose vehicle, *i.e.* a company established to carry on only one particular activity

System Marginal Price	—	A component of the pool input price and the main element of the price paid under the Pool Rules for the generation of electricity
TEN	—	Trans-European Network
TPA	—	Third party access (to gas or electricity grids)
Tranche	—	A discrete part of a borrower's overall borrowing under a credit agreement
TRDQ	—	Total reservoir daily quantity
USEXIM	—	The Export-Import Bank of the United States, the U.S. ECA
WRA	—	Water Resources Act 1991

Introduction

SCOPE

The purpose of this book is to try to explain in general terms some of the more important legal issues that arise in the course of a project financing. While it is written primarily from the point of view of English law, many of the legal problems that arise are universal and other jurisdictions may have the same or similar solutions to those discussed here.

WHAT IS "PROJECT FINANCE"?

Although this question is probably capable of a number of widely differing answers, the answer which I prefer is that project finance is financing the development or exploitation of a right, natural resource or other asset where the bulk of the financing is not to be provided by any form of share capital and is to be repaid principally out of revenues produced by the project in question.

ASSUMPTIONS

In order to keep the size of this book within reasonable bounds, I have generally assumed that project sponsors will want to carry out any particular projects through the medium of a sole purpose company and to keep their own financial support to a minimum. Project sponsors will not always want to do this, however, and may (for tax or other reasons) wish to implement a project themselves. In these circumstances, their prime objective will be to try to prevent a collapse of the project having an adverse impact on their balance sheets.

Although references in this book to the *project company* should primarily be construed as references to a vehicle company set up by a project's sponsors for the sole purpose of carrying out that project, it can in most circumstances be read as if it were a project sponsor which had decided to carry out the project itself.

I have also rather tended to write this book on the grand scale, focusing on major infrastructure projects promoted by a host government. This is not to say, however, that the book is only relevant to such projects. The law applicable to project finance is essentially the general law. Much of what is said in the context of an international infrastructure project applies equally to a domestic property development financing. I leave it to the reader to make the leap of imagination which, for example, sees in the position of a host government the position of a site owner.

Chapter 1

The Parties' Objectives

Part of the challenge of any project financing is trying to reconcile the differing objectives of the various interested parties in such a way that each party, although possibly compromising its ideal position, nevertheless generally stands to gain if the project is completed. A good understanding of what each party's general objectives are is an essential pre-requisite to any sensible negotiations. So what are the parties' objectives or, perhaps more accurately, what might they include (for a party need not necessarily have all of the objectives listed below)?

1.1 THE HOST GOVERNMENT

It can usually be fairly safely assumed that the host government's attitude to a project will be governed by some perception of what is in the public interest. A government may wish to promote a new mass transit system in its capital in order to ease congestion or to develop oil reserves to earn hard currency (through production sharing or royalty arrangements) and to provide jobs. But when a government decides to allow the private sector to develop a project (whether or not in conjunction with it) it will have at least some of the following objectives:

(a) *to satisfy the national interest and have the project completed (to the government's specification) as soon as possible;*

(b) *to bring the project back into public ownership once the private sector has received an acceptable return on its investment* — this is an important aspect of BOT (build-operate-transfer) schemes;

(c) *to have adequate safeguards and assurances that the project will be operated properly and in the public interest* — in other words, to

1

ensure that the lights do not go out or that the 08.32 train to London Bridge runs safely, on time and with tickets priced at a level that the public can afford;

(d) *to reduce or eliminate the need to use the government's own funds or borrowings* — although for certain types of project (mass transit systems in particular), a certain level of subsidy may be necessary in order to make the project viable in the first place;

(e) *to limit the undertakings given by the state* — although, in some projects, some undertakings from the state (e.g. to construct access roads to a new airport or not to compete with a new mass transit system) may be essential;

(f) *to be able to offer the ownership and/or operation of the project to other private sector entities should the original private sector participants fail to provide the required level of service or run into financial difficulties* — this may involve the host government in paying, or arranging for the payment of, adequate compensation for what might otherwise be considered to be an act of expropriation, however;

(g) *to be able to regain control of the project itself or to bring it back into public ownership as a matter of last resort should the private sector generally fail to provide the required level of service or if the project runs into otherwise insurmountable difficulties* — intervention in the running of a project is probably the more attractive of these two options for a host government since, depending on the nature and duration of the intervention, this can probably be achieved without having to pay the private sector compensation for expropriation;

(h) *to fetter the government's discretion as little as possible* — a government will wish to retain the right to pass new (and, if necessary, more onerous) laws and regulations relating to health and safety and the protection of the environment, for example. This flexibility may come at a price since it represents the ability to change the rules on the private sector after investments have been made and money lent; and

(i) *generally to transfer risk from the public sector to the private sector.*

1.2 THE PRIVATE SECTOR SPONSORS

Not surprisingly, the preponderant objective of the private sector sponsors in a project is to make profits. But monetary gain is not the only reason for private sector involvement in a project: the owner of a refinery which operates on steam may well promote an electricity co-generation project on the same site as the refinery in order to secure a steam supply (without which the refinery would have to shut down). The objectives that private sector sponsors might have include the following:

(a) *to satisfy a strategic corporate objective by completing the project* — this strategic corporate objective might be securing a steam supply (as noted above) or it may simply be to diversify into another related area of activity (for example, an electricity generating utility may wish to reduce its dependence on gas suppliers by acquiring interests in gas fields);

(b) *to extract profit* — there are various ways in which this objective may be met. For example:
  (i) by way of a simple investment return: that is, the sponsor in question sees the project in question as a simple investment opportunity with purely financial risks and rewards. Such a sponsor will extract profit by way of dividends or other distributions;
  (ii) by selling equipment or raw materials to the project company: one does not have to be particularly astute to understand why a rolling-stock manufacturer would be interested in sponsoring a light railway project or why a toll road operator would be interested in sponsoring a company to build a new tolled motorway or bridge; or
  (iii) by buying (or even possibly selling (as an agent for a commission)) the project's product;

(c) *to share the risk in carrying out a project* — a company may decide to fund a project through project finance rather than from its own resources simply because of the damage the project could do to its finances if it went wrong. Banks providing project finance are the most obvious people with whom such a company might seek to share risk, but there are other candidates. There is nothing to stop risks being transferred to product suppliers, contractors, offtakers and host governments, for example;

(d) *to carry out a project "off balance sheet"* — this essentially means a sponsor financing a project without having to show any borrowing for the project among its own borrowings in its consolidated accounts. Too high a level of borrowings will result in a sponsor having an unfavourable gearing ratio (the ratio of (consolidated) borrowings to net worth) and make it

3

more difficult for that sponsor to raise funds on the capital markets. In the past, legal structures were created which meant that a project company was not consolidated with a sponsor for accounting purposes even though that sponsor took all of the rewards generated by (but none of the risks inherent in) the project in question. In the United Kingdom, these structures have been attacked (and mortally wounded) by a combination of the legislature[1] and the accounting profession,[2] but the off balance sheet effect can still be achieved with a project company which is a true joint venture; and

(e) *to retain control of the project for as long as possible in times of hardship* — the sponsors will fear losing not only control of the project but also the value of their investment if they allow the host government to exercise its intervention powers (see section 1.1(f) and (g) above) or the lenders to enforce their security at too early a stage.

1.3   THE LENDERS

It is essential to understand that commercial banks simply providing loans to a project company cannot be treated as shareholders, despite the increased risks and rewards that they will be taking. Commercial banks lend money for a margin — if a project is enormously successful, all they are usually entitled to is repayment of their loans plus accrued interest — they usually have no "upside". "Upside" is usually the exclusive preserve of the shareholders. This absence of a share in profits and the attitude of the world's banking regulation authorities combine to make commercial banks relatively risk-averse. There is a limit to the level of risk a commercial bank is prepared to accept for the level of remuneration it typically receives in a project financing.

Against this background, the objectives of commercial banks in a project financing will usually include the following:

(a) *to make profits* — but, unlike the sponsors, these profits will be made by lending at attractive project finance margins and for attractive arrangement fees. Commercial banks cannot usually obtain extra remuneration when a project goes well;

---

[1] See ss.258 *et seq.* Companies Act 1985.
[2] See the Accounting Standards Board's Financial Reporting Standard 5 ("FRS 5"), "Reporting the Substance of Transactions", April 1994.

(b) *to assume only measurable or measured risks* — this is, of course, a function of the banks' limited share in the "upside". Banks will usually only assume risks associated with a project after a careful due diligence exercise. So, for example, they will accept the risk that an oilfield does not contain the level of reserves that everyone thinks it has only after they have received a reservoir consultant's report confirming that, in his view, that level of reserves is present;

(c) *to have control over key project decisions* — this is, not surprisingly, a constant source of friction between the banks and the sponsors in the course of negotiations. This control is usually exercised through restrictive covenants in the credit agreement. The banks' argument is that they are prepared to lend against a particular project profile in respect of which they have carried out an extensive due diligence exercise and, particularly because they have (usually) funded the greater part of the project's costs, they are entitled to prevent that project profile being changed; and

(d) *to take control of the project as soon as possible in times of hardship* — this is, of course, diametrically opposed to the sponsors' objectives (see section 1.2(e) above).

Lenders to a project company who are not commercial banks may, of course, have other or differing objectives. For example, the export credit agencies in a particular country will support a project in order to promote that country's industry and they may not, as a result, have as great a profit motive. Bondholders will share the commercial banks' objectives but will tend to be less interventionist and rely on covenants which are expressed in far more general language than those found in a loan agreement. Shareholders in a project company who lend it money may view their loans as quasi-equity (especially if they have high interest rates or interest rates which vary with profits) and will usually accept a subordinate position to other lenders.

Chapter 2

The Choice of Vehicle

2.1 THE PRE-DEVELOPMENT PHASE

The pre-development phase is the period during which the sponsor or sponsors of a project are evaluating its technical feasibility and financial viability. It ends with *financial close*, the date when all of the project contracts become unconditional and all conditions precedent to the project credit agreement are satisfied or waived.

Where there is more than one sponsor, it is common for them to enter into a *pre-development* or *project development agreement*. The purpose of this agreement is to regulate the relationship between the sponsors before there is a project. Such an agreement would typically contain provisions along the following lines:

(a) *A statement of exclusivity.* An exclusivity requirement will invariably be included where a particular project is put out to competitive tender and a number of consortia are in the process of coming together in order to submit competing bids. The purpose of an exclusivity commitment on the part of a sponsor in such a case is to ensure that he does not play "fast and loose" by being involved with more than one consortium. An exclusivity commitment might also be included in other cases and for other motives, however. The legality of such a provision is discussed in section 3.4(e).

(b) *A commitment to carry out a pre-development programme.* The parties agree to carry out an identified pre-development programme, covering the technical, contractual and financial aspects of the project. They may agree to commission or carry out feasibility studies, to search for other sponsors or investors (not necessarily the same thing), to identify potential contracting parties (such as fuel suppliers or product offtakers) and/or to develop or commission a computer model of the project's economics. The pre-development programme may also include guidelines as to how the project's

7

major contracts are to be put out to tender, its bank group selected or its professional advisers (such as its lawyers) appointed. It may also require the sponsors to agree upon a structure for the project, to form an appropriate vehicle (if, indeed, this is appropriate) and to apply for certain consents and authorisations.

Together with agreement on a pre-development programme usually goes agreement on a pre-development timetable.

(c) *An agreement as to how the pre-development costs are to be funded.* Here, freedom of contract reigns. There are no hard and fast rules and project development agreements quite often provide for one or more of the sponsors not to contribute in cash for the pre-development costs. They might have brought something else — such as essential know-how — to the party. Since there is an understandable reluctance on the part of sponsors to authorise others to go and spend their money, budgets are normally set and are expected to be adhered to.

(d) *Voting provisions.* There are usually provisions determining how important decisions are to be taken. Proceeding with the project usually requires unanimity, although objecting or reluctant sponsors can withdraw (see below) and unanimity can be achieved in this way.

(e) *Allocation of roles.* This is particularly found in larger sponsor groups. Individual sponsors (or groups of sponsors in working groups) are allocated specific roles and are mandated to report back to either all of the sponsors or a steering committee established for this purpose.

(f) *Withdrawal and abandonment.* If a sponsor feels that he no longer wishes to be involved in the project, he can normally withdraw without any particular financial penalty on giving an agreed period of notice. Clearly, if a withdrawing party was contributing, or contributing significantly, to the funding of costs during the pre-development phase, this can put an increased financial burden on the remaining sponsors, some of whom may in turn wish to withdraw. Because of the snowball effect that withdrawal might have, project development agreements recognise the obvious and provide that a withdrawal by all of the sponsors constitutes an abandonment of the project. Otherwise, formal abandonment of the project usually requires unanimity.

(g) *Confidentiality.* This is self-explanatory. Much of the information about a project in its early stages will be sensitive if not price sensitive. Press releases normally require unanimity.

(h) *RTPA suspensory clause.* As will be seen (in section 3.4(e)), an agreement which is registerable under the Restrictive Trade Practices Act 1976 (the "RTPA") but which is not so registered will be void in respect of any "restrictions" (within the meaning of the RTPA) accepted by the parties. In order to avoid bringing down the whole agreement (where severability of provisions may be doubtful), an RTPA suspensory clause states that any provision which results in the agreement being registerable under the RTPA will not take effect unless and until particulars of the agreement are furnished to the Office of Fair Trading in accordance with the RTPA.

2.2 GENERAL CONSIDERATIONS WHEN CHOOSING A VEHICLE

A vehicle will not always be required for a project. A single sponsor may decide to carry out the project himself; other sponsors may decide to participate in the project otherwise than by investment (*e.g.* they may become the construction contractor and extract profit in this way). However, where there is more than one sponsor of a project, a decision usually has to be made on the most appropriate vehicle or vehicles through which to carry out and finance the project.

The choice of vehicle will be dictated by, *inter alia*, the following considerations:

(a) *The extent to which the sponsors wish to be insulated from the risks and liabilities inherent in the project.*

(b) *The extent to which the sponsors wish to avoid moneys borrowed for the purpose of funding the project appearing on their respective balance sheets.* This is usually a concern for listed companies whose gearing ratios may be seriously distorted by the level of borrowings required to fund some of the more major projects, even if those borrowings are non- or limited recourse (see section 5.2).

(c) *The ease with which profits can be extracted by the sponsors.*

(d) *Tax efficiency.* A phrase often heard in the context of project financing is "tax transparency". When used in the context of a project vehicle, the phrase means that a shareholder or owner of or participant in the vehicle is taxed in relation to the profits and losses arising from the project as if the vehicle did not exist.[1] The issue is at its most acute in the development (or construction) phase

---

[1] In its broadest meaning, "tax transparency" means that the existence of any project vehicle is totally ignored for all tax purposes and not just in relation to profits and losses. The phrase is used in its narrower meaning in this book, however.

when a sponsor may wish to use his share of the losses building up in a project which is not yet generating revenues to reduce his taxable profits in other areas of his business.

Tax transparency is not the only tax issue when considering the choice of vehicle, but it is a preponderant one. Other tax issues arise when sponsors are considering where to set up a vehicle, including withholding tax on distributions, royalties and interest payments and capital gains or similar tax on a disposal of an interest in the project. In general terms, a sponsor will be looking to minimise the overall amount of cash lost to the taxman or, to use the market's euphemism, he will be looking for *tax synergy*.

(e) *Flexibility of management structure.*

(f) *The level of minority protection.* A sponsor's objectives in this area will depend on whether he is a majority or minority participant in the project!

(g) *The level of required publicity of the vehicle's affairs.* Sponsors may not wish to have the project's accounts made public through registration, for example.

(h) *Ease of dissolution.*

This is not a book on accountancy and so little will be said on how that might affect the choice of vehicle for a project. Before moving on to consider each of the possible vehicles under English law (and two possible contenders from European Community law), it is worth emphasising the point that sponsors should bear in mind the possibility of using multiple vehicles for a project since tax and other advantages are sometimes to be had by fragmenting the various constituent parts of a project. One of the most basic examples of how multiple vehicles can be used to good effect is the sponsor labouring under a tight negative pledge from his general corporate bankers who has to deliver a security interest over his shares in a project company to the project finance banks who will specifically finance the project in question. If the negative pledge prohibits the sponsor or any of his subsidiaries or subsidiary undertakings[2] creating security over any of their respective assets to any person other than the sponsor's general corporate bankers, he can nevertheless deliver a security interest in the shares in the project company which directly owns the project assets if he first forms — together with the other sponsors — an intermediate holding company for the shares in the project company and ensures

---

[2] See ss. 258 *et seq.* Companies Act 1985.

that that intermediate holding company is (usually by virtue of the other sponsors' involvement) neither his subsidiary nor his subsidiary undertaking. Equally, if a sponsor who wishes eventually to dispose of his interest in a project is taxed in a jurisdiction which has a high tax rate for capital gains, he may wish to hold his shares in the project company through an intermediate holding company which may be wholly-owned but which is in any event resident for tax purposes in a jurisdiction with a lower (or no) tax rate for capital gains. Any disposal of the shares in the project company will then be a disposal by the intermediate holding company and not a disposal by the sponsor.

Predictably enough, tax considerations usually dominate any discussions on the choice of vehicle for a project.

2.3   THE UNINCORPORATED JOINT VENTURE

The unincorporated joint venture is probably the most flexible form of co-operation as far as internal management is concerned. The parties are more or less free to write their own rules. The unincorporated joint venture is the invariable medium for co-operative projects in the oil and gas industry and the joint operating agreements (or JOAs) that are typically found in relation to North Sea developments have taken the various legal and commercial issues involved to a high level of sophistication.

One of the major drawbacks of the unincorporated joint venture is its lack of a separate legal personality. In a JOA, this problem is overcome by the parties (or participants) appointing one of their number to be the *operator*. The operator is, broadly speaking, in charge of the project and its management on a day-to-day basis but his actions are subject to review by an *operating committee* (comprised of representatives from each of the participants) which can in the last resort dismiss him. The operating committee also takes the major policy decisions in relation to the project. A participant's representative on the operating committee has a vote which generally corresponds to the share of the costs of the project for which that participant has agreed to be responsible. The operator will enter into the necessary fabrication and other contracts required by the project and will meet expenditure under those contracts through a system of *cash calls*. The cash call system involves the operator running a joint account for all of the participants and estimating in each month how much each participant must contribute (in accordance with its respective agreed share of the project's liabilities)

11

towards the next month's estimated expenditures (which in turn should fall within items of expenditure authorised by the operating committee). Each participant must then pay this estimated amount — the cash call — to the operator. If a participant defaults in his cash call, the other participants are obliged to pay their share of the defaulted amount (with a right of reimbursement from the default-ing party) and, after the expiry of certain notice periods, the defaulting party stands to lose his interest in the project outright (through forfeiture provisions) or to have his entitlement to lift petroleum scaled back (through so-called "withering" provisions).

The cash call system is obviously one way in which an operator seeks to limit the exposure he takes on if he contracts with third parties in his own name but on behalf of the participants (*i.e.* as principal). He can also seek to limit his liability on contracts by expressly entering into them as agent for disclosed principals. Unfortunately, practice in the North Sea is often hopelessly vague in this area and operators sometimes enter into contracts "as operator for the XYZ Group". With this formulation, it is unclear whether or not the operator is disclosing his agency or merely describing himself and, if he is disclosing his agency, whether it is an agency to act on behalf of just the existing members of the group or its present and future members. It is in the interest of both operators and the third parties with whom they contract for these issues to be put beyond doubt.

The unincorporated joint venture obviously does not in itself provide any form of limited liability, but sponsors will frequently participate in unincorporated joint ventures through sole purpose limited liability companies established especially for this purpose. If such a company's share of the joint venture's liabilities is not to appear on the sponsor's balance sheet, then that company must itself be "off balance sheet".[3] Distribution of the revenues and profits of an unincorporated joint venture are a matter for the joint venture agreement and, as the unincorporated joint venture has no separate legal personality, tax transparency is (subject to any peculiarity of overseas tax regimes) usually guaranteed. Flexibility of management structure is discussed above and the level of minority protection and dissolution are also matters for the joint venture agreement. There is no separate requirement for publicity of an unincorporated joint venture's affairs under English law.

---

[3] Although this is difficult for a U.K. group. See section 1.2(d).

2.4 THE GENERAL PARTNERSHIP

Unlike the position in certain other jurisdictions, partnerships (both general and limited) do not enjoy a separate legal personality under English commercial law. They therefore share this drawback (if, indeed, it is in practice a drawback) with unincorporated joint ventures. As a general partnership has all of its partners sharing not only in the profits but also the losses of the partnership (although not necessarily equally), it does not afford its partners the benefit of limited liability and, for this reason, where partnerships are used in project financings, the sponsors may use specially formed limited liability companies as the partners.

There are important differences between unincorporated joint ventures and partnerships, however. To take but a few, each individual partner can generally bind a general partnership when contracting with a third party,[4] the taxable profits of a partnership are assessed for the purposes of United Kingdom taxation as if the partnership were a company (with the profits and losses then allocated to each partner according to his interest in the partnership) and the maximum number of partners is still 20 outside professional partnerships.[5]

Weighing a general partnership up against the other general considerations given in section 2.2, the following results emerge. A sponsor may have to consolidate with his own accounts the accounts of a partnership in which he has a "participating interest" and over which he exercises a "dominant influence" (in each case for the purposes of Part VIII of the Companies Act 1985).[6] Profits can be extracted from a general partnership relatively easily, the management structure can in theory be relatively flexible, minority protection can be dealt with in the partnership agreement, there is no requirement for a general partnership to register its accounts or

---

[4] See s.5 of the Partnership Act 1890.
[5] See s.716 of the Companies Act 1985 and s.717 in relation to limited partnerships.
[6] This is because consolidated accounts must be prepared if a company has a *subsidiary undertaking* within the meaning of s.258 of the Companies Act 1985 and "undertaking" is defined by s.259(1) of that Act to include a partnership. By s.260(1) of that Act, a "participating interest" is defined as "an interest held by an undertaking in the shares of another undertaking which it holds on a long-term basis for the purpose of securing a contribution to its activities by the exercise of control or influence arising from or related to that interest". By s.260(2) of that Act, a holding of 20 per cent or more of the shares of an undertaking is presumed to be a "participating interest" unless the contrary is shown.

other particulars of its affairs[7] and, subject to anything in the partnership deed to the contrary, a partner can dissolve a partnership by simple notice to the other partners.[8]

A fair degree of transparency for United Kingdom tax purposes can be achieved with a United Kingdom partnership in relation to trading profits and losses. A United Kingdom partner's share of any losses that his partnership makes in a year can be set off against any taxable profits that he makes from other activities in the same year (but not in previous or subsequent years).

The position with regard to the security that can be granted by a partnership (general or limited) under English law may also influence the choice of vehicle. Although there is no conceptual barrier to a partnership creating a floating charge, it would probably be registerable (at least insofar as it purported to cover chattels) under the Bills of Sale Acts. Fresh registrations would have to be made as and when fresh chattels were acquired. The bills of sale regime is not really suited to the needs of project finance banks and the usual advice given is that a floating charge granted by a partnership is likely to be cumbersome and/or unreliable. A charge over each partner's share in a partnership would not confer any priority over the partnership's creditors and, to this extent, can be equated to a charge on shares in a company. However, not only does section 31(1) of the Partnership Act 1890 expressly state that a chargee of a partner's share in a partnership is only entitled to the charging partner's share of the partnership profits, it also states that such a chargee cannot "interfere in the management or administration of the partnership business or affairs".

2.5 THE LIMITED PARTNERSHIP

Limited partnerships were established by the Limited Partnerships Act 1907. In a limited partnership, a partner may be a "general

---

[7] Consideration needs to be given, however, to the possible implications that s.30 of the Partnership Act 1890 may have in relation to the RTPA where two or more parties are bodies corporate carrying on a relevant business in the United Kingdom. There is, by virtue of that section, an implied or indirect restriction on a partner competing with the business of the partnership in that, if he carries on a business which competes with the partnership without the consent of the other partners, he has to account to the partnership for the profits he makes. The point will, of course, not arise if the partnership agreement makes it clear that a partner is free to compete with the business of the partnership.
[8] s.32 of the Partnership Act 1890.

partner" or a "limited partner", but each limited partnership must have at least one general partner. A general partner is liable for all of the debts and obligations of the partnership without limit whereas a limited partner is only liable for such debts and obligations up to the amount he contributes to the capital of the partnership.[9] The general partner is charged with the management of the limited partnership's business; a limited partner has no power to bind the partnership but if he nevertheless takes part in the management of the business, he is liable for all debts and obligations incurred by the partnership while he so takes part.[10] The theory is that the general partner is the person who will be seen by the outside world doing business on behalf of the limited partnership and so should be generally liable for the partnership's debts and obligations. The limited partners are (or should be) merely passive "behind-the-scenes" investors. The theory is slightly corrupted by the fact that there is nothing to prevent a limited liability company being the general partner.

It would be wrong to go into too great a degree of detail in relation to limited partnerships under English law because they are very rarely found in practice. They are still regarded as something of a legal curio and tend to be ignored in favour of more well-known forms of business organisation.[11] They used to be found in projects involving United States corporations because they could produce transparency for United States tax purposes. However, the United States tax rules have recently changed and certain more conventional vehicles (including a United Kingdom private limited company) can now opt for United States partnership tax treatment.

Details of a limited partnership must be registered with the Registrar of Companies, failing which the partnership will be treated as a general partnership.[12] The particulars to be registered include a statement that the partnership is limited and the sum contributed by each limited partner.[13]

Subject to the above and to the fact that a limited partner cannot dissolve the partnership by notice,[14] a limited partnership scores in the same manner as a general partnership when weighed up against the general considerations specified in section 2.2.

---

[9] s.4 of the Limited Partnerships Act 1907. A limited partner's capital should not be withdrawn during the continuance of the partnership: *ibid.*, s.4(3).

[10] *ibid.*, s.6(1).

[11] A significant drawback for a limited partner is the lack of control he is likely to have over the limited partnership's affairs because of the fear of becoming a general partner if he is held to be "taking part in the management of the partnership business".

[12] *ibid.*, s.5.

[13] *ibid.*, s.8.

[14] *ibid.*, s.6(5)(e).

2.6 THE INCORPORATED COMPANY

A company incorporated with limited liability under the Companies Acts needs little introduction. There are, of course, other types of company under English law, including companies limited by guarantee and unlimited companies (both of which are regulated by the Companies Acts). Both of these last two types of company are theoretical contenders for the role of project vehicle but are hardly ever seen in practice. The unlimited company's main use used to be to avoid capital duty when the United Kingdom still had that form of tax. Because other forms of company are rarely encountered, this section deals only with the company incorporated under the Companies Acts with limited liability.

Such a company clearly provides a high degree of insulation for a sponsor from the risks and liabilities of a project. There are relatively few instances where English law is prepared to pierce the corporate veil. The problems (under English law) with getting vehicle companies "off balance sheet" have already been alluded to (in section 1.2(d)). The extraction of profits from a company is tightly regulated by the United Kingdom's rules on maintenance of capital[15] and, from a tax point of view, the payment of distributions is subject to the advance corporation tax ("ACT") system which can in the normal course lead to fiscal inefficiencies, albeit in some cases only short-term cash flow inefficiencies. However, for United Kingdom investors these inefficiencies can be avoided under the United Kingdom's rules relating to group and consortium relief and allied relief and it is these rules which provide the simple project company structure with a high degree of tax transparency.

If the requirements for group or consortium[16] relief are satisfied in relation to a project company and a sponsor (as a shareholder in that company) and the requisite elections are made, then trading losses incurred by (and other reliefs available to) the project company can be surrendered by that company to the sponsor (and vice versa)[17] and under similar rules dividends can be paid by the project company to the sponsor without any obligation to account

---

[15] ss. 135–141, 159–170, 171–177 and 263–281 of the Companies Act 1985.

[16] There is, strictly speaking, no such thing as "consortium relief" but only a consortium claim for group relief. "Consortium relief" is the generally used term, however. What constitutes a consortium for these purposes is divined from ss.402(3) and 413(6) of the Income and Corporation Taxes Act 1988 ("ICTA"). S.413(6) essentially requires 75 per cent or more of the ordinary share capital of a company to be owned by companies of which none owns less than 5 per cent of that capital.

[17] ss.402ff ICTA.

for ACT.[18] The surrender of losses in this way represents, from the sponsor's point of view, the transfer of a valuable asset (it can reduce his tax bill) and it is common practice for the recipient of surrendered losses to pay for them (often at a discount to their nominal value). A project company will normally incur substantial losses during the construction phase of a project (it is spending vast sums of money at a time when it is unlikely to have any income) and it would normally have to utilise those losses in reducing taxable profits over a number of years once the project facilities were completed and began to produce revenue. Payment for the surrender of those losses can represent a useful infusion of cash into the project company and hence be beneficial to the project company and the sponsors alike. It has to be remembered, however, that, if a project company surrenders any of its losses, this will bring forward the date on which it will first pay tax (as it has, by definition, fewer losses with which to stave off such date) and this needs to be properly reflected in the computer model of the project's economics.

A company's management structure is fairly rigid and formalistic as far as the powers and duties of directors and the division of competence between the board and the general meeting is concerned but this is hardly seen as an issue in practice. The rules relating to the protection of minority shareholders are relatively well developed.[19] The publicity requirements for a limited liability company are extensive and such a company is not the vehicle for sponsors wishing to have a degree of secrecy surrounding their project. A limited liability company can be wound up by means of a simple special resolution passed by its members.[20]

2.7   THE EEIG

The basis upon which European Economic Interest Groupings ("EEIGs") can be formed was established in an EC Regulation of 1985.[21] The Regulation is aimed at increasing effective co-operation across the frontiers of the European Community. Although (as a Regulation) the Regulation has direct effect under United Kingdom law, it gives Member States various options on its face and the United Kingdom's position (together with various administrative provisions) is set out in a statutory instrument passed in 1989.[22]

---

[18] s.247 ICTA.
[19] See, *e.g.*, s.459 of the Companies Act 1985.
[20] s.84 of the Insolvency Act.
[21] Council Regulation (EEC) No. 2137/85
[22] The European Economic Interest Grouping Regulation (S.I. 89/638).

The bare essentials of an EEIG are that it is a grouping comprised of at least two persons which (if companies) have been formed under the laws of a Member State and which have their administrations in different Member States or (if natural persons) carry on their principal activities in different Member States.[23] An EEIG is intended to enhance its members' profits, not to make profits itself and its activities have to be related to the economic activities of its members and must not be more than ancillary to those activities.[24] An EEIG is intended to be tax transparent: Article 21 of the Regulation states that the profits resulting from an EEIG's activities shall be deemed to be profits of its members and that losses shall be treated in a similar way and Article 40 expressly states that the profits or losses resulting from an EEIG's activities shall be taxable only in the hands of its members.

Although the Regulation states that an EEIG has the legal capacity to conclude contracts and do other legal acts (including, presumably, the granting of security) and can sue and be sued,[25] it goes on to state that it is left to each Member State to determine whether an EEIG registered at its registries[26] has legal personality.[27] This is apparently due to tax complications in certain Member States (notably Germany and Italy) relating to the requirement that EEIGs be tax transparent. The United Kingdom statutory instrument provides for an EEIG registered in the United Kingdom to be treated as a body corporate.[28] Notwithstanding an EEIG's separate legal personality, its members are jointly and severally liable (without limit) for its liabilities (although creditors are expected to pursue claims against the EEIG first).[29]

The EEIG is therefore a rather curious beast — a beast with a separate legal personality whose members are jointly and severally liable for its obligations and whose activities must be merely ancillary to those of its members. The nearest thing to it under English law is the unlimited company. Other Member States have forms of business entity which more closely approximate to the EEIG.[30] Although the EEIG is tax transparent and its profits appear to be automatically imputed to its members, it will not insulate its

---

[23] Art. 4(2) of the Regulation.

[24] *ibid.*, Art. 3(1).

[25] *ibid.*, Art. 1(2).

[26] By Art. 6 of the Regulation, an EEIG has to be registered at the designated registry in the Member State in which has its official address (the Companies Registry in the case of the U.K.)

[27] *ibid.*, Art. 1(3).

[28] Reg. 3 of the S.I.

[29] Art. 24 of the Regulation.

[30] For example, the *agrupamento complementar de empresas* in Portugal.

members from the liabilities in a project — in fact, quite the contrary: its members will be jointly and severally liable for such liabilities (although there is presumably nothing to prevent creditors (such as banks) waiving their rights to proceed against the members from the outset). As far as internal management is concerned, the Regulation requires an EEIG to be managed by one or more natural persons (subject to each Member State's rights to allow legal persons to be managers)[31] but appears to leave the detail of the management and supervisory structure as a matter to be dealt with by the EEIG's members.[32] Minority protection is very briefly dealt with in Art. 17(2) of the Regulation which provides that a unanimous decision of the members of an EEIG is required to do various specific acts (such as altering the contribution by all or some members to the EEIG's financing).[33] The Regulation provides for a certain amount of information to be published in relation to an EEIG.[34] Article 36 of the Regulation states that an EEIG is subject to national laws in relation to insolvency and cessation of payments.[35]

Article 22 of the Regulation allows a member of an EEIG to create security over his participation in the EEIG but goes on to state that "the holder of the security may not at any time become a member of the grouping by virtue of that security". The admission of new members requires a unanimous decision by all of the members.[36] Security over a member's participation will be of limited value.

The EEIG is at present a project finance virgin. The fact that it does not offer its members limited liability is probably not a particularly deciding factor since, after all, the classic unincorporated joint venture cannot offer this. What holds the EEIG back is largely its newness: banks like predictability and precedent and the EEIG at present has neither. The requirement that it must only undertake activities ancillary to those of its members will also be a hindrance but, in the proper circumstances, an EEIG might well provide an appropriate vehicle and should not be dismissed out of hand.

---

[31] Art. 19(1) and (2) of the Regulation.
[32] *ibid.*, Art. 19(3).
[33] *ibid.*, Art. 17(2).
[34] *ibid.*, Arts. 7–10.
[35] An EEIG registered in the U.K. will be wound up as an unregistered company: see r.7 of the S.I.
[36] Art. 26(1) of the Regulation.

2.8   THE EUROPEAN COMPANY

At the time of writing, the European Company is still merely a proposal from the European Commission. Their proposal is in the form of a draft Regulation on the Statute for a European Company[37] and a draft Directive on worker participation.[38] The proposal has languished amid differing views from various Member States on both draft texts.

If the present draft Regulation is finally adopted, the European Company ("Societas Europea" or "S.E.") will be a public company with liability limited by shares and with separate legal personality.[39] The cross-border nature of the EEIG is retained for the S.E.[40]: an S.E. can be formed by existing public companies merging or by existing companies forming a joint holding company or subsidiary provided that, in each case, at least two of them have their central administration in different Member States or have a subsidiary or branch office in a Member State other than that of their central administration. A public company formed under the laws of a Member State may also transform itself into an S.E. if it has a subsidiary or branch office in a Member State other than that of its central administration. Each S.E. must have a registered office in the Member State in which it has its central administration.[41]

The proposed Regulation envisages that an S.E. will be governed by the provisions of the Regulation itself, by the S.E.'s statutes (where this is expressly authorised by the Regulation) and then by the law on public companies in the Member State in which the S.E. has its registered office.[42]

An S.E. can have either a two-tier or a single tier board structure,[43] although a Member State may require S.E.s registered in its jurisdiction to adopt one form or the other.[44] The supervisory board is purely supervisory and cannot manage the S.E.[45] An S.E. can be wound up by a simple majority decision taken by the general meeting.[46] The draft Regulation does not expressly deal with either

---

[37] [1991] O.J. C176/1 (July 8).
[38] [1989] O.J. C263/69 (Oct. 16).
[39] Art. 16 of the proposed Regulation.
[40] *ibid.*, Art. 2.
[41] *ibid.*, Art. 5.
[42] *ibid.*, Art. 7.
[43] The two-tier system comprises a management board and a supervisory board. The single tier system is the single administrative board favoured by English law.
[44] Art. 61 of the proposed Regulation.
[45] *ibid.*, Art. 63.
[46] *ibid.*, Art. 115.

the method in which distributions may be made to the shareholders of an S.E. or the tax treatment of the S.E. and these matters will therefore be decided by application of the relevant national laws.

To the extent that the rules governing an S.E. with a registered office in the United Kingdom are the United Kingdom laws applicable to companies generally, much of what is said in section 2.6 relating to the use of companies as vehicles applies to an S.E. However, if the S.E. — in the proposed form or any other — ever sees the light of day, it is likely not to be used a vehicle in project financings for two reasons. First, it will suffer from the same problem of newness which afflicts the EEIG. Secondly, it is unlikely (in the absence of special circumstances) that sponsors will wish to opt for a *public* limited liability company (which the S.E. is) rather than a private one because of the stricter and more inflexible provisions of general law applicable to public companies throughout the European Community.

Chapter 3

The Contractual Framework

3.1 TYPES OF CONTRACT

The underlying contractual framework of a project is all important.
It allocates risks between the various commercial parties and so
determines the risk profile that will be presented to the project's
proposed lenders.

In addition to any pre-development agreement and any more
permanent agreement regulating the relationship between the
project company's shareholders (a shareholders agreement), a typical list of the major commercial contracts for a project would be as
follows:

(a) *A concession agreement, licence or mineral lease* or some other
    document (possibly legislation) giving the project company
    the right to carry out the project. In some projects this will
    not, of course, be needed — for example, where the project
    is to build a simple manufacturing plant and the project
    company owns the freehold to the proposed site and the
    right to build and use the plant.

(b) *A construction contract or a development management agreement.* The
    contractual arrangements for the construction of project
    facilities are infinitely varied. There would be no need for a
    master construction contract if the project company itself
    had the ability and resources to do most of the construction
    work and only had to employ outside contractors for special-
    ist aspects of the construction work. On the other hand, if
    the project company is essentially just a finance vehicle, a
    comprehensive "turnkey" construction contract (*i.e.* a con-
    tract to construct and commission all of the project facil-
    ities) might be entered into with a single contractor or
    construction consortium. The single contractor or consor-
    tium would then sub-contract work to the extent necessary.

23

As an alternative to this type of contract, the project company might appoint a project management company which would arrange for a number of contractors to enter into a series of construction contracts with the project company direct (each for a particular segment of the overall construction work).

(c) *A supply agreement,* but this would obviously not be necessary where the project company provided its own raw materials or the project was the actual extraction of natural resources in the first place.

(d) *A sales agreement,* if the project is one where a long-term sales agreement would naturally be entered into (*e.g.* an electricity generation or gas project) and sales would not be made on a spot or retail market. Even if the product was one normally sold on the spot market (*e.g.* crude oil), there might still be a long-term sales agreement if a particular purchaser wished to secure a source of supply. Long-term crude sales agreements are entered into on this basis in the North Sea: all (or part) of the crude produced from a particular field will be sold to a purchaser for a given period of time but the price payable will be the spot price on the date of each delivery.

(e) *An operating agreement.* This would not be necessary if the project company was able to operate and maintain the project facilities itself.

Other major contracts may exist in any particular project depending on the structure adopted. For example, it may be intended to isolate the lenders from a market price risk attached to a project's product by having one of the sponsors enter into an exclusive distributorship or sales agency agreement under which it will pay the project company a fixed fee.

Two of the contracts in the above list have variants which have been specifically developed for project finance. The variants are the fixed price turnkey construction contract and the "take-or-pay" sales agreement and these are discussed further below.

3.2 DEAL PHILOSOPHY

As noted above, the underlying contracts for a project will determine the allocation of risks between the various parties. If all things were equal, the project company would fight its own corner and try to pass as many risks as possible onto the sponsors and each sponsor would fight its own corner and try to pass as many risks as possible onto the project company and the other sponsors. The problem with project finance, however, is that usually all things are not equal. In large infrastructure projects, for instance, the project company is often initially just a creature of the construction companies. If, at the time the construction contracts are negotiated, the project company has no independent management and the contracts end up being rather favourable to the contractors, there is a risk that the contracts will be unacceptable to lenders when the time comes for the finance to be arranged. In cases such as this, serious consideration should be given to giving the project company effective and independent management and separate legal representation from the very beginning or at least trying to settle the contracts in a way that is not too blatantly one-sided. The alternative is for the sponsors to be forced to renegotiate the main contracts by the lenders (which may result in ill-feeling).

By contrast, many projects (especially large projects) will be structured deliberately to insulate the project company from as many risks as possible. In these cases, the project company is intended to be a mere financing vehicle and risks will be "passed through" it. In a power project, part of the price the power purchaser has to pay the project company generating the electricity will frequently be a "capacity charge" which is made up of all of the project company's "fixed" costs. Another part will be an "energy charge" which consists of the project company's fuel supply and other variable costs. Taking the pass-through concept in its purest form, if the project company has to pay a certain amount in a given period to the lenders by way of repayment of their loans and the payment of interest, an equivalent amount will be included in the capacity charge payable by the power purchaser for the same period. Equally, if the project company has to pay a certain amount for its fuel supply in a given period, an equivalent amount will be included in the energy charge payable by the power purchaser for that period. The fixed costs that would typically be passed through in this type of structure are fixed operating costs (such as salaries and insurance premia) and debt service costs, although in sophisticated structures other costs may also be included (such as a dividend "cost" to provide the project company's shareholders with a return on their investment). A direct pass-through of costs in a project where the project company is meant to be capable of running the project independently of its shareholders can be criticised because it does not encourage the project company to be efficient. If the pass-through is effectively only to one of a number of shareholders in the project company, this can also be seen as unfair. Because of this, various techniques have been developed to incentivise the project company and encourage it to be efficient. The most obvious method of achieving these ends is only to allow it to pass through some or all of its costs if it meets certain performance targets.

In a pass-through structure where the project company incurs pass-through costs in different currencies and the project company is not supposed to take any foreign exchange risk, the purchaser should either make his payments in the various component currencies or in one currency, but in an amount which will allow the project company to purchase the amounts in the other currencies which it needs. If it is not intended to pass through the foreign exchange risk, then the project company will usually be required by its lenders to effect some form of hedging (although a totally effective hedging programme may be difficult if the level of the project company's future revenue is uncertain).

It is important to appreciate that some projects require not only costs but also legal liabilities to be passed through the project company. This is often the case with large infrastructure projects based on a concession where (because of the huge risk involved) there is little or no direct sponsor support and the project company is a pure vehicle, a mere repository for contractual rights and obligations with no real technical expertise or back-up. Such a company will probably not manage the construction contract itself (it will employ a project management company to do this) and it will not operate the project itself (it will employ an operation and maintenance company to do this). In this sort of case, the lenders will get understandably nervous about any residual project risks which remain with the project company and may insist that any project-related obligation placed on the project company under the concession be passed through the company.

In other words, if the project company has to give a design warranty to the person granting the concession, the lenders may insist that it receives a warranty in identical terms from its contractor. If it is liable to pay a certain amount of liquidated damages under the concession agreement if completion of the project is delayed, the contractor must be liable to pay an equal amount of liquidated damages to it. This process is commonly referred to as attempting to make the contracts "back-to-back" and can be incredibly time-consuming.[1] Probably the only realistic way to

---

[1] In a concession-based project, one of the main back-to-back issues is seeking to ensure that, if the project company can be forced, under the terms of the concession agreement, to accept a specific price for a variation requested by the person granting the concession, the contractor must carry out the variation for the same price under the construction contract.

26

prevent this sort of process turning into a documentary nightmare is for the sponsors and other relevant parties to accept from the very beginning that they may themselves have to accept (as against the project company) obligations in the same terms as those imposed on the project company under the concession agreement. Having the project company accept an unduly onerous obligation under the concession agreement may be an expedient way of getting the concession agreement signed, but it may be storing up trouble for the future.

3.3 COMPULSORY COMPETITIVE TENDERING ("CCT")

Before moving on to consider the terms of various of the key contracts that are likely to make up a project, it is important to bear in mind that some of the most important of those contracts may have to be let following compulsory competitive tendering or "CCT". This will almost invariably be the case where the main contract to be let (in the present context, usually a concession agreement) is to be let by central or local government. The E.C.'s legislation on CCT, the United Kingdom's implementation of the various E.C. Directives and the economic justification for CCT are discussed in section 9.2(c). This section discusses general practice issues for those involved in organising a competition or a bid under any CCT rules. A competition is usually preceded by a pre-qualification round which is used to narrow down the number of participants in the competition by eliminating potential tenderers who are unlikely to have the ability and/or resources to carry out the contract in question.

The person organising the competition for the award of a contract (the "authority") will need to ensure that the competition is run fairly and within the applicable CCT rules or regulations, that the competition produces the best value for money and that the selection of the preferred bidder and the award of the final contract are as immune from challenge as possible. There is a great deal of interplay between these three objectives. For example, the best value for money in relation to a project might not actually be delivered by the specification that the authority includes in its invitation to bid or "ITB". The authority needs to encourage innovation in order to solicit bids with novel approaches which it has not thought of, but it also needs to impose some discipline on the competitive process. The classic response to this — so long as the

27

relevant CCT rules or regulations allow it — is for the authority to include in the ITB a very general specification (usually just listing the required outputs) and to invite variant bids. An authority should usually stipulate that variant bids will only be allowed if a tenderer submits a conforming standard bid. It will probably be required to stipulate this in any event by the relevant CCT rules or regulations: the point is to ensure that, if none of the variants submitted is acceptable, the authority can fall back on the standard bids and make a fair determination between them. The classic response is itself not without its difficulties: if the authority specifies that it wishes a power plant with three 100 MW turbines, can it accept a variant bid for two 175 MW turbines? Such a variant bid might be put forward by a particular tenderer who only builds turbines of the larger size. Although over the stated specification, such a bid might be very attractive for the authority because the incremental cost of the extra 50 MW of installed capacity might be very cheap. Subject to the underlying CCT rules or regulations, the answer should lie in the terms of the ITB which should allow variant bids to depart from certain less essential parts of the authority's specification so long as other key parts are complied with. A technique often used is to state certain of the criteria are *minimum* criteria, inviting tenderers to submit bids which offer better performance.

The relevant CCT rules or regulations may require an authority to award a contract to the lowest bidder or — like the World Bank guidelines (see below) or the E.C. rules (see section 9.2(c)) — allow the authority to take other factors (such as reliability of equipment and length of warranties) into consideration. If other factors can be taken into consideration, the authority clearly needs to consider the detail in which it wishes to set out those factors in the ITB. The greater the detail, the more ammunition it gives to a losing tenderer to argue that its bid met more of the criteria than that of the preferred bidder. Formal "point scoring" systems are usually not included in an ITB, although the authority will often indicate (and may often actually be required to indicate) which of the various factors it regards as more important. Although formal point scoring systems may not necessarily be included in an ITB, some authorities do actually adopt them behind the scenes. The deletion by a tenderer of certain clauses of a model contract attached to an ITB might result in a fixed amount being added to that tenderer's price, for example. Such a point scoring system — even one operated behind the scenes — is a two-edged sword. On the one hand, it may enable the authority to establish objectivity and fairness, but, on the other, it may again provide a disgruntled losing tenderer with ammunition with which to challenge the final award.

3.3 Compulsory Competitive Tendering ("CCT")

Clearly, the ITB is a critical document from the authority's point of view. It should obviously be drafted to give the authority as much flexibility in running the competition as possible and, properly drafted, it should be capable of providing the authority with a great deal of protection against challenge. One of the most frequently encountered problems with competitions is whether or not the authority can accept a bid that is late (*i.e.* submitted past the deadline contained in the ITB). The robust response is to give the authority the ability to accept late bids in the ITB itself. This may not always be possible under the relevant CCT rules or regulations, however. Another problem is the possibility that the authority may have actually produced such a tight specification that no one can submit a confirming bid. The usual solution to this is to state in the ITB that, if a tenderer really cannot submit a confirming bid, then, if it still wishes to bid, it must state the reasons why it cannot submit a fully conforming bid, submit a bid with the minimum number of changes and certify that these changes are indeed the minimum necessary. When drafting the ITB, it is important to appreciate that the ITB may itself constitute an enforceable contract, at least insofar as the rules contained within it for the running of the competition are concerned. It may be possible to state in the ITB that it is not intended to have contractual effect or, alternatively, to exclude contractual rights and remedies. Other, non-contractual, remedies (such as judicial review and the express rights of challenge required by the E.C.'s CCT legislation and implemented by domestic legislation) may not be capable of being excluded, however.

Tactics abound in competitions, particularly when the authority is not required simply to choose the lowest price. Should an authority shortlist two or more tenderers or should it award "preferred bidder" status to just one tenderer? If it shortlists two or more tenderers, to what level of detail should it seek to negotiate their bids before awarding "preferred bidder" status to one of them? Should it, for example, negotiate a final form of draft concession agreement with each shortlisted tenderer or is it safe to award "preferred bidder" status to one of them after a few rounds of clarificatory meetings, leaving much of the detail to be negotiated later? If a preferred bidder is selected, should one or more of the losing bids be kept formally in reserve and, if so, for how long (*i.e.* how long is the preferred bidder going to be given to finalise the deal)? The longer the authority keeps the tenderers "on the hook", competing against each other, the longer it is able to keep the upper hand in negotiations. In fact, the award of "preferred bidder" status can cause the authority to lose much, if not all, bargaining power,

29

particularly if a public announcement is made of the award: the preferred bidder's competitors will effectively have been stood down and the longer the detailed negotiations drag on, the more desperate the authority usually is actually to finalise the deal and not to lose face by trying to reopen the competition. From a tenderer's point of view, however, the longer he has to spend negotiating in detail before he knows that he has won the deal, the more he has to lose by way of money and effort expended on what might turn out to be a losing bid.

An area which illustrates this tension between the authority, keen to maintain its bargaining position, and its tenderers, keen to keep their development costs within sensible bounds, is the nature of any financing commitment which has to accompany any bid. The authority will be keen to see that the tenderers have underwritten finance, but each of the tenderers will usually be reluctant to provide this because obtaining a true underwriting commitment from banks will involve paying an underwriting fee and meeting the costs of an initial due diligence exercise conducted by the banks and their advisers. Tenderers usually try to offer a form of support letter from their banks in which the banks state that they have done a certain amount of due diligence and would in principle lend to support the bid in question but that further due diligence is required in order for them to give a binding commitment to lend. Tenderers usually try to persuade their banks to give such a commitment for a work fee at most. The problems for the authority are obvious: it could select a preferred bidder only to find either that that tenderer's financing collapses before financial close or that the banks have demands arising out of their fuller due diligence which will fundamentally alter the project from the authority's point of view.

There is no right answer to the above issues for an authority but it is interesting to note that there was a movement in the United Kingdom PFI deals towards appointing a preferred bidder but not making the appointment public. Losing bidders would then be told that their bids were being kept in reserve unless they wished to be debriefed as to why they had lost, in which case their bids could no longer be accepted if, for whatever reason, the authority could not subsequently achieve financial close with the preferred bidder.

The export credit and multilateral agencies[2] usually have their own requirements in relation to CCT for contracts which they finance.[3] The World Bank, for example, believes that its various

---

[2] See sections 8.2 and 8.3.

[3] International procedures tend to be rather more flexible than domestic ones. For an example of the more prescriptive approach in a domestic environment, see the provisions relating to CCT by local authorities set out in Part I of the Local Government Act 1988.

requirements in relation to the efficient implementation of projects and giving all eligible bidders an opportunity to compete can usually best be realised through international competitive bidding ("ICB"). It will therefore generally require its borrowers to obtain goods and works through ICB and it has published its own guidelines for the procedures to be followed.[4] It will cancel that portion of any World Bank loan allocated to any goods and works which have been misprocured.[5] The World Bank applies its guidelines to BOT or similar schemes[6] by either requiring that the project company is selected by ICB (in which case the project company can itself procure goods, works and services using its own procedures) or, if the project company is not so selected, that the project company procures goods, works and services using ICB.[7] The World Bank acknowledges that the selection of a project company for a BOT scheme using ICB may need a procedure comprising several stages "in order to arrive at the optimal combination of evaluation criteria". It acknowledges that the evaluation criteria for a BOT scheme may include the cost and size of any financing that is involved, the performance specifications of the facilities in question, the cost charged to the potential user or users, other income generated by the facilities and the period of the facilities' depreciation.

The World Bank's guidelines are a useful guide as to how to carry out any ICB process. By way of example, the following statements in those guidelines offer sound general guidance:

(a) The ITB must clearly state the type of contract to be entered into. The guidelines state that the most common types of contracts provide for payment on the basis of either a lump sum, unit prices, reimbursable cost plus fees or any combination of these methods. Reimbursable cost contracts are acceptable to the World Bank only in exceptional circumstances (*e.g.* where there is high risk) or where costs cannot be determined in advance with sufficient accuracy. In

---

[4] *Guidelines on Procurement under IBRD Loans and IDA Credits,* published by the World Bank (5th ed., 1995) (the "World Bank Procurement Guidelines"). See also *Procurement Policies and Rules* published by EBRD (revised March 1996), which employ a slightly lighter touch. IFC appears to take a more relaxed attitude still. Because IFC lends to the private sector (see section 8.3), it takes the view that there is less likely to be flagrant favouritism towards contractors of the same nationality. It does not therefore require the World Bank's procurement guidelines to be followed but instead simply has a general requirement that the contracts let in any of its deals must have been competitively awarded.

[5] *ibid.,* 1.13.

[6] See section 3.5.

[7] World Bank Procurement Guidelines, para. 3.13.

each such case, the reimbursable cost contract in question must nevertheless still include "appropriate incentives" to limit costs.[8]

(b) Where the ITB relates to a turnkey contract[9] or to large complex plants, a two-stage bidding procedure may be used. The first stage would require the submission of unpriced *technical* proposals on the basis of a conceptual design or performance specifications. The second stage would follow a round of clarifications on the technical proposals (which might require the issue of an amended ITB) and would consist of the submission of final technical proposals and priced bids.[10]

(c) Bid security (typically in the form of an on-demand bond) should be set at an amount which will protect the authority against irresponsible bids but which will not discourage bidders.[11]

(d) ITB's must state, *inter alia*, the schedule for completion of the works, minimum performance requirements and the warranty and maintenance requirements.[12]

(e) All prospective tenderers must be provided with the same information.[13]

(f) The authority should specify in the ITB that it requires ISO standards[14] and the specification contained in an ITB should be based on relevant characteristics or performance requirements. References to brand names should be avoided (in order to stimulate competition), but if it is necessary to refer to brand names, the words "or equivalent" need to be added after the reference.[15]

(g) ITB's should require security (in the form of a performance bond or bank guarantee) in an amount sufficient to protect the authority in the case of a breach of contract and an appropriate portion of this security should extend beyond

---

[8] *ibid.*, para. 2.2.
[9] See the end of section 3.6.
[10] World Bank Procurement Guidelines, para. 2.6.
[11] *ibid.*, para. 2.14.
[12] *ibid.*, para. 2.16.
[13] *ibid.*, para. 2.18. In practice this will mean that any questions raised with the authority by a prospective tenderer must be circulated to all other prospective tenderers together with a copy of the authority's response.
[14] *ibid.*, para. 2.19.
[15] *ibid.*, para. 2.20.

completion of the works to cover liability during any defects period. As an alternative, a percentage of the contract price may be retained until the expiry of the defects period, however.[16]

(h) ITB's should require liquidated damages to be payable if there is delay in completing the works in question or if the works do not meet guaranteed performance levels.[17]

(i) Bids must be "substantially responsive" to the requirements of the ITB and the other bidding documents; if any bid is not, it should not be considered further. A bid will not be "substantially responsive" if it contains material deviations from or reservations to the terms, conditions and specifications in the bidding documents.[18]

(j) The bid with the "lowest evaluation cost", but not necessarily the lowest submitted price, shall be selected for the award.[19] The factors (in addition to price) which will be taken into account when determining the lowest evaluated bid must be stated in the ITB and may include the payment schedule, the delivery time, efficiency and compatibility of equipment, availability of service and spare parts and any training, safety and environmental benefits. Factors other than price that will be taken into account shall, to the extent practicable, be expressed in monetary terms (which will often be impossible) or (which is more practicable) given a relative weight in the ITB.[20]

(k) An ITB should usually provide that the authority may reject all bids, *i.e.* it is not obliged to award the contract. The World Bank considers that rejection of all bids is justified when there is lack of effective competition or when all of the bids are not "substantially responsive" to the requirements of the ITB and the other bidding documents.[21]

(l) A tenderer must not be required, as a condition of being awarded the contract, to carry out work not specified in the

---

[16] *ibid.*, para. 2.38. See the comments in section 3.6(g) on bonding and retentions in construction contracts. Retentions are not normally appropriate in a BOT scheme with a concession agreement; the authority in such cases will normally protect itself by reducing the fees (or tariff) it pays if the service provided to it does not meet the required standards. Bonding is, of course, unpopular with contractors and tenderers.
[17] World Bank Procurement Guidelines, para. 2.40.
[18] *ibid.*, para 2.47.
[19] Compare the "most economically advantageous tender" concept under the EC procurement rules (see sections 9.2(c)).
[20] World Bank Procurement Guidelines, para. 2.51.
[21] *ibid.*, para. 2.59.

ITB or otherwise to modify his original bid. Tenderers must not be requested or permitted to alter their bids after the deadline for receipt of bids, although the authority may ask tenderers for any clarifications necessary in order to evaluate their bid.[22]

3.4 SHAREHOLDERS AGREEMENTS

There are really no aspects of shareholders agreements which are unique to project finance. Most of the general problems associated with shareholders agreements for joint ventures will be found in a project financing, however. There will naturally, for example, be conflicts of interests where shareholders include the construction contractor or (as happens quite frequently) the host government or one of its public entities. Minority shareholders will need protecting.

It is probably worth running through some of the general problems that will be encountered in the relationships between shareholders in a joint venture if only to give the reader a quick orientation. Some of the issues listed below may be best resolved in the project company's constitutional documents rather than a shareholders agreement, but this is a point on which to take careful advice on a case by case basis if the project company is incorporated overseas.

(a) *Contingent capital contributions.* Contingent capital contributions are becoming more popular in project finance as the banks' attitude to debt-equity ratios in projects becomes more sophisticated. Banks no longer insist on all of the shareholders' contributions being subscribed and expended before they will lend at all, but are now prepared to allow the shareholders' capital contributions to be made on a phased basis, pro rata with drawings under the banks' credit agreement, or even towards the end of the project's development stage (so-called "back-ended equity"). Back-ended equity has obvious attractions to shareholders, not the least of which is that it can help improve their rate of return from the project.

If any capital contributions are to be made (whether by way of shares or loans) after the commencement of the project, each

---

[22] *ibid.*, paras 2.45 and 2.58. This is presumably subject, however, to what the World Bank Procurement Guidelines say about a two-stage bidding procedure for turnkey contracts and large complex plants (see paragraph (b) above) where an amended bid (at least in relation to technical aspects) is expressly contemplated. Compare the more flexible "negotiated procedure" under the E.C. procurement rules (see section 9.2(c)).

shareholder will have to take a view on the other shareholders' creditworthiness. Will the other shareholders exist or be good for the money when the time comes for the further capital injections to be made? If there is unease about any particular shareholder's creditworthiness in these circumstances, some form of credit enhancement may be necessary. The most obvious (and most frequently seen) form is the provision by the shareholder in question of a bank guarantee (or standby letter of credit). The reason for the bank guarantee's relative popularity is that, although the shareholder in question will have to pay the issuing bank a guarantee fee, it will not have to tie up its own capital until the money is needed (which is the drawback of the other most usual method, the provision of cash collateral). The decision on a shareholder's creditworthiness and the level of any required credit enhancement is often taken by the host government (and not by the other shareholders) since the host government has as great an interest (if not a greater interest) in ensuring that contingent capital contributions are made.

(b) *Contributions in kind*. Sometimes the only equity contribution a party can make is a contribution in kind. This is often the case where there are local shareholders in projects in emerging markets where the usual form of equity contribution from the local shareholders is a contribution of the real estate required by the project.

Where a contribution in kind is made by a shareholder, the other shareholders will be concerned to ensure that an acceptable value is placed on such contribution since that shareholder might otherwise obtain a disproportionate return. Valuation may prove difficult in an emerging market which has a limited economy, a restricted or non-existent free market and/or exchange controls, however.

(c) *Pre-emption rights*. Pre-emption rights are one of the ways in which the private nature of a joint venture can be safeguarded. If one of the parties wishes to sell an interest in the joint venture to a third party, he is first obliged to offer such interest to the other existing parties to the joint venture. The price at which such offer is made can be the price the third party is prepared to pay or an assessed "fair" price.

(d) *Conflicts of interest*. Where a project company has or is likely to have any contract with any of its shareholders, the other shareholders will be keen to exclude the contracting shareholder from any decisions taken by the project company or its shareholders in relation to that contract.

(e) *Non-competition clauses*. An important aspect of any joint venture is that the participants in the joint venture are pulling

35

together towards a common objective and none of them should do anything to undermine the achievement of that objective. This aspect of joint ventures is often reinforced by non-competition clauses — agreements by each party not to undertake any activity in competition with the joint venture. These clauses need to be carefully considered in the light of applicable competition laws.

The main piece of United Kingdom domestic legislation is the RTPA.[23] The inclusion of a non-competition clause in a joint venture or shareholders agreement is likely to require particulars of all of the agreements forming part of the overall transaction[24] to be given to the Office of Fair Trading ("OFT") within three months of the date of the agreement. If this is not done, the non-competition clause will be void and unenforceable.[25] The agreement is then placed on a public register although part of the register is confidential[26] and application can be made to the OFT to put an agreement on the confidential section. Although there are provisions for the OFT to refer a registered agreement to the Restrictive Practices Court for a determination as to whether or not any restrictions it contains are against the public interest,[27] this is unlikely to happen in the case of normal non-competition clauses in a joint venture or shareholders agreement relating to a normal project. The RTPA will not generally apply to non-competition clauses given in relation to a project which is wholly outside the United Kingdom, even though one or more of the shareholders is carrying on business in the United Kingdom.[28]

Non-competition clauses may also fall within the scope of Article 85 of the E.C. Treaty depending on their impact on the common market and the size of the relevant project.

3.5 CONCESSION AGREEMENTS AND BOT PROJECTS

A concession is essentially a licence. In the context of project finance, it is usually granted by a governmental or quasi-

---

[23] Plans for a Competition Bill which would have repealed the RTPA in its entirety and replaced it with a general prohibition of anti-competitive agreements based on Art. 85 of the E.C. Treaty fell victim to a lack of Parliamentary time in the last session of the 1992-7 Parliament. The new Labour government has now resurrected the proposals, however.

[24] This requirement may mean that details of the credit agreement have to be given to the OFT in a project financing.

[25] s.35(1) RTPA. It is also unlawful to give effect to any relevant restrictions until the particulars have been furnished.

[26] See s.23(3) RTPA.

[27] See s.1(2)(c) RTPA

[28] See paras. 6 and 9 of Sched. 3 to the RTPA. But note that the RTPA may apply if the project involves goods to be exported from the U.K.

governmental authority. The concession is the cornerstone of the "BOT" ("build, operate, transfer") project finance model. In this model, a concession is granted to a concession holder who is required to build the relevant project facilities or piece of infrastructure, operate them for a fixed period and, at the end of such period, transfer them back to the person who originally granted the concession. A BOT project will therefore usually have a definite life and part of the skill when the projects are put out to tender is to put together a financing package which will ensure that the lenders get repaid and the shareholders get a sufficient return on their investment before the concession terminates.

A concession agreement can take many forms, but the following is a list of typical provisions that may be found:

(a) an obligation on the project company to design the relevant facilities or piece of infrastructure to a stated specification and then to construct such facilities by a stated date (often with liquidated damages being payable if this date is not met);

(b) provisions entitling the person granting the concession to vary the above specification;

(c) provisions enabling the person granting the concession (or his representatives) to visit the site and inspect progress and drawings;

(d) warranties (for example, as to fitness for purpose) from the project company relating to its construction work;

(e) an obligation on the project company to operate the facilities or infrastructure item at and to maintain them or it to stated levels for a stated period;

(f) an obligation to place a minimum amount of work with local contractors and to train local labour in the use of the facilities;

(g) an obligation on the person granting the concession to obtain (by the use of compulsory purchase powers) and transfer to the project company any real estate needed for the project;

(h) an obligation on the person granting the concession to carry out any works or abide by any undertakings which are necessary on his part for the project to be successful (*e.g.* in the context of a bridge, this may involve agreeing to build connecting roads and, in the context of a new urban transit system, this may involve agreeing to close down competing forms of public transport (such as bus routes));

(i) provisions requiring the project company, at the request of the person granting the concession, to allow other parties onto the site in order to upgrade the facilities[29];

(j) provisions for the payment of a concession fee by the project company;

(k) provisions entitling the concessionaire to charge relevant fees or fares or provisions requiring the person granting the concession to pay fees or a tariff to the project company in return for the project company delivering a service under the concession agreement;

(l) provisions giving the person granting the concession some degree of control over fees or fares charged by the project company (although this is very much dependent on the philosophy of the concession (see below));

(m) a "financial balance" clause (this is explained below);

(n) a provision requiring the project company to apply any insurance proceeds it receives for physical damage in reinstatement or repair of the facilities damaged or destroyed[30];

(o) a provision stating that the concession agreement takes priority over all the other project agreements in the case of conflict (although, of course, such a provision strictly only has effect as between the parties to the concession agreement and does not as a matter of strict contract law bind others (*e.g.* the lenders));

(p) provisions entitling the person granting the concession to intervene and run the project himself (without necessarily terminating the concession agreement) should the project company fail to carry out the project or fail to do so to the required standard[31];

---

[29] This is a feature of the U.K. government's DBFO road schemes. The fear is that, without this right, the project company can hold the person granting the concession to ransom if, for example, the telephony along a stretch of motorway comprised within a concession becomes outdated and needs to be replaced. The project company is usually able to bid to do these so-called "additional works" itself.

[30] See the discussion on this topic in section 5.8(e).

[31] This can sometimes result in the person granting the concession insisting that the other contracting parties to a project enter into a direct agreement with him. See section 6.4 for a description of the direct agreements that such parties are usually required to enter into with the project company's lenders.

(q) provisions entitling the person who granted the concession to terminate it in certain circumstances (*e.g.* breach by the project company of a provision of the concession agreement and insolvency of the project company);

(r) provisions dealing with the transfer of assets and personnel (or, possibly, the shares in the project company) at the end of the concession period (or earlier termination)[32];

(s) restrictions on the sponsors disposing of shares in the project company[33]; and

(t) a prohibition on the project company assigning its rights under the concession agreement.

A concession agreement may also contain assurances about the granting of subsidies and tax concessions necessary for the project to be economically viable, although this will depend on the nature of the government entity granting the concession and such matters may be dealt with in separate documentation with more appropriate government entities. Such matters, particularly in relation to tax, may need parliamentary (as opposed to governmental) approval and careful advice needs to be taken on the constitutional position.

Where the person granting the concession pays fees or a tariff to the project company in return for services under the concession agreement, the concession agreement will need to contain clauses which define the scope of those payments. Making or withholding payments is, after all, one of the simplest (and most effective) ways of allocating risk. This feature of a concession agreement was developed to an extremely high level in the United Kingdom government DBFO road schemes. Actually charging road users tolls for using a motorway is, for the present, politically unacceptable in the United Kingdom. The United Kingdom government nevertheless asked the private sector to fund the development of a number of roads and to take the risk on traffic flows that the private sector would have taken had the government been able to let a concession for a properly tolled motorway. The manner in which the government achieved its political and economic objectives was to pay the project company a "shadow toll", *i.e.* a toll which was dependent on

---

[32] These provisions may sometimes require the project company to ensure that the project facilities meet stated "handback" requirements and to set money aside in a sinking fund towards the end of the concession in order to defray the cost of meeting such requirements.
[33] Sponsors will normally seek to have these restrictions fall away (or significantly reduced) two years after completion by which time, they argue, the project will have demonstrated not only its integrity and economic viability but also its ability to survive independently of its original shareholders.

the number and type of vehicles using the road in question. This raised a number of complex issues. The government reserved the right to charge actual tolls on the road if this ever became politically possible but agreed that, if it did this, it would still have to pay the concessionaire shadow tolls. But actual tolling would obviously influence traffic flows. Should the concessionaire be insulated from this risk and, if so, how? What if the government introduced user-paid tolls on a motorway which led onto a motorway which was the subject of a shadow toll concession and thereby diverted traffic away from the shadow-tolled motorway? What if traffic on the shadow-tolled motorway wildly exceeded the traffic forecasters' most optimistic projections? Was it right to effectively give the private sector a massive, windfall shadow toll payment in such circumstances? Similar issues of risk allocation arise in all of the United Kingdom PFI schemes where the concession is for the provision of a service.[34]

The "financial balance" clause referred to in (m) above is a clause which seeks to put the concession holder back into the same financial position he would have been in but for the occurrence of certain risks which have been assumed by the person granting the concession. (For example, the person granting the concession may have assumed the change in law risk, *i.e.* the risk that the construction or operation of the project in question may be made more costly as a result of a change in law after the concession agreement is executed.) Financial balance clauses have to address two principal issues: first, how the extent of the damage to the finances of the project is to be calculated and, secondly, how the damage is to be put right. On the first point, the parties can either simply leave the extent of the damage to be agreed between them or, in the absence of agreement, to be resolved by litigation, arbitration or any other form of disputes resolution procedure they have provided for or try to be a little more scientific and seek to ascertain the extent of the problem by using an agreed computer model of the project's economics. Reference to an agreed computer model will not totally eliminate the possibility of dispute: it will not tell the parties how much extra a change in the design of the project's facilities will cost, but it should at least give the parties an idea of (for example) the extra amounts of interest that may have to be paid to finance the additional cost once the additional cost is agreed upon or otherwise determined. On the second point, there are various ways of redressing the balance: the person granting the concession can be required to make a compensating cash payment (in one lump sum or in

---

[34] See section 10.1 below.

instalments), the period of the concession can be extended or (if these are otherwise controlled (see below)) the fees or fares charged by the concession holder can be increased. Not surprisingly, the payment of cash compensation is likely to be the least popular form of redress for the person granting a concession.

There are two fundamental points of principle that any governmental agency involved in a BOT infrastructure project needs to decide in the context of the concession agreement and the project as a whole:

(i) *To what extent does it wish to become involved in the detail of the project and of the other project documentation?*

(ii) *To what extent (if at all) does it wish to control the level at which fees or fares are set by the project company?*

There are two aspects to the issue in (i) above. The first aspect is to do with the basic allocation of risk during the construction phase. If the person granting the concession specifies a detailed design for a particular project, the project company will be able to claim that a defect in the project's performance is due to a faulty design. Similarly, if the person granting the concession gives any directions as to how any particular piece of work should be carried out, the project company will be able to claim that a defect in performance is due to compliance with that direction. For these reasons, designs specified in a concession agreement are usually only conceptual designs, with the project company bearing the responsibility for developing a working detailed design. Sometimes there is not even a conceptual design but the project company is instead required to design a particular project or piece of equipment to meet specified "output parameters", *i.e.* a required end result such as a power station capable of generating 300 MWh in an ambient temperature range of 10°C to 30°C. Rights to give directions or otherwise to interfere with construction or operation are often treated slightly differently in that they may be reserved as a precaution but would only be exercised after taking careful advice.

The second aspect of the issue in (i) above is related in that interference in the terms of contracts that the project company enters into is another way of controlling a project.

The most robust approach, however, is for the host government simply to take the view that all of the matters that concern it (such as the basic project specification, the time for completion, etc.) should be dealt with in the concession agreement and that it is for the project company to determine what contracts it needs in order to carry out its obligations under the concession agreement. Such a view can be backed-up by including a provision in the concession

41

agreement that the concession agreement takes priority over all of the other project agreements (see (o) above) and making this provision bind all of the other parties to such agreements by requiring the project company only to enter into other project agreements which recognise this principle. The alternative approach is for the person granting the concession to approve all of the project agreements when they are first entered into and all amendments to those agreements. This can be a time consuming process and the relevant governmental officials and their professional advisers may not be close enough to the private sector documentation to express any meaningful view on the adequacy or fairness of such documentation (although they may well, of course, be able to take a view on whether or not it is at least consistent with the concession agreement). There may be instances, however, where some of the provisions of the other project agreements are of critical importance to the host government and when interference in their detailed terms is therefore essential. This might be the case, for example, where the project company is thinly capitalised and the design of the project is highly novel. Any design warranty from the project company would be of limited value and as a result the host government would be concerned to ensure that the main contractor gave the project company a proper warranty so that a company of substance would be liable to rectify any problems or pay damages (albeit to the project company) if the design was faulty.

As far as the issue in (ii) above is concerned, the attitude of the person granting the concession to the setting of fees or fares can have a dramatic impact on the project economics. What is essentially at stake is whether or not cost overruns (in both the construction stage and the operation stage) and risks such as inflation can, in the last resort, be passed on to the end-user (often the public at large). In infrastructure projects, this is a major political issue. There are, of course, various alternatives to total control and total freedom: fee and fare levels can be index-linked or subject to review by an independent regulator (although, in the latter case, a decision needs to be taken on what particular aspects of the pricing structure the regulator can review). Restricting fees and fares may mean that the person granting the concession has to pay shadow tolls (see above) or other subsidies in order to render the project viable.

Another issue on which the person granting a concession should formulate a view is the issue of whether, in a BOT project, any amount should be payable by him to the concession holder if the concession agreement is terminated by reason of a default by the concession holder. On a termination of the concession agreement in such a project, most, if not all, of the project's assets will usually become vested in the person granting the concession[35] and the question is whether this can happen without payment (as many concession agreements provide in the case of termination by reason of a default by the concession holder). The position that the concession holder is in breach and is therefore entitled to nothing may be capable of being impugned on the following grounds:

(a) It amounts to expropriation without compensation. This may be unconstitutional or be contrary to a human rights convention to which the host government is a party (*e.g.* the European Convention on Human Rights).

(b) It is effectively a penalty for breach of contract.[36] This argument will be at its strongest where the concession holder's default is relatively minor.

(c) The person who granted the concession has been unjustly enriched and the host jurisdiction's general laws on unjust enrichment require some form of payment to be made.

The absence of any payment in these circumstances will certainly be unpopular with banks since they (who will have funded the bulk of the project's capital costs) will effectively be taking an enormous risk on the concession holder's ability to comply with the terms of the concession agreement. It must be said, however, that, although unpopular, the absence of payment in these circumstances is not necessarily always fatal to a project's "bankability" (on which see section 4.3(c) below).

The inclusion of a clause providing for payment to be made in these circumstances is, by the same token, usually unpopular with the person granting the concession for various reasons. First, there is the purely emotional issue: why should the person granting the concession pay compensation when he is the innocent party and it is

---

[35] Often this is because the real estate rights are conferred on the project company by a lease (or similar interest) granted by the person granting the concession and, on a termination of the lease, all buildings and fixtures on the land become the property of the lessor.
[36] There is a more general debate about the penalty doctrine when the person granting the concession has to pay compensation on a termination of the concession agreement for his own default. The amount payable is often designed to repay the banks and provide some form of compensation for the sponsors. As it is a somewhat artificial amount, it may be capable of being impugned as a penalty. It may be possible, in certain circumstances, however, to structure the payment of compensation as the payment of liquidated damages. This will not necessarily always be effective under English law because of the requirement for liquidated damages to be a genuine pre-estimate of loss, but the courts seem to be evidencing a reluctance to re-open the commercial bargains of sophisticated parties. See *Welsh Development Agency v. Exfinco* [1992] B.C.C. 270.

the project company which is in default? Secondly, if the person granting the concession is liable to pay compensation when the project company is in default, it would be all too easy for the project company to engineer defaults when the project encountered difficulties, forcing a termination of the concession agreement with the payment of compensation. Thirdly, if compensation is payable, the person granting the concession will be forced to use public revenues when the whole point of adopting a BOT structure was to ease the pressure on the public purse. (This particular objection might be capable of being met by either paying the compensation in instalments, however, or by engineering a solution whereby the person granting the concession accepts a novation of the project company's obligations to its banks.) In addition, the person granting the concession will also feel that any attempt in the concession agreement to quantify the amount of any payment of compensation may prejudice any claim he may have against the concession holder for damages for breach of the concession agreement.

Some projects have tried to reach some sort of a compromise by providing for compensation on a project company default only to be payable for the benefit of the banks. Even if this is done, it is philosophically wrong to pay the banks the amount of their loans outstanding because this will mean that they have not taken project risk. A better approach would be to pay compensation equal to the lesser of the amount due and owing to the banks and the net present value of the project's revenues. Even with this formulation, the person granting the concession will need some protection in relation to the amount due and owing to the banks. It should only be debt lent to finance the project in question and it may be desirable to limit the amount by reference to the original amortisation profile (so that, in this latter case, the person granting the concession is not adversely affected by any rescheduling or refinancing that takes place).

There are some difficult tax issues which are often overlooked in relation to the payment of compensation on termination. The main issue is that such compensation might be treated as the realisation of an asset (the contractual right represented by the concession) and so might therefore be subject to capital gains tax. If this is correct, it might be difficult to identify a base cost in some concessions (*e.g.* where nothing is paid for the grant of the concession) and so the possible tax charge would be very large. In addition, if compensation is paid by the person granting the concession to the project company in order to compensate the project company's shareholders for the loss of their investment, the compensation is being paid to the wrong party. There may be tax payable when the relevant amount is distributed by the project company to its shareholders and this will reduce the effective value of the compensation paid. Some concession agreements have provided for the compensation to be "grossed-up" in both of the above circumstances.

As is now obvious, the concession agreement is the main instrument by which the person granting the concession can seek to keep some degree of control over the project. It is important to realise that this control can be achieved not only by the inclusion of various undertakings on the part of the concession holder, but also through the termination events. An example of the latter is having as a termination event the actual or threatened suspension by the project company's banks of the project company's right to borrow money under the project credit agreement. Such a termination event will, not surprisingly, guarantee the person granting the concession a "seat at the table" in any ensuing discussions between the project company and the banks and should ensure that he is not kept on the sidelines (one of the United Kingdom government's alleged frustrations during the apparently bitter arguments between Eurotunnel and its contractors over the escalation of the Channel Tunnel's construction costs and how they were to be funded).

3.6 CONSTRUCTION CONTRACTS

Construction contracts are simple in theory but notoriously difficult in practice. The essence of a construction contract could not, in fact, be simpler: one person (the contractor) agrees to construct a building or a facility for another person (the employer) for agreed remuneration by an agreed time. The variants on this simple theme and the scope for abuse of bargaining position (on both sides) have led to various standard forms being developed by various participants in the construction industry[37] and it is now usual in major projects for one of these standard forms to be used as at least the basis for the final construction contract. One of the features of the general standard forms is that they attempt to produce a fair and

---

[37] See, for example, the JCT (Joint Contracts Tribunal) standard forms for U.K. building contracts and the standard forms of contract produced by ICE (the Institution of Civil Engineers, the Association of Consulting Engineers and the Federation of Civil Engineering Contractors) for major civil engineering projects and by FIDIC (Fédération Internationale des Ingénieurs-Conseils), based on ICE, for major international projects. FIDIC has now published a standard set of conditions for a turnkey construction contract: *Conditions of Contract for Design-Build and Turnkey*, (1995) (the so-called "Orange Book").

balanced contract for both the contractor and the employer and, because a fixed price turnkey construction contract is intended deliberately to transfer a greater degree of risk than is normally the case onto the contractor, they will require a fairly high degree of amendment if they are to form the basis of such a turnkey contract.

The key issues relating to a construction contract for any project financing are as follows:

(a) *How will the construction arrangements be structured?* In a complex construction project comprised of various interlocking parts (involving both civil and mechanical and electrical works), the basic decision to be taken is whether to have one contractor responsible for all of the works (a "turnkey" contract (see below)) or to have the individual contractors enter into separate contracts with the employer but to have them subject to control by one overall project manager (who enters into a project management agreement with the employer). Both structures have their advantages and disadvantages: with a turnkey contract, the turnkey contractor takes a risk on the performance of the sub-contractors he has to employ to carry out the specialist parts of the works and, with a project management agreement, the employer does not have a single entity from whom to claim damages (but will have to prove that one of the individual contractors was responsible for the relevant problem and claim from that individual contractor). There is a third option which is sometimes found in major international projects which is to have all of the contracting companies (with all of their specialities) form a construction consortium which enters into the construction contract with joint and several liability on the part of all of its members. The advantages of this approach are that no one contracting company in the consortium has to assume responsibility for the performance of the others (they all do) and the employer retains his single port of call for damages and remedial work.

(b) *Who is responsible for the design of the works?* As between the contractor and the employer, the responsibility for the design can be the employer's or the contractor's. In the more traditional (and simple) construction contract, design is the employer's responsibility: his team of architects and specialists will design the office block and the contractor simply has to build it. The alternative approach is for the employer to let a "design and build" construction contract where the contractor's professional team (or an independent designer commissioned by the contractor) has to come up with the design. Both approaches are found in major projects but the latter approach is more prevalent and is in any event more suited to international competitions where governments put large

46

infrastructure projects out to competitive tender. (Readers may recall the wide variety of designs (bridge and tunnel, road and rail tunnel and rail tunnel alone) submitted by the various consortia who originally bid for the Channel Tunnel concession in the United Kingdom.) If the design is the employer's responsibility and it does not work, there will be the potential for unlimited cost overruns. If the design is the contractor's responsibility and it does not work, the contractor will (subject to what is said in the following paragraph) be liable to make the design and project work within the terms of the fixed price turnkey construction contract.

If the contractor is responsible for the design, the crucial point for the employer is whether the contractor's obligation is merely to use *reasonable endeavours* to produce a design fit for the relevant purpose[38] or to produce a design which *is* fit for such purpose. The first level of obligation will only give the employer a claim against the contractor if he can (essentially) prove negligence; the second level of obligation is one of more or less strict liability. The stricter level of obligation may well be implied by law into a design and build construction contract and, in such a contract, if the contractor wishes only to be bound by the lesser level of obligation, the only safe course is to expressly state this.

(c) *Is there a fixed price for the works?* The price for the works in a major project is normally fixed to some degree but it is important to be aware of standard price "re-openers". A contractor's price may include provisional sums (estimates for work which he was, for whatever reason, not able to price accurately at the time of the award of the contract) and a mix of fixed price items of work and items for which he is to be paid on a cost reimbursement (plus agreed profit margin) basis. Furthermore, any fixed price will usually be capable of being increased for any extra work that the contractor has to carry out because of the occurrence of risks assumed by the employer. These risks would, in a typical construction contract, include the risk of unforeseen ground conditions,[39] the risk of the discovery of fossils and antiquities and the risk of a change in law affecting the works. An example of such a change in law would be a change in the health and safety requirements for an oil rig which required parts of the rig to be redesigned and parts of the construction work already done to be altered.[40] A

---

[38] Including meeting the required output specification (if any).

[39] Unforeseen ground conditions can be classified as: (a) unforeseen soil conditions (*e.g.* sand not rock), (b) unforeseen physical obstructions (such as cables and pipes) and (c) unforeseen levels of ground contamination.

[40] In this context, see, in relation to the U.K. sector of the North Sea, the recommendations on safety contained in the report of the *Public Inquiry into the Piper Alpha Disaster* (the "Cullen Report"), Cm1310, November 1990.

fixed contract price can, of course, also be increased by the employer varying the works.

In the larger projects, it is becoming increasingly common for the contract price to be expressed in prices of the day as at the time the contractor submits his bid in response to an invitation to tender and for this base price to be escalated (up to financial close) by reference to a specified index to take account of inflation.

(d) *Is there a fixed date for completion of the works?* Again, whilst a date for the completion of the works is invariably specified, there are usually certain risks assumed by the employer (for example, unforeseen ground conditions and adverse weather conditions) which will entitle the contractor to an extension of time and, of course, a variation of the works by the employer may also lead to an extension of time.

Liquidated damages for delay (see (f) below) are calculated by reference to the construction contract's date for completion and it is therefore essential for the employer to know with certainty what that date is. For this reason, construction contracts normally contain procedures which must be followed in order to ascertain the precise length of any extension of time and it is important that the contract invokes those procedures whenever an extension of time is possible.[41] If it does not, there is a terrible trap for the employer in that, under English law, the contractor may become entitled to a reasonable extension of time at law and the delay liquidated damages provisions will become inoperable.[42]

(e) *How is completion determined? What are its consequences?* Most construction contracts work on the basis that completion will occur prior to the date on which all of the works are complete to the last detail. In civil works construction contracts, the general test is one of practical completion, *i.e.* only minor works remain outstanding which will not affect the use of the project for its intended purpose. In construction contracts involving mechanical and electrical equipment, completion is generally a two stage process. First, there is mechanical completion, *i.e.* all of the plant and equipment that was to be installed has been installed with the exception of minor

---

[41] Ignoring the special case of delay caused by the employer, an extension of time is only permitted when the construction contract expressly states it is permitted. In order to avoid the trap under English law referred to above in relation to delays caused by the employer, it is essential that any construction contract governed by English law expressly includes delays caused by the employer as one of the express events giving rise to an extension of time ascertained in accordance with the contract's procedures.

[42] Time is in these circumstances said to be "at large". The employer can still claim damages for delay under the general law if the works are not completed within a reasonable time; he simply cannot claim *liquidated* damages. See, *e.g.*, *Dodd v. Churton* [1897] 1 Q.B. 562.

outstanding items recorded on a so-called "punch list". After mechanical completion, the plant and equipment has to pass various performance tests and, if it does, completion (or, as it is more frequently called in major construction contracts, takeover) occurs. Takeover can usually be achieved if the plant and equipment merely achieves required minimum performance levels in the tests. Performance liquidated damages (see (j) below) are generally payable, however, if the plant and equipment do not perform at higher guaranteed levels.

A contractor frequently faces a dilemma if, during commissioning, it is obvious that the plant and equipment is not performing well. Should he delay the performance tests (and suffer the payment of delay liquidated damaged because takeover has not occurred (see (f) below)) in an attempt to improve performance in the meantime and so lessen his liability to pay performance liquidated damages, or should he simply get the plant and equipment to pass the minimum performance levels, thereby stemming the payment of delay of liquidated damages[43]? In order to provide some relief for contractors in these circumstances, some construction contracts contain provisions allowing the contractor to continue to work on a problem for a limited period[44] after takeover (and after he has paid performance liquidated damages) in order to improve performance and, after a retest, to claim back some of the performance liquidated damages paid. An employer needs to carefully limit these provisions to ensure that the contractor cannot interrupt the operation of the plant. Typically, if the contractor has this type of right, he can only work on the plant and equipment in order to try to improve performance during periods of scheduled maintenance.

Construction contracts sometimes provide that completion occurs when an independent third party (a contract administrator or engineer (see (l) below)) certifies that the relevant test has been met. This formulation is clearly an attempt to minimise disputes. However, construction contracts also frequently state that completion occurs simply when the tests are passed (*i.e.* it is an objective test) or when the employer's agent certifies that the tests are passed (a mixture of a subjective and an objective test).

Some projects are extremely complex and comprise various independent sections, each with a function of its own. An example of such a project is a coal gasification power project where the gasifier and the power plant are discrete and capable of functioning independently from each other. Another example is a refinery with

---

[43] The contractor will, not surprisingly, usually take the lowest cost option.
[44] *e.g.* a year.

several chemical processes in each product train. In these cases, although it is obviously important to apply tests to each discrete section of equipment, the employer may also wish to have an overall completion test to demonstrate that all of the sections are functioning satisfactorily together.

Where a project is based on a concession, the "back-to-back" exercise carried out by the banks (see section 3.2 above) may lead to the banks insisting that completion under the construction contract can only occur when completion occurs under the concession agreement. This stance is unpopular with contractors because they are not a party to and have little influence on the concession agreement.

The consequences of takeover occurring usually include:

(i) by definition, the fact that liquidated damages for delay will no longer run;

(ii) risk in the project facilities passes from the contractor to the employer;

(iii) the employer is entitled to possession of the project facilities;

(iv) the defects period starts (see (j) below); and

(v) a percentage (typically 50 per cent) of any retention from the contract price becomes payable to the contractor (or a percentage of any bond given in lieu of a retention is released by the employer) (see (g) below).

Takeover is not usually relevant to transfer of title, since title to the project facilities usually passes earlier (see (h) below)).

(f) *Are liquidated damages payable for delay in achieving completion?* Liquidated damages are damages which are agreed by the parties in advance as a genuine pre-estimate of loss. So long as they are such a genuine pre-estimate and not a penalty, a person claiming liquidated damages under English law need not prove his loss.[45]

Contractors will usually say that a construction contract without delay liquidated damages will be cheaper than one with delay liquidated damages. To the extent this is true, the contractors are clearly charging the employer a premium for taking on what they perceive (or allege) to be an additional risk.

---

[45] Some jurisdictions, however, will allow liquidated damages provisions to be re-opened (whilst, paradoxically, allowing contractual penalties). See Art. 1384 of the Italian Civil Code.

50

(g) *How is the contract price to be paid?* It is rare indeed for the entire contract price in any construction project to be paid only when the works are completed. In a major project, this would put an intolerable working capital burden on the contractor and result in a commensurate increase in the contract price he was prepared to offer.

Instead, stage payments are common: the contractor is paid as he goes along, often against the issue of interim certificates by the contract administrator or engineer involved in the construction contract (see (l) below). There is usually also a retention (commonly in the region of 5 per cent) against each stage payment. The purpose of retentions is to incentivise the contractor to remedy any defects in the works and to provide a notional fund out of which the employer can himself rectify any such defects if the contractor fails to do so. The retentions are usually payable on the expiry of the defects liability period, although sometimes part is payable earlier (typically on takeover/completion). It is not uncommon to find the contractor procuring the issue of bank guarantees or bonds to the employer in lieu of retentions. This achieves the same result for the employer (the bond will provide the notional fund referred to above) but is more advantageous for the contractor in that it enhances his cash flow (he receives the full amount of his stage payments).

Two types of stage payment are frequently used in project finance. The first is payment against actual physical milestones such as the digging of foundations or the assembly of a major piece of equipment on site. The second (which is more commonly found in civil engineering projects such as the construction of motorways) is payment against value within a predetermined "payment envelope". This second type of payment involves the contractor being paid a predetermined amount so long as the value of work on site at any time is above a minimum threshold amount (the lower limit of the payment envelope). The function of the upper limit of the payment envelope is to provide a maximum rate of payment to the contractor. Not surprisingly, banks (through their technical advisers) subject the description of any milestones and the width of any payment envelope to considerable scrutiny. They are generally concerned to ensure that stage payments are only made against true value on site. Contractors usually try to weight as much of their payments as possible towards the early phases of a job. Not only does this enable them to at least break even if a project is cancelled in the middle of its construction phase, but it can also enable them to recoup very early on the full amount of any equity contribution they have made or have agreed to make to the project. There are

51

obvious implications for a contractor's commitment to see a project through if the stage payments are weighted too heavily towards the early phases of his job.[46]

(h) *When do title and risk pass?* The position at common law with regard to title to materials is that title only passes from the contractor to the employer when they are incorporated into the works.[47] This exposes the employer to the risk that if the contractor becomes insolvent, any materials on the site may be seized by the contractor's creditors. Not surprisingly, the common law position is invariably altered in the construction contract so that title to materials passes to the employer upon delivery to the site or upon payment for those materials being made pursuant to an interim certificate.

The basic position at English law with regard to the passing of risk in materials is that risk passes when title (or, to use the term used in the Sale of Goods Act 1979, "property") passes.[48] This position is often varied in the construction contract so that risk in the project facilities remains with the contractor until takeover, although the practical impact of this is somewhat diluted since the contract will usually specify that one or other of the parties is to take out "all risks" insurance in joint names (see (k) below). Nevertheless, if the project facilities are destroyed immediately before takeover and if risk only passes on takeover, then the contractor will usually be obliged to rebuild the facilities. This is often the cause of tension between the contractor and the employer's banks because the contractor wishes to have access to any insurance moneys to fund his reinstatement obligation while the banks wish those moneys to go to prepaying their loans.

(i) *Are the contractor's obligations to be bonded?* Bonding in the present context consists of the contractor procuring for the employer an on-demand bond or guarantee from a bank or insurance company to back up either the contractor's payment obligations or his obligations under the construction contract in general. The form of the bond or guarantee is kept relatively simple in order to avoid disputes with the issuer as to whether or not he should pay and the contractor seeks to protect himself against an unwarranted demand on the bond or guarantee by the employer by specifying in the construction contract when the employer can actually make a

---

[46] This was one of the criticisms of the original construction arrangements for the Channel Tunnel.
[47] *Sims v. London Necropolis Co.* [1885] 1 T.L.R. 584.
[48] s.20 Sale of Goods Act 1979.

demand. An alternative to bonding is to increase the size of the retention.

Sometimes the amount paid to the contractor in the early stages of a construction contract far exceeds the value of the work done. This is usually where the employer has agreed to pay the contractor's mobilisation costs. In these circumstances, the contractor is often required to procure that a bank issues the employer with an advance payment bond, the amount of which reduces over time. This bond is supposed to enable the employer to recoup the amount by which he has theoretically overpaid the contractor should the construction contract be terminated before he has received value equal to the amount of his advance payments.

(j) *What warranties does the contractor give? Is there a defects period? Are there liquidated damages for performance shortfalls?* The position with regard to responsibility for design has been discussed in (b) above. Any construction contract should contain a fairly standard set of "boilerplate" warranties dealing with such matters as using only new materials. Whether the contractor also gives warranties on any plant (such as a warranty in relation to latent defects in turbines and compressors) will depend on whether the contractor is the supplier of such plant or has merely purchased such plant from a supplier. In the latter case, the contractor will either only pass on the warranty he has himself received from the supplier (in identical terms) or will avoid giving any warranty whatsoever and seek to have any warranty he has received assigned to the employer. To state the obvious, any such warranty can only be assigned if it is assignable. A contractor will, in any event, usually try to obtain "back-to-back" warranties from his subcontractors. Any resistance that banks encounter trying to negotiate amendments to a contractor's warranties can often be explained by the fact that the contractor is trying to negotiate parallel amendments with his subcontractors.

Some civil jurisdictions have a concept of "decennial liability" which gives the employer the right to sue for defects in buildings which mainfest themselves within 10 years after completion. This right is usually implied into a construction contract. Article 1669 of the Italian Civil Code is a good example:

> "*1669. Destruction of and defects in immovables.* In the case of buildings or other immovables intended by their nature to last for a long period of time, if within ten years from completion the work is totally or partially destroyed by reason of defects in the soil or in construction, or if such work appears to be in evident danger of destruction or

reveals serious deficiencies, the contractor is liable with respect to the customer and his successors in interest, provided notice of said destruction or defects has been given within one year of their discovery . . ."[49]

The issue of warranties should not be confused with the contractor's liability for defects or the contractor's liability for poor results during the running of performance tests (although these issues obviously interrelate). Subject to any exclusions the contractor is able to negotiate, he will be liable under English law (in damages and subject to the usual rules on limitation of actions) to the employer for any defects for which the contractor is responsible (which may include defects in design in the case of a "design and build" contract). The contractor has contractually agreed to produce a particular facility: if the facility is defective, he has not fulfilled his basic contractual obligation.[50] It is important to appreciate that, under English law, a defects period does not necessarily act as an exclusion clause absolving the contractor from liability for defects. Depending on the drafting, it may simply act as a period within which the contractor is entitled to enter upon the site to correct any defects himself (which is likely to be a cheaper course of action for him than having to pay for the cost of a third party appointed by the employer to remedy any defect). If a contractor wishes to be absolved from all liability for defects under an English law construction contract at the end of the defects period, he will need to state this expressly in the contract. The situation appears to be different in civil law jurisdictions where the inference taken from specifying a defects period seems to be that the contractor is only liable for defects during that period.

As noted in (e) above, a construction contract involving mechanical and electrical equipment will invariably contain performance tests and liquidated damages payable by reference to the results of those performance tests. The idea is that, if the contractor builds a plant which does not meet the employer's desired performance levels, then the employer has overpaid and requires a rebate on the contract price. This is, in very broad terms, the function of performance liquidated damages. The concept is sometimes referred to as "buy-down", *i.e.* performance liquidated damages are paid in order to bring the contract price down to more or less what it should have been for a plant meeting the lesser performance

---

[49] This translation is taken from the translation of the Italian Civil Code by Beltramo, Longo and Merryman (1996).
[50] Note in this context the extended limitation period applicable to latent defects afforded by s.14A of the Limitation Act 1980 and the Latent Damage Act 1986.

levels. It is, however, doubtful whether performance liquidated damages really ever do compensate an employer effectively for the lower performance levels. They are, by their nature, pre-assessed and an employer's actual loss may be higher or lower. In addition, a contractor will usually negotiate an absolute cap on his liability for performance liquidated damages,[51] although the employer will often have another remedy, the right to reject the plant, if that cap is reached.

Performance tests for a power plant can be relatively complex. The tests will usually include the following:

(i) *a net dependable capacity test* — *i.e.* a test to determine the generating capacity of each generating unit;

(ii) *a reliability test* — this will often be run in conjunction with the net dependable capacity test and usually requires a minimum number of hours of uninterrupted running (which in turn requires the grid to dispatch the unit in question);

(iii) *a net electrical output test*;

(iv) *a net heat rate test* — *i.e.* a test of the efficiency of the plant (the rate at which it can convert a unit of fuel into a unit of electricity); and

(v) *tests for compliance with the relevant emissions and other environmental requirements.*

All of the performance tests in (i)–(iv) above must be carried out in conformity with all of the emissions and other environmental requirements affecting the plant in order for the results to be valid.

Performance liquidated damages are generally only payable by reference to the results of the net electrical output test and the net heat rate test.[52] A fixed monetary amount (or percentage of the contract price) is usually payable for each kW shortfall in output and a fixed monetary amount (or percentage of the contract price) is usually payable for each Kcal increase per kWh of output.

In addition to liquidated damages for delay and performance shortfalls, some construction contracts for IPPs have also recently

---

[51] Usually there is a cap on the amount payable by way of performance liquidated damages, a cap on the amount payable by way of delay liquidated damages and an overall cap on the aggregate amount payable by way of all liquidated damages (whether for performance shortfalls or delay). Caps will typically be expressed as a percentage of the contract price (thereby allowing the caps to increase if the contract price escalates).

[52] If the other tests are not met, completion or takeover simply will not occur. See section 3.6(e).

begun to contain liquidated damages for failure to meet an availability guarantee. Availability is measured over time (in these cases, typically 12 or 24 months) and this type of guarantee clearly exposes the contractor to the risk that the availability of the plant deteriorates over the period of measurement not because of something he has done wrong but because of something the project company or the operator does wrong. The wording of an availability guarantee clearly needs to relieve the contractor from liability to the extent that he is not responsible for any availability deficiencies. Subject to this, a fixed monetary amount (or percentage of the contract price) is usually payable for each percentage point by which the plant's actual availability falls short of the guaranteed availability.

(k) *What are the insurance arrangements?* The insurance provisions of the various standard form construction contracts can be fairly complex but an employer will essentially be concerned to see that the contractor carries adequate insurance for any liability he may have in relation to death or personal injury and that the works are insured against "all risks". A construction contract may place the responsibility of taking out "all risks" cover on the employer and not on the contractor. This may be the case when the contract is the refurbishment of existing premises but may in any event be preferred by the employer if he believes he can get better premium rates than the contractor. ("All risks" insurance should be contrasted with insurance against "specified perils". The former type of cover insures against any physical loss or damage subject to specific exceptions (such as wear and tear, design defects and sonic booms) and is a wider form of cover than "specified perils" which is simply cover against a specified list of catastrophes (such as fire, flood, explosion and riot).)

There is a risk in having the contractor (as opposed to the employer) place the all risks policy. The insureds on a contractor's all risks policy in a project financing should be the banks and the project company in addition to the contractor and his sub-contractors. If the placing of the insurances is "contractor-led", the contractor may not appreciate the need to take the banks' requirements (in particular, as to non-vitiation) into account (as to which, see Chapter 7). This may result in a time consuming renegotiation of the insurance package after it has been placed.

(l) *Is there a contract administrator or engineer?* Certain forms of construction contract have a professional (an architect, surveyor or engineer) involved in the contract in two separate capacities: as the employer's agent and as an independent adjudicator (usually described as a "contract administrator" or "engineer") between the contractor and the employer.

The point of involving such a professional as an independent adjudicator is to minimise the possibility of disputes. Where there is a contract administrator or engineer performing this role, he is usually under a duty (owed to both contractor and employer) to act impartially. In this role, he will issue certificates dealing with matters such as whether a payment is due from the employer for work done, whether practical completion has occurred and whether or not the contractor is entitled (in accordance with the terms of the construction contract) to an increase in the price or an extension to the time for completion (and, if so, what). Whether the use of a contract administrator or engineer in this role will avoid (as opposed to merely minimise) disputes will depend on whether the construction contract provides that the certificates are to be conclusive, whether any arbitration clause includes a provision giving the arbitrator power to re-open any certificate and the attitude that the governing law of the construction contract takes to both such provisions.[53] Unfortunately, English law on the subject is not particularly clear and, for the moment, it should be assumed that a court may have at least some ability to reopen certificates notwithstanding a provision stating that the certificates are to be conclusive.

It should also be said that the concept of a contract administrator or engineer acting as an independent adjudicator is really an Anglo-Saxon concept and is not so common in civil law jurisdictions. Where there is no such independent adjudicator, the parties will have to rely on self-assessment and verification in order to ascertain whether or not a payment is due to the contractor and the construction contract will usually provide that, where the contractor is entitled to an increase in the price or an extension to the time for completion, this will be a "reasonable" increase or a "reasonable" extension. What is "reasonable" would then, in the event of a dispute, fall to be determined by an arbitrator or a court, depending on the disputes resolution procedure adopted in the construction contract (see (m) below).

(m) *How are disputes to be resolved?* There are three main options for disputes resolution in a contract. The parties can resort to:

(i)   the courts;

(ii)   arbitration proceedings; or

---

[53] See *Northern Regional Health Authority v. Derek Crouch Construction Co. Ltd* [1984] 1 Q.B. 644, where the court refused to assume for itself the power that an arbitrator had been given under a contract to re-open certificates. The case is much criticised because, if a party misses the usually strict time limits within which to go to arbitration, a certificate becomes unchallengeable.

(iii) a contractual disputes resolution procedure (sometimes (but not necessarily) revolving around referring a dispute to an expert rather than an arbitrator), the parameters of which they set themselves.

There are advantages and disadvantages to each option. For example, the courts may be a better forum for deciding difficult points of law and there is a view that judges and masters are more brutal at imposing procedural deadlines than arbitrators, but litigation is generally considered to be more expensive than arbitration or expert determination, it may be difficult to avoid a public hearing and court procedures are sometimes thought to be too inflexible (judges are reluctant to hear cases outside normal court hours, for example). The advantages and disadvantages of each form of dispute resolution can be overstated: speed and cheapness are considered to be the main advantages of arbitration, but a complex arbitration can be just as lengthy and as expensive as court proceedings.

The use of experts in a contractual disputes resolution procedure has the advantage of turning a procedure which would not necessarily produce a binding result into one which can,[54] but it is important to realise that the use of experts in this manner is a totally different legal concept to arbitration. John Kendall, in his book on expert determination,[55] sums up the essential differences under English law as follows[56]:

> "Experts are a distinct species of dispute resolver whose activities are subject to little or no control by the court, from whose decisions there is no appeal, but who may nevertheless be liable for negligence in performing . . . otherwise unreviewable functions. Arbitrators, by contrast, are subject to control by the court, some of their decisions are, at least in theory, subject to appeal, and they are immune from actions for negligence. A partnership or company can be an expert, whereas an arbitral tribunal always consists of readily identifiable individuals."

(n) *What is the position with regard to unforeseen ground risk?* In the usual course, the risk of unforeseen ground conditions is generally

---

[54] Recent English cases (*Jones v. Sherwood Computer Services plc* [1992] 1 W.L.R. 277 and *Nikko Hotels (U.K.) Ltd v. MEPC plc* [1991] 28 E.G. 86) have led to talk of experts' decisions being "judge-proof" (see Jonathan Grant Q.C., *"What makes an award judge-proof?"*, [1991] 28 E.G. 70).

[55] John Kendall, *Expert Determination* (1996).

[56] *op.cit.* p.2.

one of the employer's risks. It is his site — the contractor is merely being invited onto his site to carry out the works. However, some construction contracts do seek to transfer the risk of unforeseen ground conditions to the contractor to some degree on the basis that the contractor should take the risk of conditions that could reasonably have been ascertained by an inspection (or, in some cases, a survey) of the site before the contractor prepared his tender.[57]

(o) *Who is responsible for obtaining what consents?* This depends entirely on the terms of the construction contract, but the responsibility for obtaining planning permission and other relevant consents is (for obvious reasons) more likely to be placed on the contractor in a "design and build" construction contract.

(p) *Can the employer terminate[58] the construction contract?* Termination of a construction contract is, for the employer, very much a remedy of last resort. If he terminates the contract, he is likely to incur significant expense in bringing another contractor onto the site in order to finish the job. The typical termination provision (for contractor default) will reflect this. No further payments will be made to the defaulting contractor, who must immediately vacate the site and make available to the employer all of the necessary plans and drawings. The employer's claims against the contractor are then effectively put into suspense until another contractor finishes the work. When this occurs, the aggregate amount paid to the original contractor is added to the aggregate amount paid to the new contractor to finish the work and, to the extent that the resulting amount exceeds the original contract price, the excess (less any sums due to the contractor at the date of termination) will be due from the original contractor as a debt.

The fixed price turnkey construction contract is a concept which readily appeals to project financiers. Its two most important hallmarks are, as the name suggests, that a contractor agrees to produce a fully working and complete piece of infrastructure or project for a truly fixed price.[59] The objective of such a contract is to

---

[57] See, for example, Condition 5.7 of the *Model Form of General Conditions of Contract* (MF1) recommended by The Institution of Mechanical Engineers, The Institution of Electrical Engineers and The Association of Consulting Engineers (1988 ed., last amended in 1995), Condition 11.1 of the FIDIC *Conditions of Contract for Works of Civil Engineering Construction* (4th ed. 1987) and Condition 4.11 of the FIDIC *Conditions of Contract for Design-Build and Turnkey* (1st ed. 1995).

[58] Termination is a slight misnomer because the employer will usually need to keep the original construction contract on foot for various purposes (*e.g.* licences to use plans and drawings). What the employer is really doing is expelling the contractor from the site.

[59] Another name for a turnkey construction contract is an EPC contract, an "engineering, procurement and construction contract". This tends to be North American terminology and reflects the fact that, before the advent of turnkey construction contracts, projects used to have separate contracts for the engineering, procurement and construction phases.

get the contractor to accept as many as possible of the risks that would result in an increase in the cost of carrying out the works. Needless to say, this type of construction contract is not popular with contractors and it is rare to find a true fixed price turnkey contract. Contractors have, however, now come to accept turnkey construction contracts as a fact of life for major projects with competitive tendering.

There are numerous amendments that need to be made to a "normal" standard form construction contract in order to make it a true fixed price turnkey contract. For example, a standard form will often provide that, if the contractor discovers an ambiguity or discrepancy in the plans, he is entitled to an increase in the contract price for any work he has to undertake in order to resolve or correct such ambiguity or discrepancy. By contrast, a typical turnkey contract will provide that the contractor is responsible for checking all of the plans for ambiguities and discrepancies and that he is not entitled to any increase in the contract price if any subsequently come to light. The treatment of sub-contractors and suppliers is also critical. Not only must the contractor take full responsibility for the acts and omissions of his sub-contractors and suppliers, but he must also not be entitled to claim *force majeure* as a result of their failure to perform (unless, arguably, such failure resulted from an event which would have constituted force majeure under the turnkey contract had it occurred in relation to the contractor). The employer should also not be able to specify that the contractor uses particular sub-contractors (so-called "nominated sub-contractors") because the counterpart to this is usually that the contractor does not take responsibility for their acts and omissions (since he did not select them).

3.7   OPERATION AND MAINTENANCE AGREEMENTS

The operation and maintenance agreement is often the poor relation in a suite of project contracts and is often only turned to in negotiations after all of the other documents have been exhaustively discussed. This is actually a rather strange attitude since, if the project in question is not properly operated and maintained, there will be no cash flow. There are various ways in which the operation and maintenance ("O&M") of a project can be structured:

(a) the project company can carry out the operation and maintenance of the project itself;

60

(b) the project company can enter into an operation and maintenance agreement with a related third party, *e.g.* one of its
shareholders (or an affiliate of one of its shareholders);

(c) the project company can enter into an operation and maintenance agreement with an arms'-length third party; or

(d) the project company can share the operating and maintenance role with a third party (related or otherwise). For
instance, it could enter into an agreement with a third party
for that party simply to provide a workforce which would act
under the project company's direction.

In addition, the operating function can be split from the maintenance function. In a power project, for example, it might be
advantageous for the maintenance role to be performed by the
construction contractor (or one of its affiliates), with the project
company either retaining the operating role or contracting it out to
a third party. The greater the number of parties performing the
operating and maintenance function, the greater the risk of disputes
about liability when things go wrong. Was a particular malfunction
caused by a defect in the plant (in which case the contractor may be
responsible) or was it caused by bad operation (when the operator
may be responsible) or sub-standard maintenance (when the maintenance contractor may be responsible)?

There are advantages and disadvantages with each approach
listed in (a)–(d) above. If it is proposed that the project company
carry out the operation and maintenance role itself, it will need to
have appropriate staff with appropriate experience and qualifications and it may need to have access to a wider pool of technical
expertise. One way in which this is often achieved is to have a
technical services agreement between the project company and one
of its shareholders who possesses the necessary staff and the greater
pool of expertise. The main provisions of such a technical services
agreement would include the following:

(i) Staff would be seconded to the project company from the
shareholder in question. It is important to clarify whether
the nature of the "secondment" means that the staff remain
employees of the shareholder or become employees of the
project company. This is crucial for various reasons: if they
remain employees of the shareholder, the shareholder will
be vicariously liable for their actions and this could seriously
undermine the principle of insulating the shareholders from
the risks associated with the project; the employer of the
staff will be responsible for their working conditions and

61

employment and pension costs; and there are insurance implications (not the least of which is that the employer will in most jurisdictions be obliged to take out some form of workers' compensation insurance to cover industrial injuries).

Some jurisdictions might make seconded staff employees of the project company as a matter of law no matter what the operation and maintenance agreement says. This would typically be the case if the relationship between the project company and the staff had all the *indicia* of an employer-employee relationship. For this reason, if it is not intended for the seconded staff to be the project company's employees, the project company should have the right not to dismiss incompetent staff but to require them to be assigned to other duties by the shareholder in question.

(ii) A clear list of the services to be provided for the fees payable. Any additional services will cost. In order to avoid overcharging by the shareholder, the project company will wish it to be made clear that the shareholder is not an exclusive supplier of those services and that the project company can procure them from other sources.[60]

(iii) A statement of the fees payable. A shareholder will require the salaries (and other employment benefits) of any staff he seconds to be covered by the project company (possibly with a mark-up) and any technical assistance provided on a consultancy basis by the shareholder's own staff will usually be charged at an hourly rate. In addition, the shareholder may require a general technical services fee which is usually justified as a fee to reflect the need to keep staff on standby but which in most cases simply reflects an agreed level of profit.

(iv) An indemnity from the project company to the shareholder, indemnifying the shareholder against any liability incurred by the shareholder as a result of an act or omission of any of the seconded staff (irrespective of whether or not the shareholder is vicariously liable).

If the project company carries out the operation and maintenance role itself, there will obviously be no place to set out the level of its duties other than in the credit agreement.

If the project company enters into an operation and maintenance agreement with a related third party (*e.g.* one of its shareholders or

---

[60] Of course, the procurement and competition laws of the jurisdiction in which the project company operates may well require the shareholder not to be the exclusive provider of those services.

an affiliate of one of its shareholders), its shareholders might feel that that agreement does not need to be too rigorous since the operator will be incentivised to perform well because, in so doing, it will enhance the value of the shareholdings. An operation and maintenance agreement entered into with an arms'-length party would be stricter and would typically include the following provisions:

(a) *A statement of the level of the third party's operating and mainte-nance obligations and the standards he must adhere to.* There are two issues here. The first is whether the third party operation and mainte-nance agreement will effectively guarantee that the project will achieve certain operating levels (for example, in terms of production or efficiency) and standards (for example, in relation to noxious emissions) or whether the agreement will instead simply state that the third party has general operating obligations (such as a duty to operate the project in accordance with good industry standards) and he is bound merely to carry out those obligations "with a view to ensuring that" the project achieves those levels and standards. If the third party is prepared to accept the former, more stringent obligation (that of guaranteeing certain operating levels and stand-ards for the plant), he will have to ensure that the drafting of his obligation does not make him responsible for bad performance of the plant caused by either bad design or bad construction. The second issue is setting the correct level of service required. In the absence of specific performance targets, this is typically done (as indicated above) by referring to "Western European Standards", "good industry practice" or some similar (and admittedly rather vague) standard.

A typical definition in the context of an independent power project would be as follows:

> " *'Good Utility Practice'*
> means those practices, methods, techniques and standards that are from time to time generally accepted for use in the international electric utility industry in Western Europe and commonly used in Western Europe in prudent electric utility engineering and operations to operate and maintain equipment similar to the Project Facilities law-fully, safely, efficiently and economically in similar circumstances."

The actual day-to-day O&M standards will often be specified in an O&M manual prepared by or in conjunction with the contractor and the operator will be obliged to carry out his duties in accordance with that manual. If he does not, this will usually void the

63

contractor's warranties. This sometimes results in a requirement for the operator not to carry out any maintenance on any equipment which is still covered by such a warranty but to leave it to the contractor. In addition, there will usually be a régime for establishing a one-year and a five-year O&M plan and O&M budgets based on those plans. The plans and budgets are usually initially prepared by the project company and sent to the operator for comment. An operator can usually object and require changes (or relief from his obligations) if the O&M plan requires him to do something illegal or something which might jeopardise health and safety or if it requires him to do something which is not properly provided for in the relevant O&M budget. Otherwise, the project company determines the content of both the O&M plans and the O&M budgets.

(b) *Provisions dealing with the operator's remuneration.* The remuneration package would typically divide itself up into three parts: first, there would be reimbursement of sums which the operator had effectively paid suppliers on the project company's behalf (*e.g.* sums paid for the procurement of spares and consumables); secondly, there would be payment on a unit or hourly basis (often incorporating a small profit margin) for certain services provided by the operator (*e.g.* a payment in respect of the operator's payroll costs); and thirdly, there would be the payment of a fee which would be the operator's main profit for doing the job.

A system of penalties and bonuses would normally be linked to this basic remuneration package in order to incentivise the operator to get the best out of the project in question. For obvious reasons, the aggregate amount of penalties which the operator could incur in any year would not normally exceed his operating fee for that year (*i.e.* the main profit element of his remuneration).

(c) *Provisions controlling the operator's expenditure.* The O&M budget would be the main means of controlling such expenditure but there would usually also be provisions which required the operator to obtain the project company's consent before incurring expenditure (*e.g.* on a particularly expensive replacement part) over an above a threshold figure. It is important to appreciate, however, that arms-length third party operators will rarely — if ever — offer a project company a fixed price deal in relation to O&M. If the true O&M costs for a project in any given year exceed the O&M budget for that year, this will be the project company's problem. An O&M budget usually imposes discipline, not risk, on an operator.

(d) *Provisions dealing with whether the operator acts as principal or agent when it is procuring spares and consumables or other goods and services for the project.* There are obvious issues of credit risk here. In addition, if the operator is a substantial company in its own right with its own network of usual suppliers, it may be able to use its general purchasing power to obtain more advantageous discounts for the project company. If the operator procures goods as principal, he will then be the seller of those goods to the project company and will therefore be liable as such under the Sales of Goods Act 1979.

If the project is subject to the E.C. procurement rules (*e.g.* because it is a utility — see section 9.2(c)), there will be a clause requiring the operator to procure goods, works and services in accordance with those rules.

(e) *A procedure for mobilising the operator.* This procedure needs to be carefully co-ordinated with the contractor's activities under the construction contract. There will usually have to be a handover period during which the contractor's personnel in charge of commissioning handover the plant to the operator's personnel. A notice is usually served on the operator requiring him to get his personnel on site as soon as the commissioning is about to start. The operator is usually entitled to his remuneration on and as from the date he mobilises and gets his staff on site (and this will represent an extra cost if completion and take-over are subsequently delayed (*e.g.* for *force majeure*)).

(f) *A limitation on the operator's liability.* In addition to the usual exclusion of liability for consequential loss, the operator will normally seek to obtain a limit on his liability to the project company in any year equal to his fee for that year. His argument is that to make him liable for all the losses he might potentially cause would be totally disproportionate to the modest fee he receives. The point is usually conceded by the project company and its banks.

(g) *A termination clause.* The project company will obviously need the right to terminate the operation and maintenance agreement for poor performance and there is usually some debate and discussion as to how poor performance is best measured in each particular project. The clauses dealing with the ownership of intellectual property and the like assume great significance on a termination since the project company must be able to pass on to any successor operator all of the rights necessary in order properly to operate and maintain the project.

3.8 SUPPLY CONTRACTS

It is important to realise that one man's supply contract is another man's offtake agreement. So, where an offshore gas field is being developed by various participants to supply gas to the owner of a gas processing plant onshore, the gas sales agreement is a sales agreement for the participants but a supply agreement for the owner of the processing plant. A lot of what is said in the following sections on offtake agreements is therefore relevant to this section and is not repeated here. In very general terms, what is relevant for a project company dependent on a particular supply is security of supply and an acceptable fit of any take-or-pay obligation contained in the supply contract with the other project contracts. These two issues are discussed further in the context of "bankability" in Chapter 4.

3.9   OFFTAKE AGREEMENTS: GENERAL

A project need not necessarily have an offtake agreement in the sense of a long-term product purchase agreement since its product may only be capable of being sold on world spot markets (see section 3.1(d) above) or its revenues may simply be payments from the general public (of tolls or fares). Where a project does have an offtake agreement, it will fall within one of two categories, that is, either:

(a) it is a true sale arrangement for the product in question on arms-length terms and at market or near-market prices; or

(b) it is a pass-through sale arrangement (see section 3.2 above).

Although an arrangement under (a) above is on arms-length terms, it can still achieve a certain degree of "price underpinning" by guaranteeing the project company a certain revenue stream through the use of a take-or-pay sales agreement. The basic idea of a take-or-pay sales agreement is that the purchaser will agree to purchase over a specified period a minimum quantity of the project company's product at an agreed price. If the purchaser does not purchase (or take) the minimum quantity, then he will be obliged to pay as if he had (but usually only if the project company was able and willing to deliver the product in question). The precise nature of a take-or-pay obligation will vary from contract to contract.

The basic structure of a take-or-pay sales agreement usually presents no problem as far as English law is concerned. It is a basic principle of English contract law that the courts are not interested in the adequacy of consideration. If a utility ends up paying ten times the market price for gas it takes because of take-or-pay

66

provisions, that is the utility's problem. It has entered into a bad bargain.[61] Courts in other jurisdictions often do concern themselves with the adequacy of consideration, however, and careful advice should be taken on the enforceability of take-or-pay provisions in a sales agreement governed by the laws of such a jurisdiction.

Examples of (a) and (b) are given in sections 3.10 and 3.11. Section 3.12 discusses the fact that it is probably now possible to state with some degree of certainty how risk should be allocated in power purchase agreements in emerging markets.

3.10 GAS SALES AGREEMENTS

A good example of a take-or-pay sales agreement is the type of depletion sales agreement that was typically entered into by British Gas plc (as it then was) in relation to North Sea gas fields. This type of agreement is called a "depletion sales agreement" because the purchaser contracts to buy all the reserves of a field until they are depleted. The term of a depletion sales agreement is, as one would expect, very long. It is normally expressed to end after a fixed number of years (25 years has been seen in the past) or, if earlier, when continued production ceases to be economic. (The term "economic" can be subject to extensive definition (as is often the case in oil and gas projects) but here usually means that operating costs exceed gross revenues.)

Depletion sales agreements have actually become the exception rather than the rule in the United Kingdom as a result of the liberalisation of the gas markets there. Gas is now sold in the United Kingdom on a portfolio basis: no one field is identified as the source of supply and the seller is assumed to have a portfolio of reserves from which he is able to meet his supply obligations. The significance of this change of approach is that the seller can no longer rely on force majeure affecting his field facilities as a reason for relieving him of liability under the sales agreement. This is a common feature of depletion sales agreements, where a significant degree of risk in the underlying field, its reserves and facilities is intended to be transferred to the buyer. Depletion sales agreements are still commonly encountered in project finance in the emerging markets, however.

---

[61] Compare a take-or-pay arrangement under which a party agrees to buy cars from a new manufacturing plant and to pay a fixed amount in a year even though no cars at all are produced by the plant. Such an arrangement might fail on the grounds of total failure of consideration but the simple (and expedient) solution is to execute the arrangements as a deed.

The offtake arrangements of a depletion sales agreement would typically work as set out below. It should be borne in mind that a gas sales agreement of this type will be entered into as a condition precedent to the development of the gas field in question (*i.e.* before the relevant facilities are completed and the true characteristics of the reservoir are known). This is because the sellers will need the buyer's take-or-pay obligation in order to raise finance for the development and the buyer will not wish to wait until the development is completed before entering into a sales agreement because he wishes to secure supplies.

(a) The participants in the gas field (the sellers) have to nominate to the buyer, normally within a few months of the earliest possible date for the first delivery from the field, an initial total reservoir daily quantity of gas ("TRDQ"). The TRDQ is a base figure by reference to which the buyer makes his own nominations to the sellers for the delivery of gas. The initial TRDQ has to be nominated within a certain range (for example, between 80 and 120 million cubic feet per day) determined by an engineering analysis of the field. The bottom end of the range gives the buyer certainty that at least that level of gas must be nominated. The range itself enables the sellers to increase the initial TRDQ once more is known about the performance of the field than was known at the time the gas sales agreement was entered into.

(b) Once the initial TRDQ has been nominated, the sellers can increase the TRDQ to a higher specified figure (in our example, up to, say 200 million cubic feet per day) which will then apply during the "plateau period". (The plateau period will exist during the bulk of the operating period of the field: it more or less equates to the period during which optimum production levels can be maintained and ends when the reserves of the field deplete to such an extent that production levels start being affected.) The higher specified figure operates as a ceiling for the buyer, but otherwise he is in the hands of the sellers for the nomination of the TRDQ during the plateau period.

Not surprisingly, the sellers can begin to reduce the TRDQ at the end of the plateau period.

(c) It is important to appreciate that, while certain matters relating to a gas sales agreement must be decided upon by the sellers acting as a block (such as nominations of the TRDQ), it is general practice for each seller to enter into a separate gas sales agreement with the buyer and for there to be a so-called "common stream agreement" in which the sellers agree to act in a concerted manner in relation to those matters when exercising discretions under their own individual gas sales agreements. (It is thought to be easier for a seller to obtain project finance if he can present his lenders with his own gas sales agreement.) The use of individual gas sales agreements requires two further definitions:

(i) *The daily contract quantity ("DCQ").* This is simply each individual seller's proportion of the TRDQ.
(ii) *The annual contract quantity ("ACQ").* This is essentially a seller's DCQ multiplied by 365.

(d) Each seller has to maintain a daily delivery capacity throughout each year calculated by reference to his DCQ. The precise figures vary and a smaller capacity has to be maintained in the summer months (for obvious reasons). So, for example, whilst a seller may have to maintain a daily delivery capacity of 167 per cent of his DCQ during the winter months, he will only have to maintain a daily delivery capacity of 100 per cent of his DCQ during the summer months.

The buyer can nominate gas for delivery up to the daily delivery capacity rates and each seller will be obliged to deliver gas at the normal contract price. If the buyer wants additional gas delivered on any day (for example, because of unusually severe weather causing an unexpected increase in demand), the sellers are not usually obliged to deliver such additional gas (which is commonly described as *excess gas*) but, if they do, they are entitled to be paid at the excess gas price. The excess gas price will be at a premium to the normal contract price.

The buyer normally also agrees to nominate at least a specified percentage of the DCQ (for example, 30 per cent) on each day, although he will often have a limited right to make zero nominations (often in the summer months). One of the reasons why any right to make zero nominations will be limited is that the best way to manage a gas field and its facilities is apparently to have gas being continually produced with the minimum possible numbers of shut-downs.

(e) Apart from being used to set the parameters of daily deliveries, the TRDQ/DCQ/ACQ figures are also used to determine the extent of the buyer's take-or-pay obligation. Usually, the buyer has to pay each seller at the end of each contract year[62] for any amount of an adjusted ACQ figure which the seller could have delivered but which the buyer did not take.[63] The price paid will be the normal contract price.

The adjusted ACQ figure is achieved by deducting the following from the ACQ:

   (i) gas properly nominated by the buyer which the seller failed to deliver for any reason (including force majeure but excluding any failure by the buyer to accept delivery);

  (ii) gas properly nominated by the buyer which the buyer was unable to accept because of force majeure[64]; and

 (iii) all gas taken by the buyer in excess of previous years' ACQs (to the extent not already deducted). This will primarily be excess gas (see (d) above) but may also include, for example, commissioning gas.

The buyer's obligation to make the take-or-pay payment is his only obligation arising out of a failure to take gas in accordance with the gas sales agreement.

(f) The making of a take-or-pay payment in any given year will entitle the buyer to take in following years an equivalent amount of gas for free. This is so-called *make-up gas*. The buyer's entitlement to make-up gas is obviously designed to allow the buyer to recover his position over time. He is only entitled to make-up gas, however, after he has taken all other gas required of him in each subsequent year (*i.e.* essentially the ACQ).

(g) A brief mention should also be made of *shortfall gas*. Shortfall gas is an amount of gas equal to any gas properly nominated by the buyer which the seller fails to deliver for any reason other than a failure by the buyer to accept delivery or force majeure. Shortfall gas is bought at a discount to the normal

---

[62] Some contracts are now being concluded on the basis of quarterly take-or-pay quantities and obligations.

[63] In the second large wave of IPPs in the U.K. (which started in 1996), the gas sellers became aware that they were supplying gas to highly-leveraged, single-purpose companies and asked to be provided with letters of credit from first-class banks securing the payment of at least one year's take-or-pay obligation.

[64] This allowance of force majeure relief for the buyer means that a gas sales agreement of this sort is not a "hell or high water" commitment (*i.e.* a commitment to make payments come what may). Compare "hell or high water" charters in ship financings where charter hire is payable even though the vessel in question may have been destroyed.

contract price (say, at only 80 per cent of the normal contract price). The buyer usually has to elect to treat gas as shortfall gas, but, if he does, he loses all his other rights in relation to the seller's particular failure to deliver. The first gas delivered after such failure is usually classified shortfall gas and has therefore to be paid for at the discounted price. The buyer's right to receive shortfall gas is sometimes the buyer's only remedy for failure to deliver by the seller.

3.11 PASS-THROUGH OFFTAKE AGREEMENTS

A fairly good example of a pass-through offtake agreement is the form of pass-through power purchase agreement used in some electricity financings where (if it was adopted) the pass-through mechanism would work on the following basis:

(a) *The Contract Charge.* As noted above,[65] the project company (the generator) would be paid:

(i) a *capacity (or availability) charge,*[66] designed in broad terms to pay for the project company's fixed costs; and

(ii) an *energy charge*, designed in broad terms to pay for the cost of the project company's fuel and other variable costs.

The capacity charge and the energy charge would together constitute the *contract charge*.

(b) *The basic formula for the payment of the capacity charge.* The basic formula for the payment of capacity charge for any period (a "payment period") would be:

$$FC \times \frac{AA}{TA}$$

where   FC   is the project company's Fixed Costs for such period;

AA   is the Actual Availability achieved by the project company for such period; and

TA   is the Target Availability for such period under the terms of the power purchase agreement.

Availability is the ability (measured in MWh) of a power plant to generate electricity over time. The Target Availability figures set

---

[65] section 3.2.
[66] The reasons for an availability charge are explained in section 3.12(a).

out in the power purchase agreement at the outset (usually expressed as a percentage of the power plant's maximum possible generation over a year) might, depending on the commercial deal, be adjusted at completion to reflect the actual performance capabilities of the completed power plant. If this was the case, the project company would not take the risk that the completed power plant was not actually capable (because of a design defect or bad construction, for example) of generating as much electricity as was originally thought.

Availability for these purposes is a function of time and declared capacity. So, for example, a power plant could achieve an availability target of 90 per cent by declaring itself available at 100 per cent of its nameplate capacity for 90 per cent of the time or by declaring itself available at 90 per cent of its nameplate capacity for 100 per cent of the time. A target availability figure would typically be calculated by taking a power plant's nameplate capacity as 100 per cent and then deducting a percentage (say 4 per cent) to allow for scheduled maintenance and then a further percentage (say 4 per cent again) to allow for "unforced outages" (i.e. breakdowns) (arriving at a target availability level of 92 per cent).[67]

For the purposes of AA above, the power plant in question might sometimes be *deemed* to be available when it actually was not because of certain events of force majeure (e.g. a failure of the national electricity grid) and other circumstances. This is obviously a device to apportion risk and is discussed further in section 3.12.

(c) *Fixed Costs.* At the beginning of each operating year, the project company and the power purchaser would calculate the estimated fixed costs for that year. This estimate would be periodically updated throughout that year and the capacity charge for any particular payment period would be calculated by reference to the latest estimate of the relevant year's fixed costs apportioned to that payment period on a straight line basis. This might produce working capital inefficiencies (e.g. the project company might have to meet certain large items of expenditure before it has necessarily been put in funds through the usual capacity charge mechanism). Adjustments are sometimes made to minimise such inefficiencies. Fixed Costs for an operating year would typically include:

(i) that amount of the banks' loans due to be repaid in that year (which can be calculated in various ways but usually by

---

[67] There are, of course, other ways in which to achieve the same incentivisation on the project company. One could, for example, have the power purchaser pay the project company a base capacity fee but then have the project company pay the power purchaser penalties if it dos not achieve stated availability levels. This type of formulation is generally avoided in English law contracts, however, because of English law's aversion to penalties.

reference to a repayment schedule specified in the power purchase agreement in order to protect the power purchaser from changes to the actual repayment schedule being made by the project company and the banks);

(ii) the interest due to be paid on the banks' loans in that year (often capped at a certain rate);

(iii) amounts due to be paid in that year in relation to changes in circumstances (see (d) below);

(iv) the non-variable operating costs for that year (which, if there was an operation and maintenance agreement, would usually be calculated in an identical manner to the manner in which payments are made under that agreement);

(v) taxes payable by the project company in that year;

(vi) any insurance premiums payable in that year and any shortfall in recoveries following the occurrence of an insured event (*e.g.* a shortfall arising because of deductibles);

(vii) the project company's administrative overheads for that year; and

(viii) the equity return for that year.

(d) *Changes in circumstances.* Any increase in the project company's costs or reduction in the project company's return as a result of changes in certain circumstances would usually be passed through in the capacity charge. The circumstances typically covered would be:

(i) a change in the taxation system (excluding[68] a change in the rate of corporation tax or value added tax but including, for example, the introduction of an environmental tax);

(ii) a change in law or the conditions of any consents (for example, requiring additional health and safety measures to be taken); and

(iii) a change in the legislative environment in which the project company operates (in the case of a United Kingdom power project, this would be a change in the highly complex electricity pooling and settlement systems described in section 10.3).[69]

In some deals, an additional feature has been added into the provisions relating to change in law and this is that, if the project

---

[68] Such a change would usually be excluded on the basis that a change in the rate of such taxes was simply a risk inherent in doing business in the country in question and was not specific to the relevant project.

[69] This is discussed further in section 3.12(f).

company is unable to raise money with which to finance any modifications to the power plant required by a change in law or the conditions of any consents, then the power purchaser will, if necessary, provide the money as a lender of last resort.[70] Any money so lent is not necessarily subordinated to the banks.

(e) *The basic formula for the payment of the energy charge.* The basic formula for the payment of energy charge for any period would be similar to that set out in (b) above for the payment of capacity charge but (obviously) the references would be to the project company's fuel and other variable costs and to actual and target efficiency levels rather than to fixed costs and actual and target availability levels. ("Efficiency" is the rate at which fuel is converted into electrical power and so will be expressed in, *e.g.*, kcal/kWh).

Efficiency can be affected by (*inter alia*) poor maintenance or the use of fuel which does not comply with specification and the efficiency targets are intended to ensure that the project company maintains the plant properly and purchases fuel within specification.

An alternative formulation for the energy charge which achieves the same risk allocation is simply to pay the project company a fixed monetary amount per kWh of generation (and not per unit of fuel burned). A fixed amount per kWh of generation necessarily implies a certain efficiency level.

3.12 POWER PURCHASE AGREEMENTS: THE STANDARD RISK ALLOCATION

It is now possible to state with some degree of certainty how risks should be divided between the parties to a power purchase agreement (or "PPA") in an independent power project (or "IPP") at least in the emerging markets or in jurisdictions which are only just beginning to liberalise their electricity markets. In this respect, PPAs have become "mature" agreements, like joint operating agreements in the oil industry and credit agreements in the banking industry.

This is not to say that risks will in practice always be allocated in a certain way or that certain provisions of a PPA cannot be negotiated. However, the broad principles of a PPA can now be said to be fixed. Not surprisingly, many of the legal and commercial techniques that are used in PPAs come from other areas, for example pipeline financing.

---

[70] This is discussed further in section 3.12(g).

3.12 Power Purchase Agreements

(a) *Availability* — In order to raise project finance, the amounts payable under a PPA must be predictable. It will not therefore be acceptable if the project company is only paid for what it actually generates. Too many unpredictable factors — totally outside the project company's control — can influence what the project company generates: for example the weather, whether the country's economy is in recession or is growing and, most importantly, whether any other power plant in the country can generate more cheaply. For this reason, the capacity or availability charges[71] under the PPA must, as a general rule, be payable whether or not the project company is generating (or, to use the industry's terminology, whether or not the power plant is capable of being "dispatched").

Under most PPAs, the availability charge will sometimes be payable even though the power plant is not capable of being dispatched. This is (as noted above[72]) the concept of "deemed availability" and is the main way that risk can be transferred from the project company to the power purchaser under the PPA. The Americans tend not to use the concept of availability: they use the concept of "deemed dispatch", which is used to produce the same result.

As noted above, however, the power purchaser will protect itself by only being obliged to pay the full amount of the availability charge if a minimum or target level of availability is met (*e.g.* 92 per cent). By contrast, the project company will usually only receive a small amount as a bonus if it produces extra availability above this level.

A PPA (or any associated grid code) will usually provide for power plants to make daily declarations of anticipated availability during the following day. Payment by reference to declared availability rather than actual generation obviously opens the power purchaser up to the risk that the project company is declaring that the power plant has a greater availability than it actually has. To prevent over-declarations of this sort, the power purchaser will usually retain the right to conduct an availability test at short notice. If the project company is found to have been over-declaring (*i.e.* cheating), then it will be penalised. The penalty can take various forms. For example, all of the power purchaser's payments may be recalculated on the basis of the lower tested availability for the period from the test in question back to the previous test.

(b) *Long-Term Price Formulae* — Long-term loans require long-term contracts. The pricing provisions of a PPA need to be clear and

---

[71] See sections 3.2 and 3.11.
[72] section 3.11(b).

they need to be fixed at least for so long as any of the project company's loans remain unpaid. The price formulae used in a PPA are another method of transferring or sharing risks.

(c) *Variable Costs* — As noted above, the cost of fuel and other variable costs are usually "passed through" to the power purchaser subject to minimum or target levels of efficiency.

Most IPPs will have fuel supply agreements which contain a "take-or-pay" provision.[73] If the reason that a project company suffers a take-or-pay payment is that the power purchaser has simply not asked it to generate sufficient amounts of power (resulting in less fuel being used), this is generally considered to be the power purchaser's risk. PPAs will therefore often contain "minimum dispatch" obligations, *i.e.* minimum amounts of power that the power purchaser must require the project company to generate in order to avoid any take-or-pay obligation. Such PPAs will then state that, if the power purchaser does not require this amount of power and the project company has to make a "take-or-pay" payment as a result, then the power purchaser must pay an equal amount to the project company.

By contrast, if the reason that the project company suffers a take-or-pay payment is its own fault (perhaps because it has taken too long to carry out scheduled maintenance), this is the project company's risk. If the reason is force majeure, this is dealt with below.

(d) *Force Majeure* — The treatment of *force majeure* will now usually depend on who is affected by the relevant event of *force majeure*. If the event of *force majeure* affects the power purchaser — for example, a storm destroys the transmission lines leading away from the site of the power plant — then the power plant will be deemed to be available (and any resulting take-or-pay payment will be for the account of the power purchaser). If, however, the event of *force majeure* affects the project company — for example a storm destroys a substation within the site of the power plant — then the project company will, in the normal way, be relieved of its obligations to generate to the extent it is prevented from doing so by the event of *force majeure,* but it will not be deemed to be available. Any resulting take-or-pay payment will not be for the account of the power purchaser, although the project company should be able to negotiate significant relief from its take-or-pay obligation in the fuel supply agreement for the case where the reason it is not taking fuel is force majeure.[74] The project company can, of course, to some extent

---

[73] See section 3.9.
[74] See section 3.10(e).

insure against the consequences of certain force majeure events which might affect it.

There is an important qualification to the above. Where the power purchaser is a state-owned entity, the project company is sometimes able to argue successfully that the risk of certain political force majeure events (such as the risk of a change in law or the risk that a necessary consent or authorisation is unjustifiably revoked) should be borne by the power purchaser (with the same consequences as those set out above). In such cases, a distinction is made in the PPA between "political" force majeure and "natural" force majeure (such as fire or flood).

Another aspect of force majeure under a PPA is that, if it continues for a prolonged period, both the project company and the power purchaser will begin to suffer. If the force majeure event is natural force majeure affecting the project company, interest will mount up on the project company's debt after any available business interruption insurance has been called upon and the power purchaser will be wondering whether he needs to take steps to permanently replace his lost capacity. For these reasons, it is now becoming accepted that either party to a PPA should have the right to terminate the PPA if an event of *force majeure* renders generation by the project company impossible for more than a specified period (*e.g.* 24 consecutive months). Compensation is usually payable in these circumstances and this is discussed later.

In addition, the term of a PPA is usually extended by any period of *force majeure*.

(e) *Privatisation of the power purchaser* — Practice might vary between Asia and other emerging markets on the one hand and Europe on the other in relation to the risk that a state-owned power purchaser might be privatised. In Europe it is often only possible to protect against this risk by obtaining a form of comfort letter from the government of the day and sometimes even this is not possible. By contrast, in an emerging market with little or no track record of successful privatisation and even-handed regulation, it may be possible to negotiate that, on a privatisation, the government of the country in question has to provide the project company with a guarantee of payments due under the PPA.

(f) *Restructuring of the electricity industry* — There is also the risk that the electricity industry in which the project company operates is restructured. There might be in a particular country, for example, a "merit order" in relation to how power plants in that country are instructed to dispatch. Usually such a merit order would require cheaper plants to be instructed to dispatch before more expensive plants. On a restructuring of a country's electricity industry, this might be changed or a particularly special or protected position that the project company has in that merit order might also be threatened.

PPAs now often contain provisions which state that, where such a restructuring occurs, the PPA will be amended (for example, by increasing the availability payments) in order to place the project company in the same position that it would have been in had such restructuring not occurred. However sometimes power purchasers are able to resist a pass-through of additional costs arising on an industry restructuring and, in these circumstances, there is usually an agreement to negotiate an "equitable solution" in good faith.

(g) *Change in tax; change in law* — As noted above,[75] a change in the rate of (or rules relating to) the tax on profits to which the project company is subject is generally seen as a risk of doing business in the country in question. A change in tax laws which is intended deliberately to discriminate against the project company is not, however. PPAs therefore frequently contain provisions which attempt to protect the project company against the effects of such a change. Usually, those provisions will ultimately lead to an increase in the availability payments.

A change in law — whether of general application or intended to be discriminatory — which increases the project company's costs (or, sometimes, which reduces its shareholders' rate of return) is generally treated as the power purchaser's risk. The best example of such a change in law is a change which imposes tighter environmental requirements on the power plant such as a requirement to "retrofit" flue gas desulphurisation units to a coal-fired plant. The availability payments will usually be increased to pay (over time) for the cost of carrying out the relevant work. If the change in law only affects the project company's price of fuel or its other variable costs, then only the energy charge will be increased.

Increasing the payments that the power purchaser makes over a period of time will not, however, allow the project company to pay for any work it needs to carry out because of a change in law. It will need money to pay for the work to be done. Its shareholders will probably not want to invest more money to pay for such work and its existing lenders might also be unwilling to lend any more money. Its existing lenders could also prevent it from borrowing the necessary funds from other banks because of the negative pledge and various other restrictive covenants contained in their loan documentation.

---

[75] section 3.11(d).

For these reasons, some (not many) PPAs state that, in these circumstances, the project company must use its best or reasonable efforts to obtain the necessary funds but, if it cannot obtain them, then the power purchaser will himself lend the necessary amount to the project company. Whether any money lent by the power purchaser in this way is subordinated to the interests of the existing lenders is a matter for negotiation. Some PPAs have sought to give the power purchaser at least a pari passu right to payment; others have sought to divide the availability payments into two payment flows, giving the lenders priority over one and the power purchaser priority over the other. The latter solution is generally felt to be somewhat cumbersome and difficult to implement in practice.

One final aspect of the protection against changes in law that PPAs may contain is a provision which states that, if a change in law (*e.g.* in relation to emissions) restricts the amount of electricity that can actually be generated, the power plant will be deemed to be available (or dispatched) at the levels that would have been possible before the relevant change in law came into force.

(h) *Consents* — It used to be thought that all of the consents for an IPP had to be issued at the very beginning of the project for the entire life of the project. Although this may be possible in highly sophisticated and developed systems like the United Kingdom, it is often very difficult to achieve this in the emerging markets. Sometimes consents will only be given for very short periods of time.

To protect the project company in such a case, the PPA will often provide that the power plant will be deemed available (or be deemed to have been dispatched) if such a consent is not renewed for "unjustifiable reasons".

(i) *Foreign exchange risks* — The treatment of foreign exchange risks in a PPA will to some extent depend on whether the project company can protect itself against adverse foreign exchange movements by taking out appropriate hedging contracts. If it can, then it will be expected to bear the risk of adverse foreign exchange movements. If it cannot, then the power purchaser will bear that risk, usually through a formula in the availability charge payment provisions which increases the amount that the power purchaser must pay in local currency.

All required exchange control consents are expected to be given at the beginning of the project and to last until the end of the project. The risk of any problems with regard to the availability of sufficient hard currency in the host country, the transferability of hard currency from the host country or the convertibility of the local currency will not usually lie with the project company in that suitable assurances or undertaking's will normally be required from the host country's government or central bank.

(j) *Interest rate risks* — The risk of an adverse increase in floating interest rates is only very rarely treated as the power purchaser's risk. It is usually simply assumed that the project company will be able to project itself against this risk (*e.g.* by using commercial hedges or obtaining fixed rate loans).

(k) *Reliability of fuel supply* — The project company is generally expected to take the risk of short-term interruptions in its fuel supply. It can, after all, protect itself against short-term interruptions by (in the case of a gas-fired plant) having adequate supplies of back-up fuel or (in the case of a coal-fired plant) having adequate stockpiles of coal.

The treatment of more serious interruptions will depend on whether alternative fuel supplies are readily available. If they are, the project company will be expected to bear the risk of such interruptions. If they are not, the power plant will be deemed to be available (or be deemed to have been dispatched).

(l) *Interconnections* — If certain connections need to be made to the power plant in order for it to be able to generate and those connections are outside its control (for example, the transmission lines to the power plant need to be built by the power purchaser), then, if those connections are not made in time, the power plant will be deemed to be available (or be deemed to have been dispatched) in any event. Failure to connect a fuel supply pipeline may be an exception to this rule. The project company might be expected in some cases to take the risk that such a connection was not made.

(m) *Compensation on termination* — If a PPA is terminated because of a default by the power purchaser, then it is generally accepted that both the banks and the project company's shareholders should be compensated. So long as the total amount of compensation does not exceed the net present value of the project's revenues, the project company should be paid sufficient to repay all amounts due and owing to the banks and to compensate its shareholders for the loss of their investment.

If a PPA is terminated because of force majeure, then compensation is usually payable in relation to amounts owing to the banks but the project company's shareholders will not usually receive any compensation: the risk of prolonged force majeure is considered to be their risk.

If a PPA is terminated because of a default by the project company, then no compensation is usually payable. This is, of course, the same concept as that discussed in section 3.5 above in relation to concession agreements. As noted there, banks and export credit agencies usually do not like this type of provision, but the counter-argument put forward by power purchasers is that the banks can ensure that their loans are repaid by exercising their security or "step-in" rights and saving the project. This, of course, requires the step-in rights to be effective.

When compensation is payable by the power purchaser on a termination of the PPA, it is usually payable in a lump sum. Some power purchasers are beginning to resist this, however, and to insist on such compensation being payable in instalments.

(n) *Limits on liability* — PPAs will usually exclude liability on the part of either party for "consequential" losses, *i.e.* loss of profit. A PPA would not be bankable if the project company could lose millions if it failed to provide electricity that it was called upon to generate. However, sometimes a project company is made liable for consequential losses caused by its gross negligence or wilful misconduct and this is normally accepted by banks. Making the project company liable for consequential losses in these circumstances probably has more to do with keeping the project company honest than giving the power purchaser a right to compensation that it requires since the power purchaser will usually have statutory limits on the amount of its own liability to its consumers.

(o) *Exclusion of background law* — Some legal systems have provisions of law that will automatically apply to any contract, including a PPA, although sometimes they can be expressly excluded. These provisions can introduce uncertainty into a contract. A good example is the type of "financial hardship" clause[76] which enables a party to apply to a court for his contract to be changed if something unforeseen is causing him financial hardship.

The above risk allocation will not hold good in all respects in jurisdictions with a developed private power generating industry such as the United Kingdom and the USA. The current trend in the United Kingdom is to try to leave an ever increasing amount of risk with the project company and, if this cannot be achieved, to pass risk through to contractual counterparties other than power purchasers. As is pointed out in Chapter 10, the United Kingdom electricity pool price used to be perceived as too volatile a revenue stream with which to obtain funding for IPPs in the United

---

[76] See, for example, Art. 1467 of the Italian Civil Code, the text of which is set out in section 4.2 below.

Kingdom. As a result, virtually all IPPs in the United Kingdom which closed prior to 1997 were financed without bank loans or, alternatively, a contract for differences (a "CfD") was entered into between the project company and one or more of its shareholders or regional electricity companies. CfDs act as a hedge: the project company's counterparties essentially agree to guarantee a fixed price per MWh of availability in return for receiving any pool receipts in excess of that fixed price. There is currently talk in the market as to whether or not banks can now be persuaded to finance a "merchant plant" in the United Kingdom, *i.e.* a plant which relies solely on its pool receipts and which does not have a CfD.[77] The main reasons for this appear to be a lack of capacity or willingness on the part of the regional electricity companies to enter into CfDs and a reluctance on the part of developers to surrender the "upside" of projects to the counterparties to CfDs. Although the position is very fluid, the current view on merchant plants appears to be that the pool has possibly not quite been long enough established for them to become regular events (although merchant plants will be possible for the right type type of project)[78] but that it may well be possible to reduce the hedge provided by a CfD (from 100 per cent of the power plant's availability to (say) 75 per cent). The extent to which banks can be persuaded to accept unhedged pool price risk may well be determined by the proportion of the funding which the sponsors are prepared to commit by way of equity. The banks' appetite will presumably increase in direct proportion to the sponsors' willingness to contribute extra equity in order to improve upon the traditional 85:15 or 80:20 debt:equity ratio for a United Kingdom IPP. In addition, there is currently talk of trying to persuade suppliers of gas to United Kingdom IPPs to accept that part of the price for their gas is linked to the pool price and/or to persuade banks and project companies that (because of an over-supply of gas) the energy charge component of a CfD should no longer be a pass-through of the project company's actual fuel costs but a fixed amount (leaving with the project company the risk that it cannot find sufficient gas at the right price).

One of the ways in which developers seem to be finding the additional equity required for a merchant plant is by pressurising

---

[77] Some current schemes even envisage gas-fired power plants determining whether to generate electricity for pool receipts or simply to sell their contracted gas supplies (because they might be able to earn more by simply selling their gas). The banks will generally want to place careful limits on when such gas sales can be made.

[78] The United Kingdom's first merchant plant financed on a project finance basis was Destec's Indian Queens project in Cornwall (140 MW) which achieved financial close in 1996. 35 per cent of its output was still subject to a CfD, however. The first large-scale merchant plant in the United Kingdom (230 MW) was AES's project at Barry in South Wales which achieved financial close in February, 1997.

turbine manufacturers into providing subordinated debt (so-called *vendor financing*). A manufacturer who agrees to do this is essentially funding the purchase of his own equipment and having to share in the risk of the long-term good health of the project. This somewhat aggressive move on the part of developers has proved possible because of the fierce competition among the limited number of turbine manufacturers worldwide to sell their turbines. The developer will try to force the manufacturer to accept a fixed interest rate on the subordinated debt which is considerably lower than the developer's target return on equity. In this way, a developer is able to provide the banks with relatively cheap quasi-equity without giving away too much of the "upside". The requirement to provide vendor financing will obviously be imposed on the manufacturers in the invitation to bid for the turnkey construction or equipment supply contract.

One final technique for the financing of power plants needs to be mentioned: the tolling agreement. The basic idea behind a tolling agreement is that one party, the toller (typically a gas company), will provide fuel to the project company for the project company to convert into electricity on behalf of the toller. The project company is effectively providing the toller with a simple service for which he is to be paid a fee. The project company holds itself ready to generate and the toller tells it when it wishes the project company to burn its fuel. The fuel never belongs to the project company nor, in strict theory, does any amount it receives for the sale of electricity.[79] Both belong to the toller. The fee the project company receives will, however, be similar to a capacity charge (see section 3.11) and the amount of the fee will depend on the levels of plant availability and efficiency. A tolling structure is usually adopted for a project where the fuel supplier has agreed to accept a large proportion of the power price risk and wants a simple documentary arrangement.

---

[79] Tollers will normally insist that the electricity revenues fall outside the scope of the banks' security.

Chapter 4

Bankability

4.1 GENERAL

"Bankability" is, as it sounds, the acceptability or otherwise of a project's structure as the basis of a project financing. What this Chapter seeks to do is to offer suggestions both on what must be included in the underlying documentary framework of a project in order to ensure bankability and on what may be included (or excluded) without prejudicing bankability. Bankability is an art, not a science. It is a very fluid concept, changing rapidly as market practice and sentiment change. It can also be a very deal-specific concept: what is an acceptable balance of risks for one project may not be acceptable for another project with slightly different strengths and weaknesses.

An understanding of banks' attitude to risk can provide a useful insight into some aspects of the ethereal concept of bankability. Bank's credit committees hate surprises and crave predictability. As a general rule, they will not accept risks which are either incapable of proper assessment or analysis or which are potentially open-ended in their effect. Banks will accept the risk that an oilfield may not have sufficient recoverable reserves because reservoir engineers can be commissioned to tell them the likely level of recovery. They will accept the risk that crude oil prices might collapse because analysts can (allegedly) predict trends based on a wealth of historic price data. They can accept the risk of a limited delay in construction because a contractor is prepared to be liable for liquidated damages in this event. But they cannot, for example, take the risk of a change in law in a project where the cost consequences cannot be passed on to the consumer or an offtaker. The change of law risk is a "wild card": there is no way of knowing whether the risk will actually materialise or, if it does, what the extent of the changes will be.[1]

The manner in which this Chapter carries out its analysis of bankability is to take the issue of consents (or, to use the United States phrase, "permits") and each of the project contracts discussed in the previous Chapter and to state the lenders' optimum position in each case. We then look at how this optimum position can be diluted without affecting bankability.

Before commencing the individual analysis, there are probably some general requirements which must be observed in order for any project structure to be bankable. The following is a tentative and probably incomplete and controversial list of these sacred cows:

A. Banks should not take the risk of a change in law.[2] This is subject to what is said about taxes in B below.

B. The project should not be exposed to the possibility of discriminatory taxation.[3] Banks will take the risk of general taxes (*e.g.* general corporate taxes) but will not take the risk that their particular project is singled out for discriminatory taxation.

C. Sponsors should not seek to extract distributions or quasi-distributions prior to the date for the first repayment of the loans or if there is a default or event of default under the project credit agreement.

D. Pre-completion revenues should be applied against the project's capital expenditures (thereby reducing the amount that needs to be funded by the banks).

E. There must be a good faith attempt to share risks. The project company must not be viewed as simply a dumping ground for all of the residual risks that neither the host government nor the sponsors wish to take. There must be some attempt made to pass risks through and away from the project company.

F. Sponsors should not push the capitalisation of their vehicle companies to unacceptable (*i.e.* unacceptably low) limits.

---

[1] Much of this reasoning also applies to sponsors, although they will probably be able to accept a greater degree of risk than banks (because of their potentially greater returns). One of the mistakes made by the United Kingdom government departments in the early days of the PFI was to assume that the private sector could take any risk — it was simply a matter of pricing. Some risks (such as change of law) cannot be priced, however.

[2] It is difficult, as far as English private international law is concerned, to seek to insulate a party from the change of law risk simply by stating that a contract is to be governed by the laws of a chosen country as they existed *at the date the contract was signed.* For a further discussion on this point, see *Dicey and Morris on The Conflict of Laws,* (12th ed. 1993) pp. 1218–19.

[3] See section 3.11(d)(i) and the related footnote.

G. The project company is either not to be liable for consequential loss (most importantly, loss of profits[4]) flowing from a breach by it of its obligations under a project contract or, if it is to be so liable, its liability in this respect must be capped. (The reason for this is that being liable for consequential loss could quickly bankrupt the project company. The point is usually argued for on a reciprocal basis, *i.e.* the other parties to the project contracts do not have to be liable to the project company for consequential loss either).

H. The project company should generally not be responsible for the detailed design of the project.

I. The other parties to the project contracts should not be allowed to terminate those contracts simply because the banks are enforcing their security over the project company's shares or assets.[5]

In addition, although more of a strong preference than a sacred cow, banks will want the project contracts to tell the whole story and not to be subject to terms implied by background law which can distort the allocation of risk as it appears from the face of the contracts. Examples of such implied terms from civil law jurisdictions are provisions of the civil code which allow a court to "equitably reduce" liquidated damages in certain circumstances[6] or to order variations which it thinks are necessary in order for the contractor to carry out the works.[7] Sometimes the parties can contract out of these provisions, but sometimes they cannot. A point often overlooked in common law jurisdictions is that the parties to a contract may have general rights to terminate the contract for breach and that the termination rights specified in a contract are not therefore necessarily exhaustive. If this is a concern, a simple provision can be inserted stating that the specified termination events are the only events which will entitle a party to terminate the contract.

A similar strong preference for banks is that monetary limits on liability under a project contract should be index-linked.

---

[4] The phrase "consequential loss" does not necessarily include loss of profits under English law despite the view of some commentators. See, *e.g.*, the unreported case of *British Sugar plc v. NEI Power Projects Ltd*, Alliott J., December 20, 1996. Liability for loss of profits should always be specifically excluded. It should also be made clear in a power purchase agreement that the project company will not be liable for the cost to the power purchaser of obtaining replacement capacity.

[5] This is one of the purposes of the direct agreement. See section 6.4.

[6] See Art. 1384 of the Italian Civil Code.

[7] See Art. 1660 of the Italian Civil Code.

4.2 FORCE MAJEURE

A few words should first be said about the concept of *force majeure*. *Force majeure* is a commercial law concept (alien to loan agreements) which exonerates a party to a contract from the consequences of a failure to perform his obligations caused by supervening events. One of the first alleged distinctions that any law student learns between common law systems and civil law systems is that the former embrace the notion of strict liability for breach of contract whereas the latter base their liability for breach of contract on fault (*i.e.* wilful wrongdoing or negligence). This distinction between the world's two great systems of law can be exaggerated. Consider the following examples (contrasting English and German law):

(a) *Two parties conclude a long-term contract for the supply of steam for heating purposes at a fixed price. Rampant inflation renders the supply uneconomic.*

These were the facts of a German case in the 1920s.[8] The *Reichsgericht* increased the price specified in the contract, ruling that not to do so would have been an unacceptable disregard of the principles of good faith, justice and equity. Contrast that decision with statements from the House of Lords that a bargain struck between parties would not be affected by "a wholly abnormal rise or fall in prices[9]" and that "the argument that a man can be excused from performance of his contract when it becomes 'commercially' impossible seems to me a dangerous contention which ought not to be admitted unless the parties have plainly contracted to that effect".[10]

(b) *Parties agree that one will sell the other certain fungible goods, available on the market. In one case, the seller's supplier lets him down and the seller is unable to deliver the goods contracted for on the due date. In another*

---

[8] RGZ 100, 130. From a socio-economic point of view, the German position is relatively unsurprising given the hyper-inflation which beset the German economy in 1922 and 1923. In January 1922, there were 192 marks to the dollar; in November 1923, 4,200,000,000,000. An interesting parallel to this German case can be found almost half a century later in Lord Denning M.R.'s judgement in *Staffordshire Area Health Authority v. South Staffordshire Waterworks Co.* [1978] 3 All E.R. 769. In that case, quite clearly influenced by the high United Kingdom inflation rates in the 1970s, Lord Denning was quite open in his intention to allow a contract to be terminated solely by reason of what he viewed as excessive inflation. He did not seek to expand the doctrine of frustration in order to achieve this, however.

[9] *British Movietonenews Ltd v. London and District Cinemas* [1952] A.C. 166, 185. In that case it was also expressly stated (also at p. 185) that a "sudden depreciation of currency" would not frustrate a contract, even though it was unforeseen.

[10] *Tennants (Lancashire) Ltd v. C. S. Wilson & Co. Ltd* [1917] A.C. 495, 510.

case, the goods subsequently become unavailable and cannot be procured, even with the expenditure of additional money by the seller.

German law's starting proposition in relation to sales of fungible goods, as specified in the German Civil Code, is that the seller bears the entire risk of procurement.[11] In the first case cited above, German law would hold the seller liable in damages. So would English law.[12] However, German law's venture into the realm of strict liability has its limitations and the German courts have held that the seller would not be liable in the second case cited above (where the goods in question cannot be procured even with the expenditure of more money).[13] Upon examination, however, English law's position may not in fact be that different. On the facts of the second case cited above, it is possible that an English court might hold that one of the heads of the doctrine of frustration applied (either impossibility or failure of purpose (see below)).

Most observers would still tend to agree, however, that, in contractual relationships between commercial parties, English law has a clear and marked predisposition towards imposing strict liability for breach. Subject to the doctrine of frustration (which is discussed below), the only way for a commercial party to be sure of avoiding strict liability for breach of contract under English law is for him to expressly exclude it. This is, of course, the purpose of the *force majeure* clause: it is an attempt to convert the basis of liability for breach of contract from strict liability to fault.

Before dealing with a typical *force majeure* clause, it is necessary first to say a few words about the doctrine of frustration under English law.[14] This doctrine will operate to discharge a contract if, after it is concluded:

(i) performance becomes impossible[15]; or
(ii) performance becomes illegal; or
(iii) events outside the control of the parties defeat the purpose of the contract.

The so-called "coronation cases" are examples of (iii) above. In the most famous, *Krell v. Henry*,[16] a contract for the hire of rooms

---

[11] para. 279 BGB, a free translation of which is: "If the goods in question are generic, then, as long as such goods are available, the debtor is liable for his inability to deliver even though this may not be due to his fault".

[12] See, *e.g.*, *Barnett v. Javeri & Co* [1916] 2 K.B. 390.

[13] RGZ 88, 172; RGZ 107, 156.

[14] Those seeking an extensive discussion on frustration and *force majeure* should turn to Treitel, *Frustration and Force Majeure*, (1st ed., 1994).

[15] Note that the United States takes a softer approach: it has a doctrine of discharge by reason of impracticability (as opposed to impossibility).

[16] [1903] 2 K.B. 740.

overlooking the route of Edward VII's coronation processions on the days on which the processions were to take place was discharged when the coronation was postponed because of Edward VII's illness. This limb of the doctrine of frustration is generally thought to be very narrow, however.

The role that foreseeability of the supervening event plays in the doctrine is a little unclear, but most commentators accept that, with some qualifications, foreseeability of the supervening event will preclude frustration. If the event was foreseeable, there is a rebuttable presumption that the parties entered into their contract accepting the risk that the event might occur.

Frustration operates to terminate the contract at the time of the frustrating event and to discharge the parties from future performance. This could theoretically lead to inequities since, on the one hand, rights which accrued before frustration remain enforceable whilst, on the other, rights which would have accrued in the future but for the frustration will not accrue. Common law struggled to deal with the inequities and the legislator intervened with the Law Reform (Frustrated Contracts) Act 1943. Under that Act:

(a) all sums payable under the contract before the time of discharge cease to be payable and (save to the extent that the court allows the payee to retain all or any part of the same to cover any expenditure incurred in or towards performing the contract) all sums paid prior to such time are recoverable by the payer[17]; and

(b) where one party has, by virtue of a partial performance of the contract by the other party, obtained a valuable benefit (other than the payment of money) prior to the time of discharge, the court has the power to order that the party who has obtained the benefit pay back an amount not exceeding the value of the benefit.[18]

Civil law systems usually have an "unforseeable circumstances" doctrine which is of more general application than the English law of frustration with its three limbs outlined in (i)–(iii) above. Consider the following Article from the Italian Civil Code (under the heading "Excessive Onerousness")[19]:

"*1467. Contract for mutual counterperformances.* In contracts for continuous or periodic performance or for deferred performance, if

---

[17] The Law Reform (Frustrated Contracts) Act 1943, s.1(2).
[18] *ibid.*, s.1(3).
[19] The translations of the provisions of the Italian Civil Code are taken from the translation by Beltramo, Longo and Merryman (1996).

extraordinary and unforeseeable events make the performance of one of the parties excessively onerous, the party who owes such performance can demand dissolution of the contract, with the effects set forth in Article 1458.

Dissolution cannot be demanded if the supervening onerousness is part of the normal risk of the contract.

A party against whom dissolution is demanded can avoid it by offering to modify equitably the conditions of the contract."

The relevant part of Article 1458 provides:

"*1458. Effects of dissolution.* Dissolution of a contract for non-performance has retroactive effect as between the parties, except in the case of contracts for continuous or periodic performance, with respect to which the effect of dissolution does not extend to performance already made (1467)."

Article 1467 is clearly wider than the English law doctrine of frustration: it applies to any "extraordinary and unforeseeable events" which simply make the performance of the contract by one of the parties "excessively onerous". Furthermore, it effectively gives the court power to modify the terms of the contract. Not surprisingly, banks — with their desire for predictability — do not find this acceptable. The parties can agree to exclude the operation of Article 1467, however, and banks lending to major Italian projects have to date generally insisted that this is done.

The concept of *force majeure* found in project contracts is generally based on the concept of forseeability and, to this extent, is more akin to Article 1467 and similar provisions in civil law jurisdictions than to the English law doctrine of frustration. A typical *force majeure* clause would state that, if a party was prevented or hindered from performing his obligations under the contract in question by *force majeure*, he would be bound to notify the other parties to the contract and to use all reasonable endeavours to find a way of recommencing performance but, in the meantime, would not be held to be in breach to the extent he was not able to perform his obligations by virtue of *force majeure*. (Note that, unlike Article 1467 of the Italian Civil Code, there is no ability to alter the problematic contractual obligations; non-performance of them is simply excused.) *Force majeure* is usually initially defined in a general way as something outside a party's control with a list of specific events then being set out either by way of illustration or as an exhaustive list. Whether these events constitute an illustrative or exhaustive list is obviously one way in which risk can be apportioned between the parties.

91

It is important to understand that the effect of a properly drafted *force majeure* clause is to make a party who might otherwise be in breach of contract not to be in breach if the reason for his non-performance is *force majeure*. Any termination event in a contract which is phrased along the lines of a party being "*in breach* of his obligations" will therefore (quite properly) not apply to a party who is unable to perform because of *force majeure*. However, a termination event which talks about a "*failure* to perform" might well apply. This would be an incorrect result: *force majeure* is intended to make the parties to a contract mark time. If they are concerned about all or part of the contract being in suspense for too long a period because of *force majeure*, they should include a specific termination event dealing with sustained *force majeure*.

A fairly typical definition of *force majeure* would read as follows:

" '*Force Majeure*'
means any event, act, fact or circumstance beyond the direct control of the party invoking *force majeure* and which such party could not have avoided by using reasonable care, including, without limitation:

    (1) strikes or other industrial action;

    (2) war (whether or not declared) or other hostilities (including terrorist action, sabotage, vandalism and riot, insurrection or other civil commotion);

    (3) blockade or embargo;

    (4) adverse natural phenomena (including lightning, earthquake, subsidence, heave, landslip, collapse, hurricane, storm, fire, flood, drought, accumulation of snow or ice, meteorites and volcanic eruption)[20];

    (5) epidemic;

    (6) impact by any vehicle, vessel or aircraft and the effect of pressure waves caused by devices travelling at supersonic speeds;

    (7) explosion, radiation and chemical contamination;

    (8) change of law or regulation (including a change in the interpretation of the same and a change in the terms of any official authorisation or consent); or

---

[20] The references in this paragraph to earthquake, subsidence, heave, landslip and collapse will need careful consideration in the wider debate of who is to bear the risk of unforeseen ground conditions. It would in most circumstances be odd, for example, to stipulate in a turnkey construction contract that the contractor took this risk but then to allow him to invoke such events as *force majeure*.

(9) any act of God.

For the avoidance of doubt, lack of funds does not constitute *force majeure*."

The definition has endless permutations, however. For example, certain events may be capable of constituting *force majeure* for one party but not for the other. Sometimes events which are expressly excluded from *force majeure* are more important than the examples given in a definition of what is included. In a power purchase agreement, for example, lack of fuel may be expressly excluded from the definition of *force majeure*, thereby making it clear that the project company has to bear the risk of an interruption in its fuel supply.

Some contracts include equipment breakdown as *force majeure* but this may be going too far. If the reason for the breakdown is bad maintenance of a pipeline system by the pipeline operator, he should not be able to escape liability for the breakdown by invoking *force majeure*.

Force majeure is sometimes used in the context of "financial balance" clauses (see section 3.5 above) or similar clauses which require one party to compensate the other in some way for the effects of *force majeure*. In these circumstances, the party liable to pay compensation usually does not wish to do so if the other party could have taken out insurance to cover any losses caused by the *force majeure* event in question. The correct way to achieve this result in the drafting is to add a suitable proviso in the relevant substantive clause, not to qualify the entire definition of *force majeure*.

One of the analyses that banks will carry out in relation to the underlying project contracts is the effect of the so-called "disaster scenario". In the case of a power project, they will ask themselves what would happen if, let us say, the power plant was unable to generate because the host government's national grid system was inoperative because of a strike or other industrial dispute. What would the effect of this be under the power purchase agreement? If the effect was that the project company received no revenues, would it still be liable under any take-or-pay provisions contained in the fuel supply contract? If so, how would it find the funds with which to make any such payment?

These thought processes have led to banks trying to ensure that the definition and treatment of *force majeure* is identical in each of the project contracts. While this is a laudable objective, it cannot always be achieved and there is in any event an appalling drafting trap for the unwary. It should be remembered that *force majeure* only excuses a party from performing under a contract to the extent that performance under *that contract* is hindered or prevented. So, if the power plant in the current example was coal-fired, a strike which shut down the national grid would not necessarily mean that the project company could not take delivery of coal. If the power plant's stocks were low and storage space plentiful, the project company's ability to accept delivery of coal would not be hindered or prevented. If the project company wished to be relieved of its obligations to accept coal in these circumstances, this would have to be specifically catered for.

4.3   REQUIREMENTS FOR BANKABILITY

(a) *Consents*. The optimum position for the banks in relation to the consents and authorisations required for a project is as follows:

(i)   All consents should be issued for the duration of the project.

(ii)   The terms of the consents should be subject to as little variation by regulators as possible.

(iii)   The consents should not terminate if the banks enforce their security (which includes selling shares in the project company if they have security over the shares in the project company). Ideally, the consents should run with the project (and not the project company) so that they will inure to a purchaser from the banks following an enforcement.

(iv)   The permits should be fully transferable (this overlaps with point (iii) above).

Banks will need persuading before relaxing any of (i)–(iv) above, although they are prepared to accept various shadings of risk depending on the jurisdiction in which they are dealing and the track record of the various regulators and issuing authorities. For example, the problem that a particular consent or licence may be capable of being terminated if the banks enforce their security may be overcome by the issuance of a suitably-worded comfort letter from the relevant issuing authority. In addition, it may be possible to pass onto another party the risk of not obtaining or renewing a consent and/or the risk of a change in the terms and conditions of a consent. This could be achieved in a concession agreement where the person granting the concession paid the project company a tariff by providing that the tariff still had to be paid even though the project company was not providing the relevant service so long as the reason the service was not being provided was an *unjustifiable* refusal to grant or renew a consent or an *unjustifiable* alteration of the terms and conditions.[21] This technique has been used in the past to persuade banks to lend to projects with very short-dated consents (*e.g.* three years).

(b) *The shareholders agreement and the sponsors' contributions.* The optimum position for the banks is:

    (i) The sponsors should provide all of their equity contributions up-front.

    (ii) The sponsors should provide cover for cost overruns.

    (iii) The sponsors should provide cover for any gaps in insurance coverage.

As far as (i) above is concerned, paying in equity contributions over time or even back-ending those contributions[22] will be acceptable so long as the banks are happy with the creditworthiness of the entities due to make those contributions or receive some form of credit enhancement (such as a bank letter of credit) if they are not.[23] In addition, banks will expect any equity contribution not yet made to be capable of being called in on the occurrence of an event of default or potential event of default under their loan agreement. Insisting that the trigger is a potential event of default (as opposed to an actual of default) is unpopular with sponsors, but the banks argue that they need access to the funds in order to sort out any problem and stave off the occurrence of an actual event of default. This is nevertheless a harsh position, and if the point has to be conceded, the sponsors should try to negotiate that the reference to potential events of default must only be to the more serious events.

(ii) above will depend very much on the project in question and extent to which the sponsors wish the financing to be without recourse to them in any way. In developed jurisdictions with a project with known risks, (ii) is likely to be very much the exception

---

[21] See section 3.12(h) for the use of this technique in power purchase agreements.

[22] Of course, back-ending a sponsor's equity contributions will allow a sponsor who is also the contractor in a project to fund those contributions out of the payments he receives under the construction contract.

[23] The New York project finance market has developed an interesting variant which has the project finance banks effectively bridging the sponsors' equity contributions. The banks lend during the construction phase an amount equal to the sponsors' equity contributions on the strengh of a guarantee from the sponsors. The sponsors then make their equity contributions to the project company on the earlier of completion of the project or an agreed long-stop date and these equity proceeds are used to repay the banks' loans. As noted in section 3.4(a), back-ending the sponsors' actual equity contributions allows them to increase their IRR (because they do not have to use their own funds until much later in the life of the project).

rather than the rule. However, if the banks are making a cost overrun facility available, then the sponsors will be expected to make equity injections each time such bank facility is used with loans and equity being contributed in the same ratio as the general debt:equity ratio for the project.

(iii) is included as an example of how problems with insurance might be solved. In 1993, the London (if not the European) insurance markets had difficulty with insuring more than a few gas turbines (destined for power plants) in marine transit at any one time. In 1992, the insurance market was unwilling to provide cover for General Electric's new 9F turbine during the commissioning phase (since the design was untested). For their part, the banks financing the projects in the United Kingdom using those turbines were unwilling to have no cover during the commissioning phase (the time when any complex machinery is liable to go wrong and cause damage) and one of the solutions suggested in order to allow the projects to proceed was that the sponsors effectively stood in the insurers' place by providing loans to the project company to repair any damage caused during commissioning.

Banks may seek to pass insurance gaps onto other parties (making them effectively insurers) or to structure out of problems. Using the above example related to insurance for turbines in marine transit, it may be possible to structure the acquisition of a turbine by the project company so that risk does not pass to the project company until the turbine reaches its port of destination. The latter course would almost certainly have an effect on the price for the turbine, however, because the problem would be shifted onto the manufacturer.

(c) *The concession agreement.* The optimum position here is as follows:

(i) The terms of the concession should be fixed for the life of the project.
(ii) There should not be any unduly onerous terms imposed on the project company, *e.g.* a high level of liquidated damages if completion is not achieved by a fixed date if the project company is unable to pass-through all of those liquidated damages to its own contractor.
(iii) The grantor of the concession should accept the change in law risk. So, for example, at the very least the concession period will be extended if the construction of the project is delayed because new regulations come into force requiring a re-working of the design or the retrofitting of new environmental protection equipment.

(iv) The concession period should be extended by any period of *force majeure*.
(v) The concession should not terminate simply because the banks enforce their security.
(vi) The arrangements for termination of the concession (when permitted) should not be expropriatory and any compensation to which the project company is entitled should always be sufficient to repay the banks (even if the concession is being terminated for default by the project company).
(vii) On an enforcement, the banks should be able to freely transfer the concession to a third party.

(i) is fairly essential. As far as (ii) is concerned, banks may be prepared to accept fairly onerous terms in a concession agreement so long as the project company is able to pass through a fair degree of the risk to other contracting parties with acceptable creditworthiness. As noted above, it will be difficult for banks to accept that the project companies should accept the change in law risk and they will be concerned to know how any actual expenditure brought about by a change in law is to be funded and amortised. Whether or not banks are concerned as to whether or not the concession period is to be extended by *force majeure* will very much depend on the length of the original concession period and the projected final maturity of the loans. (v) is essential. As far as (vi) is concerned, whether or not banks can get comfortable with other arrangements in relation to termination compensation will depend upon how any base compensation payments are to be calculated (usually by reference to the net present value of foregone revenue) and the level of protection that those base compensation payments give them. As noted above (see section 3.5), banks will sometimes accept that there should be no compensation if the concession agreement is terminated by reason of the project company's default (although this will usually require a good direct agreement (see section 6.4) and a high degree of confidence on the part of the banks as to the ability of the project company to carry out the project and comply with the terms of the concession agreement). The deal struck on compensation for termination for other reasons is usually that the compensation should be sufficient to repay debt and equity (and provide some return on equity) in the case of termination by reason of a default on the part of the person granting the concession and that it should be sufficient to repay debt in the case of termination for *force majeure* (subject to a

97

possible limit calculated by reference to the project's NPV to ensure that the banks still take some aspect of project risk[24]).

Banks will usually reluctantly accept that, at least where the project is of national importance, the person granting the concession has a veto over the identity of the concessionaire, although it is sometimes possible to limit such person's control to satisfaction with the technical and financial capability of any proposed new concessionaire.

(d) *The construction contract.* The banks' shopping list for the construction contract is fairly predictable:

(i) The construction contract must be turnkey. No aspect of the construction and design should "fall between the cracks". So, for example, if the contractor is basing his design on any plans or data supplied by the project company, the contractor should be given the opportunity to verify the accuracy of the same but must take responsibility for them, even though they were supplied (or even prepared by) the project company. Similarly, there must be no nominated subcontractors or equipment specified by the project company (or, if there are, the contractor must take responsibility for the same).

(ii) There should be a fixed price, incapable of being reopened, and the price should be paid in one lump sum on completion.

(iii) Completion must occur within a fixed period.

(iv) The *force majeure* events should be limited.

(v) Where there is a concession agreement, the contractor should only be able to claim *force majeure*, an increase in price or an extension of time to the extent that the project company is able to claim *force majeure*, an increase in price or an extension of time on the same grounds under the concession agreement. In addition, completion under the construction contract can only occur when completion also occurs under the concession agreement.

(vi) Liquidated damages should be payable if completion is not achieved by a fixed date and those liquidated

---

[24] Although an adjustment would need to be made if a default by the person granting the concession had had an adverse effect on the NPV. The reason for the NPV limit is referred to in section 3.5.

damages should be adequate and at least cover interest payable on the loan for a reasonable period.[25]

(vii) There should be no contract administrator or engineer, but an employer's agent instead. (The point here is that, as an employer's agent would be the agent of the project company, he should be made subject to the restrictions on his principal contained in the project credit agreement (*e.g.* restrictions on agreeing to variation orders). An independent contract administrator or engineer cannot really be made so subject without corrupting his role as an independent arbiter between the parties).

(viii) There should be no (or large) limits on the contractor's liability.

(ix) The contractor should give extensive guarantees and, if the contractor is to be released from liability for defects after a period, that period should be long (in a domestic transaction the starting position is usually two years for mechanical and electrical works and five years for civil works) and only run from the passing of a well-defined completion test.

The above "wish list" is seldom achieved for the understandable reason that few contractors are ever prepared to offer those terms. Banks may be satisfied with a project management approach to construction so long as they receive technical advice that all aspects of the design and works are covered by the individual construction contracts and are persuaded that the overall position with regard to limits on liability, liquidated damages and warranties is acceptable.[26] The position with regard to liquidated damages under a project management approach will rarely provide as much protection as under a turnkey construction contract. As each individual contractor could, for example, cause delay, each individual contractor should in strict theory be liable for the full amount of delay liquidated damages that a turnkey contractor would be expected to pay (see below). Imposing this liability on an individual contractor

---

[25] Banks essentially see liquidated damages as a revenue stream which substitutes for the project's real revenue stream in the event of delay. However, the way the construction industry sometimes operates is that liquidated damages are simply to be set off against the final payment(s) due to the contractor. If it is intended (as it usually is in project financings) that the contractor must actually pay cash, any provision in the construction contract along the above lines should be amended accordingly.

[26] Even with a turnkey construction contract as opposed to a project management agreement, the banks will need to be satisifed by their technical adviser that the specification is complete and will truly produce a turnkey project.

in a project management situation would be entirely disproportionate to his contract's value, however.

As far as a fixed price is concerned, banks will accept that the contractor should not take the change of law risk as far as the price of the works is concerned so long as they are satisfied that the overall project structure insulates the project company from that risk to a high degree (see above). They will, however, expect any of the standard price re-openers to be justified (for example, must there be any provisional sums?). Banks will accept that the high theory of the lump sum payment is really unobtainable and that the construction contract may instead have stage payments so long as these are made on sensible milestones being achieved or by reference to the value of work done (see section 3.6(g) above) and so long as some price retention (or a bond in lieu thereof) is included. They will object to stage payments being made which bear no correlation to the value of works done and which smack of the contractor trying to extract his profit early.

Banks will normally accept the construction period being extended for *force majeure* and certain other risks (*e.g.* antiquities) subject to their usual due diligence exercise. They are also prepared to allow the project company to take unforeseen ground risk so long as they can be satisfied that the risk is a low one (through sight of appropriate surveyors' reports). Banks dislike wide *force majeure* clauses and normally, for example, expect a contractor to take responsibility for his own workforce in terms of industrial action. However, their ultimate position on the construction contract's *force majeure* provisions may well depend on the consequences of *force majeure* for the project as a whole. So, for example, extending the construction period for *force majeure* would be acceptable so long as the banks could be sure that any period by which the project company had to achieve completion under the concession agreement was extended in the same circumstances by a similar period. In this connection, it is difficult to persuade banks away from the position stated in (v) above and, if this is the case, contractors should argue for the right to be joined in any dispute procedure under the concession agreement so that they can ensure that their point of view is heard in the forum that will decide whether or not they are entitled to *force majeure* relief, an increase in price, an extension of time or the issue of a completion certificate. Sometimes in concession-based projects, banks go further and request a general provision to be included in a construction contract stating that the contractor can only claim from the project company what the project company is able to claim (and actually receives) from the person granting the concession. To the extent this type of provision applies to damages and indemnity claims, there is a technical problem in that the provision may deprive the project company of any loss for which to claim from the person granting the concession in the first place. The way to solve this problem is probably to treat it as a timing issue and to state that the project company is only obliged to make a payment to the contractor when the project company receives the corresponding payment from the person granting the concession.[27] Another general provision banks will often request in concession-based projects is a provision stating that the contractor will perform his obligations so as not to cause the project company to be in breach of the terms of the concession agreement.

Banks will accept a contract administrator or engineer if they have to, but will try to prevent him overriding the more important of their reserved discretions[28] in a direct agreement with him.

Banks will normally expect a contractor to suffer some degree of pain with liquidated damages if completion is not achieved by a fixed date but will be prepared to accept sensible limits on a contractor's liability. The banks' position on product or performance guarantees and warranties will largely depend upon the technical advice that they receive. A lesser degree of warranty protection will obviously be more acceptable if the technology involved is proven.

(e) *The operation and maintenance agreement.* The optimum position for the banks corresponds with that of the project company and is as follows:

(i) The operator should be given proper incentives to run the project properly and efficiently in order to maximise the project company's profit.

(ii) Conversely, the operator should be subject to tough penalties if certain operating targets are not met.

(iii) The banks should be able to remove (or bring about the removal of) the operator for poor performance.

The balance of incentives and penalties will need to be negotiated on a project by project basis and it is impossible to make any generalisation about them other than that the banks will expect the point at which incentives become penalties to be a point comfortably above that at which repayment of their loans is put in jeopardy. If the operation and maintenance agreement is between the project

---

[27] This solution was originally suggested to the author by Hilary Wilson of Trafalgar House/ Kvaerner.

[28] See section 5.8(i)(iv).

company and a related company and it does not, as a result, include a system of incentives and penalties (see section 3.7 above), the banks will expect to have some control over the operation and maintenance budget (since there is no incentive on the operator to operate efficiently).

It will be difficult to deny the banks the right to require the dismissal of the operator for poor performance although this is usually done by allowing the banks some control over the exercise of the termination right that the project company has under the operation and maintenance agreement. The banks are sometimes afforded this control prior to the time when they enforce their security. If the operator is a related company, the banks may also insist on a break clause in his operation and maintenance agreement which would allow them to terminate the agreement without cause if they stepped in. This would allow the banks either to renegotiate the agreement to put it onto arms'-length terms (*e.g.* proper incentives and penalties) or to replace the related company with a more motivated third party.

(f) *The supply contract.* The main issues for the banks in a supply contract are those that will also pre-occupy the project company, namely:

(i) Security of supply and the remedies for unwarranted interruption of supply.
(ii) The fierceness of any take-or-pay obligation imposed on the project company.

Banks' reactions to both issues will depend on a number of factors, including the availability of alternative supplies (for example, gas oil for gas-fired power plants). There are projects which have been banked where the parties have accepted that the only remedy for failure to supply gas should be the right to receive shortfall gas (see section 3.10(g) above). As far as any take-or-pay provisions are concerned, banks will expect a high degree of overlap between the supply contract's definition of *force majeure* and that contained in the other project contracts.

(g) *The offtake agreement.* The banks' reaction to the terms of an offtake agreement depends to a large extent on the identity of the offtaker (is he also a shareholder?) and whether the offtake agreement is an arms-length market price arrangement or a pass-through arrangement (see section 3.9 above). In the former case, the banks will be concerned to see that the project company is offered true market terms and that the offtaker's credit-standing is acceptable. While the creditworthiness of the offtaker will also be an issue in

102

the latter case, the banks' analysis here is more complex. The optimum bankable position is:

(i) A full pass-through of capital and energy costs.

(ii) Any pass-through should be effected in matching currencies (so that the project company does not bear any residual foreign exchange risk).

(iii) There should be an extensive assumption of the *force majeure* risk by the offtaker (the offtaker should effectively "stand still" notwithstanding the fact that the project company cannot produce the required product).

Banks are happy, however, to link a pass-through of costs to various targets being achieved so long as they are satisfied with the levels at which those targets are set. They are more sensitive with regard to the currency risk (this is considered as a fundamental principle of sound lending), although there are, of course, often various hedges that can be taken out by the project company in the bank market. The assumption by the offtaker of *force majeure* risk is part of the general issue relating to *force majeure* discussed above. In PPAs in emerging markets, banks will seek the standard risk allocation already extensively described in section 3.12.

4.4 LENDERS' SECURITY CONCERNS

Some concerns the potential lenders to a project might have on the underlying contracts have been touched on above. Apart from those (and apart from having to satisfy themselves on how acceptable the general apportionment of risk is), the lenders' main legal concerns on the underlying contracts are likely to be:

(a) ensuring that they can take effective security over the contracts; and

(b) ensuring that all of the key contracts remain in place in one form or another if and when they enforce their security.

In order to meet the first concern, each contract over which the lenders propose to take security should be capable of being charged or assigned to the lenders by way of security and any consents required from the other contracting parties for this to occur must be obtained. It should be noted that, if a contract is governed by English law and is stated to be non-assignable, that contract probably cannot be charged or assigned by way of security by one

103

party without the other party's consent.[29] If such consent is not forthcoming, the most that can be obtained (subject, in the case of project companies incorporated in England and Wales, to some difficult arguments about the powers of administrative receivers in relation to English companies [30]) is a charge on the proceeds of the contract. A charge on the proceeds of a contract is subject to an obvious limitation: it does not confer on the person entitled to the charge the right to generate the proceeds in the first place (for example, by making a demand for payment) and the proceeds may therefore never arise. In order to meet the second concern, it will be necessary to examine the termination clauses in each underlying contract. Not surprisingly, there will usually be provisions entitling the other contracting parties to terminate the contract if the project company is insolvent, if any security it gives is enforced or if another party obtains control of its shares. If these provisions are left to stand in the major underlying contracts, there is clearly a risk that the lenders will be held to ransom — they will not be able to take enforcement action without opening themselves up to the possibility of a renegotiation of the contracts' terms. For this reason, lenders will usually seek to have the provisions amended or to have the other contracting parties enter into direct agreements with them (see section 6.4).

---

[29] See, *e.g.*, *Helstan Securities v. Hertfordshire County Council* [1978] 3 All E.R. 262.

[30] The main argument is that the power to carry on the business of a company conferred on an administrative receiver of a company by para. 14 of Sched. 1 to the Insolvency Act 1986 is an overriding statutory power and that the nature of an administrative receivership could be subverted if a party contracting with the company could effectively put certain rights out of the administrative receiver's reach. The argument against this is that a contracting party should be free to stipulate that the contract in question is truly personal to the company and that, if this contract is a major asset of the company, this may simply mean that any receiver appointed over the company's assets cannot be an administrative receiver in the first place (because he cannot be appointed over the whole or substantially the whole of the company's property for the purposes of s.29(2)(a) of the Insolvency Act 1986).

Chapter 5

The Credit Agreement

5.1 BASIC TERMS

A typical term (as opposed to "on-demand") loan agreement[1] in the London bank market (whether the lender was a single bank or a syndicate of banks and whether or not related to a project financing) would contain the following provisions:

(a) *General conditions precedent.* Various general conditions precedent would have to be satisfied before any bank was obliged to lend any money. These would include the delivery of certified copies of the borrower's constitutional documents, of any relevant board and shareholder resolutions and of any key documents and the delivery of legal opinions confirming, inter alia, that the loan agreement was within the borrower's powers and had been properly authorised.

(b) *Conditions precedent to each drawdown.* In addition, at least two standard conditions would have to be satisfied on the date that any drawdown request or drawdown was made: first, that no event of default (see below) or event which, "with the giving of notice, lapse of time or fulfilment of any other condition",[2] would constitute an event of default (a "potential event of default") had occurred and was continuing on that date and, secondly, that no representation or

---

[1] Loans that are repayable on demand rarely (if ever) constitute the core funding for a project because they are not sufficiently committed.

[2] The point of the reference to a potential event of default is to prevent a bank from being forced to "lend into a default". If a borrower has negotiated a grace period of (say) two business days before a non-payment by him under a loan agreement constitutes an *actual* event of default, the wording relating to "lapse of time" in the definition of potential event of default will permit a bank to refuse to lend money on the date the borrower fails to make the payment (and not simply on the date two business days thereafter). If a potential event of default draw-stop applies in the construction period of a project, this will rapidly lead to a full-blown event of default because the project company will usually lose the ability to draw down funds to pay interest and a non-payment event of default will result.

warranty made or deemed to be made or repeated on that date under the loan agreement was incorrect. Although the second condition is found in virtually every term loan agreement, it is probably otiose because the breach of a representation or warranty is invariably an event of default.

(c) *Drawdown mechanics.* It is London market practice that the borrower cannot request a loan denominated in a currency other than sterling (a "Eurocurrency") any later than two business days prior to the proposed date of drawdown. By contrast, if the borrower wishes to draw down in sterling, he can theoretically request the loan up to 11.00 a.m. (London time) on the proposed date of drawdown itself. (This is because the banks may have to go into the London interbank market themselves to borrow any Eurocurrency to on-lend to the borrower and the market will only deliver the Eurocurrency two business days later. By contrast, sterling is (or is deemed to be) readily available to all banks in the London market.) The above notice periods for drawdown will be longer if the loan agreement is a syndicated one (for purely logistical reasons — the agent bank will need time to contact each member of the syndicate).

(d) *An interest clause.* Interest on sterling loans is sometimes charged at a margin over base rate. (The size of the margin will depend on the bank's view of the riskiness of the loan.) Where interest is charged by reference to base rate, the loan agreement should stipulate which bank's base rate is being used (particularly if the loan agreement is syndicated). There may be a London base rate for a very limited number of other currencies (in particular United States dollars when lent by the London branches of United States banks).

However, interest on sterling loans may also, and interest on Eurocurrency loans usually will, be charged at a margin over LIBOR (the London Interbank Offered Rate). LIBOR is the rate at which banks can themselves borrow money from other banks in the London interbank market. When interest is charged by reference to LIBOR, the theory is that each bank is itself borrowing money to lend to the borrower (so-called "match-funding"). Although a loan agreement may be drafted in this way, some banks do not actually match-fund on a loan by loan basis but actively manage their funding exposure and seek to balance their borrowings with their lending commitments across the board.

Banks will usually only obtain funds in the London interbank market with short maturities. One year is generally speaking the longest maturity that they will or can obtain for the purpose of funding their commitments under a term loan agreement. The market quotes rates for a range of shorter maturities, however: one, two, three and six months are the most common. The short-term nature of the interbank funding that is available means that a bank will usually have to borrow funds from the interbank market on a number of occasions during the course of a term loan. The borrower is usually able to select the maturity of each borrowing his banks are to make: he does this by specifying each "interest period" that is to apply to his loan. Interest is generally paid at the end of each interest period and this enables the banks in turn to pay the interest then due on their own interbank borrowings. They repay the principal of each interbank borrowing with the proceeds of another interbank borrowing (save to the extent the borrower actually makes a repayment). This process of repaying one interbank borrowing with the proceeds of another interbank borrowing is called "rolling-over".

If the borrower repays or prepays principal otherwise than on the last day of an interest period in a matching amount, the banks may incur losses in that, whilst they are themselves still incurring interest on their matched borrowing from the interbank market, they are no longer receiving interest from the borrower with which to meet the same. These losses are called "breakage costs". Whether or not banks actually incur them will be determined by whether or not they can redeploy the funds repaid or prepaid in the interbank market and achieve a return at least equal to the interest they are having to pay. The borrower has to indemnify banks against any breakage costs.

(e) *A repayment clause.* A term loan may be repayable in one lump sum (this is referred to as a "bullet repayment") or in instalments of fixed or variable amounts.

(f) *Margin protection clauses.* Ignoring income from arrangement fees and the like, banks make their profit when lending money out of the margin they charge as part of the interest rate. Banks will express the interest rate as "one per cent over LIBOR" — one per cent is the margin and LIBOR reflects their cost of funds, *i.e.* what they must pay the person in the interbank market who provided them with the matching funds. If a bank suffers an unexpected cost connected with making a loan, this will obviously erode its margin: it has to pay the LIBOR element of any interest it receives from the borrower to its match-funder in the market come what may.

Three main types of margin protection clause are included in loan agreements as a result. Their inclusion is invariable market practice. A borrower may not consider them fair, but they seek to address apportionment of risk as between the borrower and the bank, not fairness. The three types of clause are:

(i) *The gross-up clause.* This clause provides that, if a deduction has to be made by law from any payment the borrower makes to the bank (and the main instance of this would be a withholding tax on an interest payment), then the borrower has to "gross up" the payment so that the bank receives, after the relevant deduction, the same amount that it would have received had the deduction not been made. (This enables the bank to pay, out of moneys received from the borrower, the precise amount due to his match-funder on the interest payment (or rollover) date.) The bank will usually eventually get a credit under a double taxation treaty for the tax withheld and this leads to an understandable cry of foul from the borrower: not only has he had to pay extra interest, but the bank has received a windfall. This in turn usually leads to a debate over whether or not to include a so-called "tax credit reimbursement" clause (usually in fairly weak terms) in the loan agreement.

(ii) *The increased costs clause.* This clause deals with the possibility that a change in practice or regulation by bank regulatory authorities or a change in law may make it more expensive for a bank to lend money (either generally or to this particular borrower). If this occurs, the clause requires the borrower to compensate the bank for the increased cost or reduction in return.

(iii) *The market disruption clause.* This clause can best be explained by reference to its historical origins. The Eurocurrency market in London grew up in the 1960s and 1970s as a result largely of the Arab states depositing with London banks enormous amounts of the dollar revenues they earned from the sale of oil. The deposits were made with London banks because they were able to offer higher rates of interest than their United States counterparts. There was at the time a certain amount of nervousness that the Eurocurrency market might only be an evanescent phenomenon and, as a result, the first Eurodollar term loan agreements included provisions stating what was to happen if the lenders suddenly became unable to obtain dollar deposits on the London interbank market for match-funding purposes because the Eurodollar market simply disappeared overnight (*i.e.* the dollars fled elsewhere). The solution adopted was that, in these circumstances,

108

the banks would fund their participations from whatever other reasonable sources they chose (for example, from the United States domestic market or from the Paris interbank market) and the borrower would be obliged to pay interest at the normal margin over the banks' cost of funds from these other sources. Today's market disruption clause is pretty much the same and it is important to appreciate (as is obvious once the origin of the clause is known) that it should really only deal with disruption to the interbank market generally and not with problems affecting individual banks. The history behind the clause has become so lost in the mists of time, however, that it is now even found in London-based sterling loans.

(g) *The illegality clause.* This clause states that, if it becomes illegal for a bank to continue to make loans or otherwise participate in the loan agreement, the borrower must prepay the loans made by that bank and the bank's obligations will be terminated.

(h) *Representations and warranties.* The representations and warranties in a loan agreement serve in practice a totally different purpose from the representations and warranties in a commercial contract such as an agreement for the sale and purchase of a business. Although the banks will in theory be able to sue for damages for breach of a representation and warranty in a loan agreement, they are not in the main interested in a damages claim — if things go wrong, they simply want their money back and the best way to do this is to give them a debt (and not a damages) claim. This is done by making the breach of representation and warranty under the loan agreement an event of default (see below). The representations and warranties are often made "evergreen", *i.e.* they are made to repeat at various times throughout the life of the loan (for example, on drawdown and interest payment dates) with reference to the facts and circumstances then subsisting and in this way they are made to afford the banks a degree of continuing protection.

(i) *Undertakings.* A loan agreement will contain various undertakings from the borrower, ranging from the purely informative (an undertaking to deliver annual accounts) to the financially protective (the negative pledge, *i.e.* an undertaking not to create security). The three key undertakings in a corporate (as opposed to a project) credit agreement are the negative pledge, an undertaking not to dispose of assets (subject to certain exceptions) and an undertaking on the part of the borrower not to change its business. The purpose of these three undertakings is (put crudely) to keep the borrower the way he was when the bank decided he was an acceptable credit risk and entered into the credit agreement.

(j) *Events of Default.* The problem with a term loan for a lender is that, if the borrower goes into liquidation prior to the final maturity date, the lender, if he relied on the repayment clause alone, would only be able to make a contingent proof in the liquidation (as the principal of his loan would not yet be due for repayment). This is, not surprisingly, considered totally unaccept-able and all term loan agreements should contain a clause dealing with events of default and acceleration in order to overcome the problem. If an event of default occurs, the bank can "accelerate" the loans, *i.e.* declare them to be immediately due and payable. (A bank is usually afforded other remedies on the occurrence of an event of default: it can cancel its commitment to lend entirely and (some-times) it can by notice to the borrower turn the term loan into a demand loan.)

Events of default in a typical loan agreement will include non-payment, breach of representation and warranty, breach of cove-nant, insolvency and "cross-default". Cross-default is essentially the occurrence of a default under any of the borrower's other borrow-ings or financial obligations. A cross-default is meant to be an indication that the borrower is in serious financial difficulties. It is at its most important in an unsecured loan where a lender will need the ability to accelerate his (unsecured) loan at the same time as any other lenders are able to do the same. If he cannot do this, the other lenders will be able to accelerate before him, obtain final judgement before him and then execute against the borrower's assets before him, effectively putting him in a subordinate position even through they too might have been unsecured.

There are, of course, typically various other clauses in a loan agreement (such as a clause dealing with how payments are to be made and an indemnity against stamp duties), but the above are the most important clauses for our purposes. It is not the intention of this book to explain how a borrower would normally seek to negotiate the above clauses (for example, by introducing concepts of materiality into the representations and warranties and by seeking a number of days' grace before an event of default for non-payment can occur). However, there are specific points to make in relation to a project financing on virtually every clause referred to in (a)–(j) and these are discussed in detail in section 5.8 below. The interven-ing sections deal with more general issues relating to the credit agreement in the context of a project financing.

5.2   THE NON-RECOURSE OR LIMITED RECOURSE CONCEPT

The general principle behind "non-recourse" or "limited recourse" transactions is that the lenders are only entitled to look to certain assets of the borrower for repayment of their loans and the payment of interest. It is important not to think just in terms of loans — the non-recourse or limited recourse concept can be applied to other forms of financing as well (such as finance leases). As far as loans are concerned, however, non-recourse or limited recourse deals are only really possible where the lenders are given security over the assets in question. Without security, other creditors may be able to have access to the assets upon which the lenders are relying and, if this risk ever materialised, the basis upon which the lenders went into the deal would be corrupted.

The simplest way for a sponsor to obtain financing on a non-recourse or limited recourse basis is for him to form a sole purpose company (which may or may not be a subsidiary) for a project, to raise all of the finance necessary for the project through that company and to grant the lenders full security over every asset that the company owns. This is known as "de facto" non- or limited recourse: although the rights of the lenders to take action against the borrower are not qualified, there is in practice (so long as there is no reason to lift the corporate veil) no recourse through to the sponsor shareholder. Although *de facto* non- or limited recourse has now more or less become the "norm", especially where there are many sponsors involved in a project, it is not always appropriate. For tax reasons, a sponsor may not wish to start up a project in or transfer a project to a separate company[3] and in such circumstances he will seek to "ring-fence" the assets comprised in the project and restrict the project lenders' rights so that they can only look to those assets for payment. Whilst just offering the lenders security over the project assets seems sufficient for these purposes, it is not, since the sponsor, as borrower, will be under a personal covenant to repay the project loans. If the loans go into default, the project lenders will not only be able to enforce their security over the project assets, they will also be able to sue the sponsor on his covenant to pay and, by enforcing that covenant through the courts, eventually have access to his other assets. However, it is possible to qualify the

---

[3] He may be generating profits and he may wish to offset interest accrued on the project loans against those profits. In some jurisdictions, this will only be possible if the profits occur and the interest accrues in the same legal entity.

borrower's covenant to pay so that, even on an enforcement of that covenant, the lenders will only be able to look to the project assets. This results in what is known as "de iure" non- or limited recourse and this is the principal subject of the remainder of this section 5.2.

There is much discussion about the difference between "non-recourse" and "limited recourse" finance. "Non-recourse" is generally understood to mean that the lenders can in all circumstances only have recourse to the assets in question and never to the borrower. In other words, their only remedy for non-payment is an enforcement of their security and they can never simply sue the borrower on a personal covenant to pay. It would be wrong to say that this type of finance is never found, but it is rare.

The main problem with non-recourse deals from the lenders' point of view is that they are usually prepared to restrict their remedies to enforcing their security over an asset only if the borrower does what is expected of him in relation to that asset. This is part of the general allocation of risks between the borrower and the lenders. So, for example, a particular set of lenders would be prepared to restrict their remedies to an enforcement of their security over a particular construction project so long as the borrower diligently complied with an obligation to build the project. Limited recourse deals are therefore deals which offer the borrower some degree of immunity from personal suit but which try to preserve rights against the borrower if he does not comply with his part of the bargain, *i.e.* if he does not comply with certain obligations to the lenders in relation to the development and operation of the project in question. (*De facto* non- or limited recourse financings effected through a sole purpose company are, of course, in their purest form non-recourse (and not limited recourse) financings as far as access to the sponsors and their assets is concerned.)

The problem that limited recourse deals have, however, is defining what rights the lenders have against the borrower if he does not comply with his project-related obligations. One solution is simply to make the loans full recourse in the case of any such non-compliance, but this "sudden death" situation is often seen by borrowers as an extreme solution. An alternative is simply to allow the lenders to sue the borrower for damages for breach of the relevant undertaking or representation and warranty in the credit agreement. While such an action would be subject to all the general limitations on a claim for damages (such as causation, remoteness of damage and mitigation of loss) and may therefore be of limited monetary use to the lenders, it would constitute a full recourse claim against the borrower and may as such be enough to secure the borrower's co-operation in rectifying the problem.

The following is an example of a fairly well-developed limited recourse clause in a syndicated credit agreement. It relates to a loan where the borrower is a company in England and Wales and the banks do not have security over all of the borrower's assets which includes a floating charge. (This example has been chosen because it leads to the most complex type of limited recourse clause since the lenders may not be able to block the appointment of an administrator[4] and the assets within their security might therefore be disposed of, not on an enforcement of their security, but by an administrator in the course of an administration.)

"5. LIMITED RECOURSE
5.1 Statement of limited recourse

(a) Notwithstanding any provision to the contrary in any Finance Document (but subject to Clause 5.2 (Breach of warranties)), the liability of the Borrower to pay Limited Recourse Payments at any time shall be limited to amounts equal to:-

  (i) Net Revenues; and/or

  (ii) the aggregate amount (without any deduction for or on account of any set-off or similar right exercisable against the Borrower) payable to or to the order of the Borrower in respect of Compensation (but only insofar as the same does not constitute proceeds of insurance which the Agent is satisfied will be applied in reinstatement of the Project Facilities in accordance with this Agreement); and/or

  (iii) the aggregate amount (without any deduction for or on account of any set-off or similar right exercisable against the Agent or any Bank) generated by the enforcement of the Security Interests created or evidenced by the Security Documents (and including,

---

[4] If loans made by a lender are secured by a charge which was created as a floating charge (or by a floating charge and other security interests) and such charge (or charges) are over *the whole (or substantially the whole)* of the chargor's property, then any receiver appointed by that lender will be an administrative receiver (see s.29(2)(a) of the Insolvency Act 1986) and, if such a receiver is appointed over a company's assets, a court is bound to dismiss a petition for the appointment of an administrator in relation to that company (see s.9(3) of the Insolvency Act 1986). But, if a lender's security does not include a floating charge or covers only part of the company's property, that lender cannot prevent the appointment of an administrator because any receiver he appoints will not be an administrative receiver. Borrowers sometimes refuse to give "full floaters". This is often the case in the North Sea where a borrower may own interests in a number of fields, not just the interest that is the subject of the project financing and he is reluctant to jeopardise his ability to project finance the other interests by granting security over them to banks other than those providing the project finance for such other interests. The "featherweight floater" has been developed to meet both parties' requirements, however (see Chapter 6 and section 6.2 in particular).

without limitation, the proceeds of any set-off against the Control Accounts); and/or

(iv) the aggregate amount (without any deduction for or on account of any set-off or similar right exercisable against the Borrower and/or its administrator and/or the Agent or any Bank) of the proceeds of any disposal by an administrator of all or any part of the Borrower's interest in the Project; and/or

(v) (except to the extent falling within sub-paragraph (iv) above) the amount of any deficiency of the sort referred to in Section 15(5) of the Insolvency Act 1986 arising on any disposal of the kind referred to in sub-paragraph (iv) above.

If the amounts listed in sub-paragraphs (i)-(v) above are insufficient to pay all Limited Recourse Payments in full for any reason other than a breach of any obligation referred to in Clause 5.2 (Breach of warranties), the Borrower shall have no liability to make up the insufficiency.

(b) Paragraph (a)(i) above is not intended to allow or require (and shall not allow or require) effective claw-back into Net Revenues which arose in Past Calculation Periods when calculating whether a Limited Recourse Payment is actually payable on any date. For these purposes, a *Past Calculation Period* in relation to any date is any Calculation Period which has ended before that date except for, if that date is on or between a Calculation Date and a Repayment Date, the Calculation Period ending on that Calculation Date.

(c) Any amount not payable or paid when due by virtue of Clause 5.1 (Statement of limited recourse) shall nevertheless be and be deemed to be outstanding under this Agreement for the purposes of enforcement of any Security Interests.

5.2 Breach of warranties and undertakings

The limitation in Clause 5.1 (Statement of limited recourse) shall not limit or affect the Borrower's liability in respect of the breach of any representation, warranty, covenant or undertaking contained in any Finance Document (except to the extent any such undertaking is an undertaking to pay any Limited Recourse Payment)."

The above example clause introduces some interesting features of the drafting of a project finance loan agreement which should now be explained.

(a) *Calculation Periods.* (See Clause 5.1(b) in the example; Calculation Periods are also relevant for the definition of Net Revenue (see below).) In order to provide a mechanism to give the limited recourse concept practical effect, time whilst the loan is outstanding is divided up into (typically) six-month periods known as Calculation Periods. A repayment date typically falls within a short period of time after the end of a Calculation Period and the loan agreement usually provides that the maximum amount of the repayment due on that repayment date is the *Net Revenue* in relation to the immediately preceding Calculation Period.

(b) *Net Revenue.* (See Clauses 5.1(a)(i) and 5.1(b) in the example.) Net Revenue in relation to a Calculation Period is an amount equal to the total receipts from the project in question in or in respect of such Calculation Period less the expenses of the project in or in respect of that Calculation Period.

(c) *Set-off.* Note how the drafting is careful to ignore any set-off the borrower may be able to exercise against the Agent or the Banks and any set-off a third party may be able to exercise against the borrower in defining the limits of the borrower's liability. If any amounts so set off were not in effect added back, there would be the possibility that all of the banks would have their claims against the borrower reduced by set-offs for transactions which were nothing to do with the project in question.

(d) *Claims are essentially limited to Net Revenue, Compensation and any amounts recovered on an enforcement of security.* (See Clause 5.1(a)(i)–(iii) in the example.) This is the crux of the limited recourse clause. *Compensation* constitutes essentially insurance proceeds and nationalisation proceeds.

(e) *The administrator provisions.* These are in Clause 5.1(a)(iv) and (v) of the example. They are not necessary if the lenders have security (comprising at least one floating charge) over the whole or substantially the whole of the borrower's property (see footnote 4 and section 6.2). Clause 5.1(a)(iv) recognises the fact that, if an administrator is appointed, there may not be recoveries on an enforcement as such but all or a substantial amount of recoveries may be effected by the administrator. The banks' claims against the borrower need to be increased to take into account any such recoveries. Clause 5.1(a)(v) makes the risk that an administrator makes a disposal for a price less than the open market price a risk that the borrower bears (since the amount of the banks' claims against the borrower are increased by the amount of any shortfall). In this way, error or misfeasance by an insolvency practitioner is

115

made not to constitute "project risk" (*i.e.* a risk arising out of or inherent in the project that the banks are prepared to accept).

(f) *Limited Recourse Payments.* There is a school of thought which says that the only payments which should have the benefit of the limited recourse shield are payments of principal and interest. Other payments (such as indemnity payments under the loan agreement) should not have this benefit.

(g) *No claw-back.* The Calculation Period system allows money to be released to the borrower once a surplus is established at the end of each Calculation Period (*i.e.* after all capex and opex that is then due has been met and all amounts then due to the banks have been paid). Clause 5.1(b) in the example establishes the principle (which can be varied although which often is not) that once any moneys are released they are always released — they cannot be "clawed-back" by the banks.

(h) *Preserving the debt.* Clause 5.1(c) in the example makes it clear that, just because the limited recourse provisions operate so that the borrower does not have to pay an amount on a particular day, this does not mean that payment of that amount is waived. It remains outstanding to be paid if and when the limited recourse provisions so permit. Other precedents have mechanics which treat amounts that cannot be paid because of the limited recourse provisions as "carried forward amounts" — they are carried forward until they can be paid.

(i) *Damages claims preserved.* The exclusion of claims for damages for breach of representation and warranty and for breach of an undertaking has been discussed earlier in this section 5.2.

Not all limited recourse clauses are as complex or as well-developed as the example set out above. In some non-recourse United Kingdom property financings, the non-recourse concept has been established simply by stating that the only remedy that the lender has for non-payment is the enforcement of his security (which, for obvious reasons, does not include a separate covenant to pay).

5.3   SOME GENERAL ISSUES

(a) *Should the credit agreement be limited recourse?* It is tempting to think that limited recourse provisions need not be included in a credit agreement if the borrower is a sole purpose company whose only assets are the project that is being financed. If the company cannot repay its loans, then the only assets to which the lenders will have recourse will by definition be the assets comprised in the project in question. However, this may be dangerous if the project company is a subsidiary of one of the sponsors, since a non-payment by the project company of amounts owed to its lenders may lead to a cross-default in its parent's own credit agreements. Including limited recourse provisions in the project company's credit agreement might provide some degree of protection against this by providing that an amount should not become due under the credit agreement unless there is project cash flow to make the payment. (This sort of provision would usually be coupled with provisions preserving the debt (see section 5.2(h) above).) This is unlikely to provide complete protection, however, because the project company's credit agreement will probably have some form of mechanism (such as a cover ratio or a schedule of maximum outstandings) which will bring about an event of default if the loans are not repaid broadly in accordance with the lenders' original expectations (and an event of default occurring in relation to a subsidiary's borrowings would usually be a cross-default in a parent company's own borrowings).

Probably the only safe way to protect a parent company from this sort of problem is therefore to ensure that, when it negotiates its own borrowings, its own cross-default provisions do not apply to "project borrowings", being either project finance arranged by sole purpose subsidiaries with no financial support from other group members or borrowings on an express limited recourse basis by any group member (including the parent company itself).

(b) *In which currency should the loans be denominated?* The classic dilemma is an oilfield financing in the United Kingdom sector of the North Sea where a substantial part of the construction costs will be in sterling but the revenues will be in dollars. Whereas a borrower would need sterling to pay his share of the construction costs during the construction phase, lenders generally like to match the currency of their loans to a borrower to the currency in which he receives the bulk of his revenues. This is to some extent an intractable problem in this type of financing and hedging is often only a partial solution (particularly in limited recourse transactions (see below)). Borrowers should in any event be wary of accepting standard multi-currency options in their credit agreements for they will usually be tied to one particular currency (the "base currency") and, although drawings may be made in other currencies, adjustments will usually be made at the end of each interest period which will effectively link the amount of those drawings to the base currency.

(c) *Does the credit agreement give flexibility for future lower cost financing opportunities?* What is meant here is not the ability to effect a wholesale refinancing of the loans made under the project credit agreement (a topic discussed in section 11.2), but the ability to bring cheaper means of finance alongside those loans. If this is desired, it is obviously a topic which needs to be discussed with potential lenders from the very beginning. The flexibility envisaged is really the ability to draw down not just loans under the proposed credit agreement but also letters of credit which can be used to support a finance lease, a fixed rate loan from another lender (such as the European Investment Bank) or even a bond issue. Using letters of credit in this way allows the project risk to remain with the original banks and allows the borrower to offer bank risk to a lessor or long term fixed rate lender. The precise interrelationship of the financings usually has to be worked out on a case by case basis but, if any of these alternative forms of finance might be available to the borrower during the life of a loan, banks are usually prepared to include at least framework provisions for the drawing of letters of credit in the credit agreement.

5.4   NPVs AND COVER RATIOS

Project credit agreements frequently have "loan-to-value" ratios. The simplest form of this type of ratio is where the asset in question (over which the lenders have security) has a capital value — most individuals in the United Kingdom are all too well aware of bank and building society rules that restrict the amount that banks and building societies will lend on a house mortgage to a certain percentage of the value of the house. Where the asset in question, however, does not have a strict capital value but is an asset which will simply generate cash over a number of years, loan-to-value ratios will be calculated by reference to the net present value ("NPV") of the anticipated revenue stream.

Putting real estate developments to one side (since slightly different rules apply), the NPV of a project is usually calculated by making various assumptions as to the variables which would affect the project's cash flow (such as product prices, operating costs and foreign exchange rates) and then projecting what the project's net cash flow will be on those assumptions. The aggregate net cash flow is then discounted at a discount rate to produce a net present value. The calculations are done using a computer programme, but what comes out of the programme is obviously determined by what goes into it.

A project's NPV will change over time (as more is learnt about the project and as product prices and interest rates fluctuate, for

118

example) and so, where NPVs are used in a credit agreement, it is important to provide for a method by which the NPV can be periodically updated. This means that the lenders and the borrower not only have to agree on a suitable computer program (or model) to use throughout the life of the credit agreement but also on a procedure which will come up with the figures that are to be fed into that program. A common starting point for negotiations on the procedure to be adopted in any particular credit agreement is that the lenders will provide the financial assumptions (*i.e.* assumptions as to the discount rate and any relevant foreign exchange rates) and the assumptions as to product price but that the borrower will provide the more technical assumptions (*e.g.* as to capex and opex levels). Various alternative solutions may be introduced in the course of negotiations. For example, independent experts may be decided upon as the persons to provide assumptions on matters such as tax or (in the case of an oilfield project) the level of reserves and rates of production. Discount rates may be fixed by reference to the yield on government securities. In addition, where the borrower retains the right to provide certain assumptions, the lenders may insist on having rights of challenge.

In order to simplify the computer model, value added tax is usually ignored. After all, the difference between a project company's VAT inputs and outputs is usually an amount due from or to the relevant taxation authorities. Where it is an amount due to the taxation authorities, that amount should be self-funding: it should be capable of being funded by the surplus of VAT receipts over VAT payments. (To a large extent, this is the point of VAT: each business is effectively a tax collector for the government.) Where, however, a project company's VAT position comprises a series of VAT refunds due from the relevant taxation authorities (which often occurs during the construction period), the project company may have a real working capital need in order to bridge receipt of the refunds from the authorities. Any working capital facility put in place as a result and drawings under such facility are usually modelled.

Whilst the procedure for agreeing upon the relevant assumptions should be clearly set out in the credit agreement (or a related document), setting out the discounting procedure in the credit agreement may not always be best practice. The computer models can sometimes be extremely sophisticated and any attempt to write their mathematical routines into a credit agreement can prove disastrous. In these circumstances, it is probably better simply to state in the credit agreement that the NPVs will be calculated using the relevant computer program and to ensure that a non-corruptible copy of the program is stored in safekeeping. If this route is adopted, however, it is important to state in the credit agreement whether that program or the credit agreement will prevail in the case of conflict.

A credit agreement will usually provide for the NPV of the project in question to be redetermined every six months. This usually ties in with six-monthly repayment instalments in the repayment phase of a project, where it is important to have up-to-date cover ratios. The work on agreeing assumptions obviously has to be done in advance of each repayment date and this is usually provided for. At the end of the various procedures, the computer print-out setting out the NPV and the various cover ratios produced on the agreed assumptions is variously termed a "banking case" or a "borrower's forecast".

Cover ratios themselves have a number of possible applications in a credit agreement. There may be an event of default if a specified cover ratio is breached and the borrower's ability to draw down loans and/or to withdraw funds freely from a proceeds account (see section 5.5 below) may be suspended if a cover ratio is not met. In addition, the interest margin payable by the borrower at any given time may vary depending on the level of one or more cover ratios at that time (but see section 5.8(c) in relation to section 3 of the Partnership Act 1890).

It is important to understand the various types of cover ratio that can be used and how they differ from each other:

(a) *The project life cover ratio.* This is in theory a ratio of the NPV of the projected revenues over the life of a project (the "project life NPV") to bank debt outstanding on any particular day. In practice, it is not quite this because banks will usually build in a safety cushion and ignore revenues after a certain date. For example, in oil and gas financings, banks will ascertain the date on which 25 per cent of the original reserves of the field in question remain to be produced and any project life cover ratio will operate on the basis of an NPV which takes into account revenues up to (but not beyond) that date (often termed the "End Date" or the "25 per cent Reserves Date"). This technique not only protects the banks from relying on potentially more speculative future revenues (recovery from oil and gas reservoirs can apparently get much more difficult as depletion draws near), but it can allow the banks to take a more robust approach towards abandonment costs. (The idea is that these are matched by the — albeit slightly speculative — revenues arising after the 25 per cent Reserves Date.) The 25 per cent Reserves Date (or similar date) is obviously an important assumption for the purposes of the computer model.

(b) *The loan life cover ratio.* This obviously contrasts with the project life cover ratio. It is a ratio of the NPV of the projected revenues during the period it is estimated that the bank debt will remain outstanding (the "loan life NPV") to bank debt outstanding on any particular day.

(c) *The drawdown cover ratio.* This is a ratio of the loan life NPV to the maximum amount that is likely to be borrowed from the banks (the "peak debt amount"). If this cover ratio is used, it will be a condition precedent to the drawdown of any loan that the required drawdown cover ratio is not breached. It is important to realise that the making of a loan can in strict theory never cause a breach of the drawdown cover ratio since the drawdown cover ratio is a creature produced by the forecasting regime in the credit agreement: the denominator is not the amount of bank debt actually outstanding at any time, but the maximum amount that it is estimated will be outstanding. Where a credit agreement contains a drawdown cover ratio, the peak debt amount is again an important assumption for the purposes of the computer model.

(d) *The repayment cover ratio.* This is simply a cover ratio used to determine how much needs to be repaid under a credit agreement on any given repayment date. It is a ratio of a project or loan life NPV to bank debt actually outstanding. A borrower would be required to repay such an amount as would ensure that, after such repayment, the repayment cover ratio was at its required level (say 1.75:1 in an oil financing). The way that the repayment cover ratio is calculated and defined means that it can also be used in the events of default: it will be an event of default if, at any time, the repayment cover ratio is below another (lower) level (say 1.4:1 in an oil financing).[5] In such a case, the repayment cover ratio is being used as a *default cover ratio.* Default cover ratios can also sometimes contain a forward-looking element and provide that there will be a default if the banking case or borrower's forecast shows that the repayment cover ratio *will be* below the required level on a future calculation or repayment date. If this is the case, both the numerator and the denominator of the ratio are being taken from the computer model's print-out.

(e) *The annual debt service cover ratio (the "ADSCR").* Whilst the above ratios relate to the NPV of a project's *projected* revenues, the ADSCR relates to a project's *historic* revenues and measures the

---

[5] A borrower's market has recently seen some default cover ratios in power projects fall to 1.1:1 or even lower.

extent to which those revenues have been sufficient to meet (or "cover") the project's debt service obligation (the repayment of principal and the payment of interest). It is therefore a ratio of the project's actual revenues over the 12 month period prior to each date on which the ratio is tested to the project's debt service obligations during the same period.

Some sponsors seek to negotiate that the project company's cash balances should be taken into account in the ADSCR. This is not in strict theory correct because the ADSCR is meant to be a test of current performance and any cash balances will have been built up as a result of past performance. The point is sometimes conceded by banks, however, and, if conceded, makes the ADSCR less of a snapshot test and forces banks effectively to look at performance over a longer period.

An ADSCR is, by definition, incapable of being tested in the first year of a project's performance. This is often overlooked in the drafting. Where banks are alert to the point, they usually require an intermediate test after the first six months.

Some project credit agreements also contain a forward-looking ADSCR test. Where this is the case, the banks will look at the computer model's ADSCR projections for future years in a manner similar to the way they would test a forward-looking default loan life cover ratio (see (d) above).

NPVs can also be used as the basis for a hybrid form of financing known as a "borrowing base" loan. In this type of financing (typically used for an oil and gas group which has a number of discoveries), the banks are prepared to lend on an unsecured basis an amount equal to a percentage (say 66.66 per cent) of the aggregate NPVs of the group's oil and gas interests "brought within the borrowing base". Only interests which are free of security can be brought within the borrowing base and certain other criteria also often have to be met. For example, exploration acreage cannot be included (its value is too speculative) and interests in gas fields can only become "borrowing base interests" if the borrower has executed a long-term gas sales agreement in relation to the gas. Borrowing base interests are subject to a negative pledge, although they can usually be sold or transferred so long as after such sale or transfer the banks' loans are less than or equal to the new borrowing base (*i.e.* (in the present example) 66.66 per cent of the aggregate NPV of the remaining borrowing base interests). There are usually various companies within the relevant group who may borrow against the borrowing base, but, if this is the case, logic dictates that each must guarantee borrowings by the others (and the provision of such a cross-guarantee is usually one of the preconditions of a new member of the group acceding to the credit agreement as a borrower).

From a purist point of view, a borrowing base loan is only as good as the banks' ability to identify all of the possible liabilities of the group and include them in the NPV calculations. Without security to protect them against other (as yet unknown) creditors, the banks may actually be overlending. The way banks seek to guard themselves against this risk, of course, is only to lend a percentage of the aggregate NPV of the borrowing base interests.

5.5   CONTROL ACCOUNTS

A control account is what its name suggests: a bank account withdrawals from which are controlled to some degree by the lenders. Banks will have security over any control accounts maintained in connection with the credit agreement.[6]

The types of control account that might exist in relation to a project credit agreement are as follows:

(a) *A disbursement account.* The proceeds of all loan drawdowns and of all equity subscriptions would be paid into a disbursement account and withdrawals would be permitted to fund construction costs (including any applicable value added tax) and interest during construction (or "IDC") (which would typically be "rolled up" and, in the absence of project cash flows, funded by the banks themselves). A disbursement account is used when banks require a fairly high degree of control over disbursements. Withdrawals can sometimes only be made against proof that the relevant expenditures have been incurred or are likely to be incurred within a fairly short space of time (*e.g.* 30 days).

(b) *A proceeds account.* All project revenues (including value added tax) would be paid into a proceeds account and withdrawals would be permitted to meet repayments of principal and payments of interest under the credit agreement and payments of capex (if

---

[6] *Re Charge Card Services Ltd* [1987] Ch. 150 causes a problem where security is to be taken over a bank account maintained in England and Wales. The case is authority for the proposition that a bank cannot itself take security over an account maintained with it (but must instead rely on rights of set-off). The rule established by the case is in practice more honoured in its breach than in its observance and this aspect of the case is generally thought to be bad law.

any), tax (including payments of VAT to the relevant taxation authorities) and opex. Payments of capex and opex would be inclusive of value added tax. Subject to certain restrictions, the borrower would also be permitted to withdraw surpluses from the proceeds account for his own use or to pay dividends.

(c) *A compensation account.* A proceeds account would capture revenue items (including any liquidated damages for delay payable by a construction contractor). A compensation account would capture capital payments such as the proceeds of any physical damage insurance, any performance liquidated damages payable by a construction contractor, any compensation for expropriation and, in the case of an oil or gas field financing, any compensation paid on a redetermination of the field. (A redetermination of a field's boundaries could reveal that more of the field lies under an adjacent licence area than was originally envisaged with the result that the licensees in that area owe their neighbouring licensees a cash payment to reflect the fact that the neighbouring licensees have funded more of the costs of developing the field than they should have.) The purposes for which withdrawals are permitted from a compensation account vary depending on the type of receipt and are often subject to negotiation. For example, the banks will initially insist that any physical damage insurance proceeds should be applied in prepaying their loans whilst the borrower will insist that they should be applied in reinstatement of the destroyed or damaged facilities. This is discussed in more detail in Section 5.8 below. Performance liquidated damages (or, at least, a percentage of such liquidated damages) would normally be applied in prepaying the loans, however.

(d) *A debt service reserve account.* Money would typically be transferred from the proceeds account to a debt service reserve account in order to establish a reserve which could be used to meet repayments of principal and payments of interest under the credit agreement if other funds were not available (for example, because there was an unexpected shut-down of production). Establishing a reserve equal to the anticipated principal repayments and interest payments over the next six months is not unusual. An alternative technique for building up a debt service reserve is to try to ensure a minimum balance on the proceeds account (by stating that the borrower can only withdraw for his own use funds in excess of the required minimum balance).

(e) *A maintenance reserve account.* A maintenance reserve account would typically be required by banks where the maintenance cycle of the project in question was such that there were large maintenance

124

costs which recurred after intervals of years (five or six years in the case of power plants). Banks would be concerned in these circumstances to ensure that cash was effectively put aside each year to build up over the years a cash reserve equal to the estimated maintenance costs in the year such costs were to be incurred. One issue frequently raised by borrowers in relation to a maintenance reserve account is the extent to which it may also operate *in extremis* as a debt reserve account. If there is cash sitting in the maintenance reserve account and the borrower has no other funds with which to make a payment due to the banks, why can it not use that cash to make such payment (subject to paying back into the maintenance reserve account out of project revenues at the first available opportunity any cash so withdrawn)?

The sponsors might themselves want certain accounts to be opened by the project company to protect their own interests. One technique often used is for the project company to open a distributions account which is not the subject of any security in favour of the banks and into which amounts are paid which may be used, in accordance with the terms of the project credit agreement, to pay distributions in due course. This enables the sponsors to have money leave the banks' security net before it can actually be physically distributed to them as shareholders (*e.g.* because of general company law restrictions on the payment of dividends).

Lenders often believe that withdrawals from a proceeds account can be prioritised (by which they usually mean that payment of amounts due to them will be made in priority to other payments). In fact, this is not particularly easy to achieve because the timing of payments tends to produce its own priority. Take the case of a project company which has sufficient funds in a proceeds account to make a payment to a supplier at the beginning of a month but not to make a payment due to the lenders at the end of that month. If the company nevertheless reasonably expects to receive revenues in the course of that month, it is hard to see why, in the normal course of events, the project company cannot pay the supplier (although, of course, the expected revenues may not arrive and the lenders may not receive their money). For these reasons, project costs (and particularly opex) can normally be withdrawn from proceeds accounts whenever they arise (with the lenders seeking protection in the form of minimum balances on the proceeds account or debt service reserve accounts). To the extent that there is a priority of payments,[7] this is usually (in the absence of different classes of

---

[7] Often referred to as a "cash flow waterfall" or cascade.

debt) as between the lenders and the project company with regard to payments of debt service on the one hand and amounts that the project company can freely withdraw on the other. Even this more limited form of prioritisation can lead to a certain rigidity, because, in its purest form, it really requires the project company only to be able to withdraw funds from the proceeds account on debt service dates (since it is only then that one can be sure that the project company is not receiving money in priority to the lenders).

If large amounts of cash are likely to accumulate on control accounts, stronger borrowers try to negotiate a right to require the cash to be invested. The points for the lenders here are to ensure that the investments are of good quality (usually equity investments will not be allowed) and of an appropriate maturity and that the lenders have security over any investments that are made. Some project credit agreements go further and state that the borrower may actually withdraw cash against either a bank standby letter of credit in an amount equal to that withdrawn or a shareholder guarantee to pay cash back into the control accounts if and when it is needed. The former is preferable since the latter may only give rise to a damages (as opposed to a debt) claim.

5.6 LEASING

Many project finance techniques can be adapted to finance leases and it has already been seen how letter of credit options in project credit agreements can give a borrower flexibility to bring a finance lease into the general financing arrangements for a project. Due regard should be had to the lenders' security position if this actually occurs, however, since part of the project's assets (and possibly a key part) will be owned by a finance lessor. If a finance lessor does not have the benefit of a letter of credit from the lenders and has project risk himself, some form of intercreditor arrangements between the lenders and the lessor will be essential.

The usual reason for resorting to finance leasing is because it is tax efficient. Project companies will inevitably enter the operating period with substantial carried-forward tax losses which, unless they are surrendered for value to shareholders (if this is possible in the jurisdiction in question),[8] are only of use to the project company when it starts generating otherwise taxable profits. A finance lessor (usually a subsidiary of a bank) will have profits against which

---

[8] See section 2.6.

capital allowances may be set. In return for being allowed to use the capital allowances associated with the relevant leased equipment to reduce its group's overall tax bill, the finance lessor charges the lessee (the project company) a rental payment which effectively includes a lower interest cost than the project company would have been able to achieve with a straightforward bank loan.

Finance leasing can also be used as a means of overcoming limitations in a particular jurisdiction on the granting or enforcement of security (as to which see section 6.3 below). A lessor by definition owns the leased equipment. Terminating an equipment lease extinguishes the lessee's right to use the lessor's asset whereas accelerating a secured loan is only the first step in the potentially difficult process of the lender being able to dispose of the borrower's asset.

5.7   HEDGING

Hedging is the protection of a borrower from adverse movements in currency exchange rates, interest rates and commodity prices. Hedging (and so-called "risk management") has become a billion-dollar business. Whilst there are some exceptionally complex hedging instruments now available in the financial markets, project financiers have to date remained fairly conservative and the types of hedging instruments most commonly encountered are the relatively simple forward foreign exchange agreement, the "zero cost cap" and the interest rate swap.

It may, of course, be possible to hedge a project company's risks otherwise than through the use of financial instruments. For example, it might be possible to hedge a gas-fired United Kingdom merchant plant's exposure to the electricity pool[9] by linking the price that the project company pays for its gas under its gas sales agreement to movements in the pool price. It might also be possible to protect a project company involved in a concession-based project against movements in LIBOR or any other floating interest rates applicable to its debt by providing that the tariff payable under the concession agreement is linked to movements in LIBOR or such other rates. It is preferable to hedge a project's risks through the project contracts if possible since this should avoid some of the complexity, exposure and sometimes also the cost associated with hedging by means of financial instruments.

---

[9] See sections 3.12 and 10.3.

Turning to the types of hedging instrument made available by financial institutions which are most relevant to project finance, a forward foreign exchange agreement is an agreement whereby one party agrees to buy on a future date a fixed amount of one currency with another currency at an exchange rate agreed at the time the agreement was entered into. (Similarly, for commodities, a forward sale agreement is an agreement to buy a fixed quantity of a commodity (such as oil or gold) on a future date at a price agreed at the time the agreement was entered into.) A cap is an agreement whereby one party (in the following example, a bank) simply agrees to pay another (the project company) the amount by which interest rates or commodity prices exceed an agreed rate or price. A "zero cost" cap is a cap coupled with a "floor", *i.e.* an agreement whereby the project company agrees to pay the bank the amount by which interest rates or commodity prices *fall below* an agreed rate or price (such rate or price being set below the rate or price agreed for the purposes of the cap). The cap is at zero cost (to the project company) in these circumstances because the cost of buying the cap is offset by the price received from selling the floor. An interest rate swap is similar: on a number of dates ("settlement dates") in the future (typically set at six-monthly intervals), one party will pay to the other the amount of floating rate interest that will have accrued payable on an agreed nominal amount over the six months prior to each settlement date and will receive back the amount of interest that will have accrued payable on the same agreed nominal amount over the same six-month period at an agreed fixed interest rate. The documentation for interest rate swaps usually provides for a net payment to be made by one party to the other on each settlement date rather than for each party to make gross payments to the other.

Counterparties will frequently hedge their own exposure to make payments under hedges that they commit to by entering into equal but opposite hedges in the market. So, if a bank were to agree with a project company to buy dollars with sterling on a fixed future date at a rate of £1: $1.50, the bank might decide to hedge its own position by agreeing with another financial institution ("Institution A") to buy sterling with dollars on the same date at the same (or a slightly more advantageous) rate. In this way, the bank could be sure that it would be able to procure the necessary sterling to pay to the project company so long as the project company fulfilled its part of the bargain on the future date. If the project company were to go into liquidation before the settlement date, the bank would be unlikely to receive the relevant payment from the project company on that date but it itself would still be committed to make a payment to Institution A. In order to crystallise its position (and in order to have an actual (as opposed to a contingent) debt for which to prove in the project company's liquidation), the bank would in these circumstances "close out" its hedge with the project company. In fairly simplistic terms, this would involve the bank cancelling its obligations to the project company and entering into a replacement hedge with another financial institution ("Institution B") at the best rate it could then obtain for settlement on the settlement date. If this meant that the bank had to agree to buy dollars with sterling at a rate of £1: $1.40, then it would make a loss: it would have to find another 10 cents in order to meet its obligations to pay $1.50 for each £1 sold to it by Institution A (each £1 sold to it by Institution A would only generate $1.40 from Institution B). This loss would be passed onto the project company under the bank's swap documentation.

Some of the difficult issues that arise with hedging in the context of project finance are as follows:

(a) *Settlement risk*. If a project company is involved in an oilfield financing in the United Kingdom sector of the North Sea, it may (as noted in section 5.3(b) above) borrow in sterling to pay its share of construction costs notwithstanding the fact that its revenues (from the sale of oil) will be in dollars. In order to hedge against currency exchange rates, it may decide to sell some of its anticipated dollar revenue stream forward in exchange for sterling. (This will involve agreeing with a counterparty that, on a specified future settlement date, the project company will deliver a fixed amount of dollars to the counterparty and the counterparty will deliver a fixed amount of sterling to the project company. The exchange rate for the future settlement date is, as noted above, fixed when the hedge is entered into.) But what happens if the project is delayed and the anticipated dollar income has not arisen by the settlement date? If the hedge has value for the project company (which will be determined by reference to the actual rates of exchange prevailing on the settlement date), the project company will make a windfall profit. But if the hedge has value for the counterparty, the project company will owe the counterparty money but have no means with which to pay. For this reason, lenders should insist that hedge counterparties enter into an intercreditor agreement with them regulating their respective rights and obligations in these circumstances. An intercreditor agreement should also place limitations on the hedge counterparties' rights to take independent action generally (since otherwise the hedge counterparties could "close out" their hedges whenever their own (often market standard) documentation entitled them to, with adverse consequences for the project's economics). A frequent compromise position is that a hedge counterparty can close out his hedge for non-payment or where it is illegal for him or the project company to perform their respective obligations under the hedge but that he can otherwise only close out when the lenders accelerate. Banks sometimes reserve the right to make payments under the hedge documentation themselves in order to avoid a premature close out.

(b) *Should hedge counterparties share in the lenders' security?* Hedge counterparties may insist on this, but, if they do and the lenders' credit agreement is limited recourse, should the hedge counterparties also accept that their hedges are limited recourse? If the hedge counterparties share in the security and accept that their hedges are limited recourse, should they have, in the context of a syndicated credit agreement, a vote reflecting their hedge exposure when the banks are being polled for a decision? (Market practice on this latter point, incidentally, tends to be that they should not. Among the reasons usually given for this is that the hedge counterparties' exposure under a hedge will fluctuate daily (quite possibly in their favour) and to give them a vote could lead to unpredictable and unfair results.)

(c) *If the hedge counterparties share in the lenders' security, should the hedge counterparties be entitled to make windfall profits on a closing out?* As noted above, if hedge counterparties close out their hedge, they may suffer a loss and their documentation will provide that the project company must indemnify them against this loss. Equally, however, the hedge counterparties may make a profit when they close out. The standard form of hedge documentation could, if one option is selected, allow the hedge counterparties to retain such a profit. If the banks have agreed to let the hedge counterparties share in the security granted by the project company in order to protect the hedge counterparties against a possible loss on a closing out, should the hedge counterparties agree to share any profit on a closing out as a *quid pro quo*? Banks normally insist that they do and, in order to achieve this, the hedge documentation should provide for "full two-way payments" on a termination or closing out[10] and any profit arising on a closing out should be paid to the project company and put into a recoveries pool and shared out. In addition, because the profit is payable to the project company on a closing out, the banks

---

[10] The option to select in the Standard ISDA form (published 1992) is the *Second Method* (see section 6(e)(i)(3) and (4) of the form and the option in paragraph (f)(ii) of Part 1 of the standard Schedule to that form).

must ensure that the security documentation includes, as an asset over which security is taken, the project company's rights under the hedge documentation.

(d) *How should hedges be factored into cover ratios (if at all)?* There are two (interrelated) aspects to this. First, if a project company has swapped a floating rate of interest under its credit agreement for a fixed rate (for example), should the NPVs be calculated on the basis of the fixed rate? If so, should the project company's contingent liability to make a compensatory payment (on a closing out) to the swap counterparty (depending on the movement in rates) be taken into account in the denominator of any cover ratios? If yes, should the gross or the net amounts payable by the project company be taken into account? Usually, swapped interest rates are incorporated into the computer model at the swapped rate and contingent liabilities are ignored. The rationale for this is that the computer model is intended to be a tool forecasting the health of the project as a going concern and not a tool for analysing liabilities on a liquidation.

It is also important to ensure that any hedging instrument is properly reflected in the mechanical provisions of the project credit agreement. For example, if the project company has hedged its exposure to floating interest rates through an interest rate swap, one of the permitted withdrawals from the proceeds account must be payments by it under the swap. In addition, the project company should only be allowed to draw down under the project credit agreement to capitalise interest (during the construction phase) at the swapped rate, since the balance of each interest payment should come from the swap counterparties.

5.8 NEGOTIATING A PROJECT CREDIT AGREEMENT

This section explains aspects of a project credit agreement which have not so far been addressed in this Chapter and looks at various positions that can be taken by the project company and the banks during the course of negotiations over a typical *project* credit agreement. This section does not seek to explain how to negotiate the general terms of a credit agreement.

(a) *Conditions precedent to each drawdown.* It is important to appreciate that, under a normal syndicated credit agreement, if an event of default occurs, each individual member of the bank

131

syndicate is entitled to refuse to contribute its share of loan drawdowns whilst the event of default · is subsisting (see section 5.1(b) above). This contrasts with the position on acceleration where, typically, a positive decision to accelerate the loans has to be taken by the majority banks (more often than not defined as banks to whom 67 per cent of all of the loans outstanding are owed). One individual bank can therefore bring about a funding shortfall during the construction phase of a project and, in so doing, precipitate a crisis.

This right of an individual bank to refuse to lend during the subsistence of an event of default is generally considered to be a fundamental tenet of syndicated lending: a bank should not be dictated to by other banks with regard to whether or not to lend during the subsistence of an event of default — it is the bank's own credit decision. Unfortunately though, this attitude can have the effect of paralysing progress on a project to the detriment of all parties. If there is a "technical" (*i.e.* a relatively minor) event of default, why should one bank — which may have slow and bureaucratic internal procedures to go through — have the ability to bring down the project? In addition, if one bank is no longer comfortable with the credit risk of the project, why should it be allowed to use the occurrence of a technical event of default to hold the other banks to ransom and pressurise them into purchasing its participation in the credit agreement? These arguments essentially centre around the "club" nature of a project financing and are really arguments which, if they are to be put forward at all, should be put forward by the banks in their discussion amongst themselves. For obvious reasons, however, they are often adopted by the project company and some project credit agreements do provide that the decision as to whether or not to continue lending during the subsistence of an event of default is one that is taken by the majority banks.

A project credit agreement will frequently contain additional conditions precedent to each drawdown to those found in a standard credit agreement. One of these has already been discussed — compliance with a drawdown cover ratio (see section 5.4(c) above). Another is a condition that, as at the proposed date of drawdown, the borrower has sufficient funds available to it (including unutilised commitments under the project credit agreement itself) in order to achieve completion. This usually involves some mechanism for calculating the remaining cost to complete (*e.g.* a certificate from a technical consultant appointed by the banks). The banks will be concerned that any funds which the borrower claims are available to it for the purpose of this condition precedent are properly committed. This particularly applies where the borrower claims that funds will be made available by its shareholders but it is also an issue for certain types of bank funding: should money available by way of overdraft (which can usually be cancelled at any time by notice from the bank providing the overdraft) be included, for example?

(b) *Drawdown mechanics.* For ease of administration, banks (particularly in syndicated deals) like to lend in relatively large amounts. If the minimum drawdown amounts and multiples are too high, the borrower may find himself forced to borrow in advance of his cash requirements and this has an interest cost. Banks may also (again for administrative convenience) try to limit the frequency of drawings. It is essential, however, for the drawdown mechanics to fit the borrower's anticipated cash needs as much as possible and some accommodation can usually be worked out.

Banks are usually concerned only to lend against progress on the project as and when milestones are achieved (see the comments on stage payments in sections 3.6(g) and 4.3(d)). Because of this (understandable) concern, banks sometimes require that a technical consultant appointed by them approve the amount of each drawing. This is desperately unpopular with contractors who see this as unwarranted interference in the construction contract by an outside professional. Their objections are even more vociferous where the construction contract provides for a contract administrator or engineer (see section 3.6(l)) since the banks' technical consultant would simply be duplicating the work of that contract administrator or engineer. It is probably fair to say that, where there is a contract administrator or engineer responsible for issuing interim certificates, the involvement of the banks' technical consultant in approving loan drawdown amounts in advance is unnecessary (although he may still serve a useful role in this respect in reviewing the achievement of milestones after the event). Where there is no contract administrator or engineer, the point is more arguable, although the banks might be capable of being persuaded that they should make payment simply against a certification from the borrower that the relevant milestone has been met, with their technical consultant again having an *ex post facto* monitoring role. The borrower is, after all, the employer under the construction contract and should have the same interest as the banks in ensuring that payments are only made against the achievement of milestones. (The banks may take some convincing of this, however, if the contractor is one of the borrower's shareholders!)

Project credit agreements (particularly where the project is overseas) will often provide that the banks must make payment to the contractor direct against presentation of documents, with any

133

such payment automatically constituting a loan to the borrower under the credit agreement. In these circumstances, the drawdown mechanics function in a similar way to letters of credit and the banks and the borrower should analyse their positions accordingly and seek appropriate protections.

Some project credit agreements will require the borrower to give formal drawdown requests in order to pay interest during construction. It is submitted that this is unnecessary and that the credit agreement should simply provide that the banks will automatically lend the amounts necessary to fund interest during construction under their own credit agreement without the borrower having to give a formal request.

(c) *The interest clause.* As has been noted above (in section 5.4), the margin payable by the borrower may vary depending on the level of one or more cover ratios. Despite occasional protestations to the contrary by banks, there is no practical reason why the margin cannot change in the middle of interest periods so that the borrower gets the immediate benefit of an improvement in the relevant cover ratios (although this will also mean that he will suffer the immediate burden of a deterioration in those cover ratios).

There is a possible technical problem under English law with an interest rate which varies with the profits of the borrower. Section 3 of the Partnership Act 1890 states:

"In the event of any person to whom money has been advanced by way of loan upon [a contract . . . that the lender shall receive a rate of interest varying with the profits arising from a business] . . . being adjudged a bankrupt . . . the lender of the loan shall not be entitled to recover anything in respect of his loan . . . until the claims of the other creditors of the borrower . . . have been satisfied."

Although the above is contained in the Partnership Act, it is of general application.[11] It does not just apply to loans to partnerships; it treats a loan where interest varies with profits as creating a form of quasi-partnership in itself.

If a loan falls within section 3, the consequences for the lender are clearly serious: he becomes a deferred creditor, ranking behind all others. It should be noted, however, that case law[12] has softened

---

[11] Despite the reference to bankruptcy, s.3 applies to companies: see *Re. Theo Garvin Ltd* [1969] 1 Ch. 624.
[12] See *Badeley v. Consolidated Bank*, (1888) 38 Ch.D. 238 (in relation to s.5 of Bovill's Act 1865, the precursor to s.3 of the Partnership Act 1890).

the effect of section 3 in the case of a secured loan by stating that it does not prevent a lender enforcing his security and retaining the proceeds of such enforcement. The territorial reach of section 3 is also a little unclear although it is obviously intended to protect United Kingdom consumers. It would therefore clearly apply where the borrower was subject to a winding up in the United Kingdom but it is unclear as to whether or not the choice of English law as the governing law of a credit agreement with a non-UK borrower would in itself be sufficient to import section 3. The risk cannot be ruled out.

The question remains, however, whether varying the margin applicable to a loan by reference to the level of typical project cover ratios would in any event bring a loan within section 3. Clearly, varying the margin by reference to a loan life cover ratio will not bring a loan within section 3: a loan life cover ratio is meant to be a test by reference to capital value. Varying the margin by reference to the ADSCR is more difficult, however, since the ADSCR can be seen as a crude measure of profitability and it could therefore *prima facie* bring a loan within section 3. This would, however, be a rather strange result since the mischief that section 3 is meant to address is a loan where interest increases when profits increase. In a project loan, interest will *decrease* when profits increase. There appear to be no cases on the point, but it would be a strange decision indeed if a court held that such a loan, where interest *decreases* with increasing profits, was within section 3 notwithstanding the bald wording of the Section.[13]

In addition, the overdue (or default) interest clause in a project credit agreement should always be looked at to ensure that interest does not accrue at the higher rate provided for in that clause simply because there are insufficient cash flows from the project to make any particular payment. The higher rate should only apply where the borrower has cash available to make a payment but fails to do so. Insufficient cash flow itself is simply a project risk which the banks should accept and they should not compound the problem by charging interest at the default rate.

---

[13] The United Kingdom tax position offers an interesting parallel. The United Kingdom, in common with many other jurisdictions, will generally, where interest on a loan varies with the profits of the borrower, treat that interest as a distribution. Section 209(2)(3)(iii) of the Income and Corporate Taxes Act 1988, for example, defines "distribution" as including "interest . . . in respect of securities of a company . . . under which the consideration given by the company for the use of the principal . . . is to any extent dependent on the results of the company's business". Elsewhere in that Act, however, some relief is given for what could otherwise be adverse tax consequences where the loans in question provide for the rate of interest to be *reduced* in the event of the results of the borrower's business improving: see para. 1(5E) of Sched. 18 to that Act.

(d) *The repayment clause.* Repayment clauses in project credit agreements are many and varied, but, irrespective of whether or not there is a limited recourse clause (see section 5.2 above), they will usually contain some limitation centring on the project's actual cash flows. They are often "cover ratio driven", *i.e.* the amount to be repaid is determined by reference to a cover ratio (usually a loan life cover ratio — see section 5.4(b) and (d) above).

A typical repayment clause might read as follows:

"5. REPAYMENT
5.1 Amount of each repayment instalment
On each Repayment Date, the Borrower shall pay to the Agent, by way of repayment of the loans, an amount equal to the lesser of:
(a) the Dedicated Percentage of the Net Revenues for the Calculation Period which ended immediately prior to that Repayment Date; and
(b) all amounts outstanding under this Agreement on that Repayment Date.

5.2 The Dedicated Percentage
The Dedicated Percentage to be applied on any Repayment Date is the lesser of:
(a) 100 per cent; and
(b) the greater of:
　(i) such percentage as will result in the Loan Life Cover Ratio being 1.75:1 immediately after that Repayment Date; and
　(ii) 50 per cent."

The use of the "Dedicated Percentage" concept is more or less a market convention — it could strictly speaking be dispensed with as a drafting matter. The use of Calculation Periods is explained in section 5.2(a) above.

In Clause 5.2 of the typical repayment clause set out above:
　(i) paragraph (a) obviously applies the general limitation that the banks are not to receive a greater amount than the net revenues generated by the project;
　(ii) paragraph (b)(i) sets out how the amount of each repayment instalment will be calculated in the normal course; and
　(iii) paragraph (b)(ii) applies a minimum Dedicated Percentage notwithstanding paragraph (b)(i) — even though a project might be going well so that little or no

136

repayment need be made in order to keep within the required Loan Life Cover Ratio, banks do not trust the future and will often require (as here) that a minimum percentage of the project's net revenues be applied in repayment of their loans on each repayment date.

It is important to realise that the effect of a limited recourse clause or a repayment clause which is limited by reference to a project's net revenues is simply to limit the ability of the banks to sue for a greater amount to be repaid to them. It protects the borrower's other assets (if any) and prevents it becoming insolvent (and hence liable to be wound up) because it is not meeting its debts as and when they fall due (because the quantum of the debt owed to the banks is, if necessary, reduced). It does not mean, however, that the banks cannot take any action if the effect of those clauses is that the amounts paid to them by way of repayment are less than those they anticipated when they agreed to enter into the credit agreement. There will usually be an event of default that will apply if repayments fall too far behind those originally anticipated: usually this will either be the breach of a default cover ratio or the failure to reduce outstandings under the project credit agreement to specified maxima which apply on the various repayment dates. The occurrence of an event of default will allow the banks to exercise their security. The theory is — and it is accepted that this may be very theoretical — that, if the borrower is unable to run the project so as to repay the banks broadly as originally envisaged, the banks should be given the opportunity of taking over the running of the project in order to do so (through the enforcement of their security). As we shall see later (in Chapter 6), not all jurisdictions possess security systems which allow the holders of security to take control of a project, however.

(e) *Mandatory prepayment of insurance proceeds.* Project credit agreements often provide that, if any of the major project facilities are destroyed or damaged and the project company subsequently receives a major insurance recovery, then the project company must use the insurance moneys to prepay the loans if the lenders so require.[14] The lenders' position is that, whereas they were prepared to finance the original project on its original timetable, the damage or destruction has now pushed the timetable back and in essence created a new project. If the project company wants funding for that, it should approach new financiers. By contrast, the project

---

[14] This type of clause is known as a "head-for-the-hills" or "cut-and-run" clause.

company, fearing "short-termism" on the part of the lenders and having already paid one set of arrangement fees, is anxious to lock the lenders into the project for as long as possible. There is no real universal solution to this problem, but it should be borne in mind that some physical damage insurance policies will only pay out on condition that the insurance proceeds are used in reinstatement of the destroyed or damaged facilities and delay in start-up and business interruption insurance (if it is available) is to some extent meant to hold lenders harmless against the financial effects of an extended project timetable. If lenders are particularly concerned about this issue, they should insist that the amount insured under the delay in start-up and business interruption insurances is sufficiently high (subject to reasonable considerations of cost). If, however, a compromise is reached which has insurance proceeds over a specified figure being applied in prepayment of the loans (but otherwise used in repair or reinstatement), the drafting of the threshold figure should make it clear whether it is calculated on a reinstatement or indemnity basis. The reinstatement basis of payment is the "new for old" basis with which home policyholders are familiar and is only paid out if repair or reinstatement is to occur. By contrast, the indemnity basis merely compensates the policyholder for the value of the item destroyed or damaged.

The battle over the use of physical damage insurance proceeds does not necessarily only involve the project company and the lenders. Where there is a concession, the person granting the concession will be concerned to ensure that, if the project facilities are damaged or destroyed, any proceeds are applied in repair or reinstatement as soon as possible. If the concession holder has to raise fresh finance with which to fund the repair or reinstatement, this will introduce delay and it will be that much longer before the bridge, airport terminal or other piece of infrastructure the subject of the relevant concession is once again available to the public. Furthermore, the contractor may have accepted, under the construction contract, that, if the facilities are damaged or destroyed whilst he is responsible for them, he will rebuild them. The reason that contractors accept such an obligation is because they believe that they (and not the banks) will receive the proceeds of any physical damage policies. In the larger and more complex projects, there may be no alternative other than to have a separate insurance agreement between all of the interested parties.

(f) *The margin protection clauses.* This is another area where (in a syndicated credit agreement) arguments based on the "club" nature of a project financing may sometimes prevail. The main argument is that, if each individual member of the bank syndicate can (for example) claim immediate reimbursement of any increased costs it suffers (see section 5.1(f)(ii)), then, if one member suffers an increased cost but the others do not, that member will in effect be receiving prior treatment as far as the project's cash flows are concerned. If this argument is accepted, the credit agreement usually provides that an affected bank's entitlement to the relevant payments will accrue but only be paid (in priority to distributions or the allocation of free cash flow to the borrower) when there is surplus cash flow.

(g) *The illegality clause.* Similar arguments to those referred to in (f) above can be applied to the borrower's obligation to prepay a bank affected by illegality. Again, if these arguments are accepted, the usual solution is to provide that the prepayment can only be made if and to the extent that there is surplus cash flow. This should not pose any particular problem for a bank since it would be highly unlikely for a change in law to require loans already advanced to be prepaid in the first place: usually, banks are simply prohibited from making any further credits available.

(h) *Representations and warranties.* A project credit agreement will contain various representations specifically relating to the project — for example, a representation that all consents necessary for the carrying out of the development in question have been obtained. Secured credit agreements often contain a representation that the security documents create the security they purport to create, ranking as set out in those documents. Borrowers often take exception to this since they (correctly) point out that their loans can be made capable of being accelerated because the lawyers acting for the banks were negligent in their preparation and perfection of the banks' security. The usual riposte to this is that the representation has nothing to do with fairness but everything to do with the allocation of risk. The argument on the banks' side is that the banks have executed the credit agreement on the basis that it is secured (and the borrower has had the benefit of an interest margin priced accordingly). If the security is flawed or does not exist, the banks are justified in having the right to ask for their money back (by accelerating the loans for breach of a representation). The banks' argument has more force in a limited recourse credit agreement where security is essential to the logic of the loan structure (see section 5.2 above).

A particular problem arises when a project achieves financial close with a single bank or group of banks who have agreed to act as underwriters but who intend to syndicate the loans after financial close. This method of achieving financial close is usually decided upon in order to achieve financial close quickly and the underwriting bank or banks have no need themselves for an information memorandum: they have been in the thick of structuring and negotiating the financial aspects of the deal.[15] A wider syndication to the general bank market will require an information memorandum, however, and, even though the underwriting banks may prepare it, it is market practice for the borrower to take responsibility for the contents of an information memorandum in the terms of a warranty contained in the credit agreement. As the information memorandum in such a case will not exist on financial close when, at the very latest, the credit agreement be signed, it is difficult to agree the terms of a warranty otherwise than in very general terms. To protect himself, a borrower will seek to negotiate a representation and warranty which simply vouches for the accuracy and completeness of the information that it supplies to the underwriting banks after financial close for the purposes of their preparing the information memorandum. A borrower will argue that he cannot give any representation and warranty in relation to the accuracy and completeness of the final information memorandum because this is prepared by the underwriting banks and they may package or use his information in a manner he does not agree with and does not want to take responsibility for. The underwriting banks, on the other hand, want the borrower to take responsibility for the final information memorandum because otherwise there may be a residual liability on them as the people who prepared it. The borrower's position is often the fairer one because, in order to make the banks' position fair, the borrower would need to be given a degree of editorial control over the contents of the final information memorandum which is likely to be unacceptable to the underwriting banks.

(i) *Undertakings.* A project credit agreement will bristle with undertakings. In an attempt to bring some order out of the chaos otherwise caused by simply listing undertaking after undertaking, the undertakings are sometimes divided up into positive undertakings (those things the borrower must do) and negative undertakings (those things the borrower must not do). This is, of course, slightly disingenuous because most undertakings can be expressed in both ways — an undertaking not to create security over an asset can be drafted as an undertaking to ensure that that asset is free from security interests.

---

[15] They may have seen a preliminary information memorandum prepared by the sponsors, however, as part of a competition run in order to choose the project's banks.

Many of the additional undertakings found in a project credit agreement will focus on the fact that the project in question is often highly dependent on certain of the key project contracts. Sometimes the only project assets that the borrower owns are rights under contracts (as in North Sea or mining projects involving joint ventures). Other undertakings will have the borrower burying the banks under an avalanche of information and paper, notionally in the cause of keeping them informed as to the progress of the project.

The following is a list of the types of undertaking that are likely to be included in a project credit agreement but which would be unusual in a corporate credit agreement:

(i) *An undertaking to comply with the terms of the project contracts.* This is self-explanatory.

(ii) *An undertaking on the project company diligently to pursue its rights under the project contracts.* This is intended to ensure that the project company will, if necessary, sue its shareholders if they are the other contracting parties under the project contracts.

(iii) *An undertaking not to amend the project contracts.* This should, of course, be made subject to a degree of materiality. It is unreasonable for the banks' consent to be required for every change to the project contracts.

(iv) *An undertaking to exercise or refrain from exercising certain discretions contained in the project contracts if so required by the banks.* These discretions are sometimes referred to in the course of negotiations as the "reserved discretions". What goes on the list of reserved discretions is usually the subject of heated debate as the project company usually takes the view that it is the person best suited to run the project and interference in the project contracts by the banks will only introduce delay. It is necessary to keep a sense of proportion when deciding on the reserved discretions and really only the more major discretions which can influence the essential economics of the project should appear on the list. The banks do, after all, usually have other checks and balances in a project credit agreement (such as their cover ratios and the various general project-related undertakings). In relation to a construction contract, the following will usually find their way onto the list of reserved discretions: the project company's right to issue variation orders with a value in excess of an agreed amount, its right to approve variations suggested by the contractor, its right to suspend the works and its right to terminate the construction contract. Others may find their way onto the list depending on the particular sensitivities of the project and the concerns of the parties involved in the negotiations: for example, the banks may be very concerned to agree the identity of any sub-contractors and accordingly wish to control the project company's approval of any sub-contractors under the terms of the construction contract. The project company's right to require the subscription of further equity under an equity subscription agreement will invariably be included on the list.

(v) *An undertaking to carry out the project in accordance with good industry practice.* This undertaking is self-explanatory but is probably too vague to give the banks much control save in the case of blatant abuse. In the case of a North Sea project where the banks are making finance available to one of the participants, that participant's ability to influence what the operator does is limited and this undertaking (and certain others) are usually changed so that the participant is merely obliged to use his vote on the operating committee[16] to ensure, so far as is possible, that the project is carried out in accordance with good oil or gas field practice.

(vi) *An undertaking not to abandon the project unless it is uneconomic.* Clearly, it would be unfortunate if the borrower abandoned the project when the banks still had amounts owing to them and believed it was economic. Whilst the banks would usually be entitled to enforce their security if the borrower abandoned the project and possibly (if their security gave them this right) take over the running of the project themselves, this will be the least favoured of the banks' options: they will prefer to keep the borrower and his management systems in place as long as possible. This usually leads to negotiation over the precise meaning of the term "uneconomic". What the parties will be trying to identify in words is the time that the project's cash flow turns negative (*i.e.* the costs of running the project exceed its gross revenues) with no prospect of them ever turning positive again. A typical definition might read as follows:

---

[16] As to which see sections 2.3 and 10.2(a)(ii).

" '*Uneconomic*'
means that Net Revenues are negative for three successive Calculation Periods and, in the reasonable opinion of the Agent, are likely to remain negative even if further capital expenditure were to be incurred in order to enhance production (and after taking into account the cost of financing such expenditure)."

The reference to cash flow being negative for three successive Calculation Periods is meant to eliminate temporary problems (such as an unexpectedly long shut-down for routine maintenance and repairs) and the reference to further capital expenditure is obviously intended to try to make the borrower explore cost-effective ways of extending the project's economic life.

(vii) *An undertaking to remain a sole purpose company.* This is only appropriate, of course, where this is what is intended.

(viii) *Undertakings specific to the project in question which arise out of the banks' due diligence review.* Examples of this type of undertaking are: first, an undertaking in a power project for the project company to carry out maintenance of the power plant so far as is practicable at the same time as the owner of the transmission lines that export power away from the plant carries out maintenance; and secondly, an undertaking in a coal-fired power plant to maintain coal stockpiles at agreed minimum levels.

In addition to the above, there will usually be an undertaking not to pay dividends or make other distributions if certain cover ratios are breached. Whilst similar undertakings are found in corporate credit agreements (where the ratios in question are likely to be ratios such as a gearing ratio), project finance banks also often insist that any reserve accounts are funded to the required levels before allowing any distributions to be made.

Insurance provisions are dealt with separately in section 7.3 below.

(j) *Events of Default.* The fact that banks might have accepted a particular risk in a project does not necessarily preclude them having an event of default if that risk arises. The distinction is between the banks accepting a risk in that they will agree to lend money knowing that the risk might arise and accepting a risk in that, not only will they agree to lend, but they will also agree to have no rights or remedies if that risk arises. In a typical project, banks will usually accept risks in both of the above senses, through more usually the former.

Events of default that one might find in a project credit agreement (in addition to the breach of any relevant cover ratios (see section 5.4 above) and the usual events of default found in any credit agreement) include:

    (i) failure to achieve completion by a long-stop date;

    (ii) destruction or damage to all or a substantial part of the project facilities;

    (iii) cessation of production (for example, because of *force majeure*) for a sustained period;

    (iv) abandonment of the project;

    (v) nationalisation of the project facilities;

    (vi) a change in law which adversely affects the project's economics;

    (vii) (in a project which relies on ECA support) an ECA's guarantee (whether for political risk or otherwise) no longer being in full force and effect;

    (viii) non-renewal or revocation of a material consent or authorisation;

    (ix) termination of a material project contract;

    (x) legal proceedings being brought alleging that any of the project contracts were awarded in breach of any applicable public procurement rules[17] (in case these proceedings could result in such contract being declared void or the project company having to pay damages to a disgruntled competitor who was not awarded the contract);

    (xi) a party to a direct agreement[18] notifying the agent bank that it intends to terminate the project contract to which it is a party[19];

    (xii) non-availability of the required insurance cover (including, subject to negotiation, non-vitiation cover[20]);

    (xiii) failure by the sponsors to provide equity in accordance with the shareholders agreement;

---

[17] See section 9.2(c).

[18] See section 6.4.

[19] The reason the banks need this event of default (which borrowers maintain is precipitous) is so that they have the right at this stage to enforce their security, take over the project and, if they deem it necessary or appropriate, cure any default under the project contract in question in order for the project contract not to be terminated.

[20] See section 7.2.

(xiv) the shareholdings in the project company changing at all prior to a specified date (typically two years after completion, when the project should have established its financial integrity[21]) or any of the sponsors reducing their shareholdings in the project company below specified levels thereafter; and

(xv) a cross-default on the major project parties (including the contractor for so long as he still has liabilities under the construction contract).

To the extent that the banks have the benefit of money on debt service reserve accounts, a point often made by borrowers is that events of default relating to the project (such as cessation of production) should not take effect until that money has been used up. Their argument is that a debt service reserve account is intended to cover shortfalls in revenue due to problems with the project and, if they allow money to be held back in this way, they should get the benefit of deferring when the event of default occurs. After all, the banks are still receiving payment in the intervening period. The borrowers' objective is, of course, to buy time in which to sort out the problem themselves. The counter-argument is that, if there is a problem with the project, there is a problem with the project and the banks need to force the borrower to the negotiating table immediately through the medium of an event of default and the money on a debt service reserve account is required to service the loans during the negotiating period. The borrower (so the banks say), should not get the benefit of the banks' careful prudence in setting money aside as collateral.

Borrowers should seek to negotiate events of default along the lines of (viii) and (ix) above so that an event of default only exists if, after the expiry of a stated grace period, the relevant consent or authorisation is not renewed or a replacement project contract (with a counterparty acceptable to the banks) is not entered into.

Borrowers often bridle at events of default like the one in (xii) above on the basis that it is a matter beyond their control. The banks' response is the predictable one that such events of default serve to allocate risk, not attribute fault. The absence of adequate insurance is particularly problematic in a project financing where the only recourse the banks ultimately have may be to the project's assets or — if they are damaged or destroyed — to insurance proceeds representing those assets.

---

[21] This may be determined by reference to benchmark cover ratios.

The event of default in (xv) above may, insofar as it includes a cross-default on the sponsors, seriously undermine the several nature of their participation in a project. The same may be said of the event of default in (xiii) above. In either case, financial difficulties in one sponsor may jeopardise the entire project. A partial solution to this is for sponsors to negotiate that, if one of their number fails to provide equity in accordance with the share-holders agreement or breaches some other obligation in connection with the project, the other sponsors will have the right to cure the default themselves within a specified period and that the event of default should only occur if they have not done so on the expiry of that period. This type of right would obviously have to be included in the shareholders agreement and — so far as this was possible — in any other relevant agreement.

5.9   INTERCREDITOR ISSUES

Many project financings require funds to be provided from several sources. All projects will have some mixture of debt and equity but there may be different classes of share capital and various layers of debt. A large infrastructure project may require loans not only from commercial banks but also from one or more multilateral or export credit agencies[22] and the essential commercial terms of those loans are likely to be different (in that, at the very least, the agencies' loan maturities are likely to be longer). In addition, some of the lenders may be subordinated to others and there may be a financial lease or bond issue involved. Some lenders may be secured and others not (*e.g.* banks simply providing working capital). Not sur-prisingly, lenders will want to ensure that their position *vis-à-vis* other lenders is clear from the outset and this is usually done in an intercreditor agreement.

The intercreditor issues that arise in project financings are fairly similar to those that arise in other types of structured financing. An intercreditor agreement will usually address issues such as whether all of the categories of lenders have to agree before any of them can accelerate their loans or take enforcement action and whether or not any category of lenders is to have the right to veto any proposed exercise of a discretion under any other lenders' credit documenta-tion. For example, should each set of lenders have to give its consent to a proposed major variation order under the construction contract

---

[22] See Chap. 8.

(providing each set of lenders with a veto) or are decisions to be taken by polling all of the lenders "across the board", with all lenders being bound by a decision of the majority? Intercreditor agreements will often also contain provisions ("pro rata sharing" provisions) which provide for all of the lenders to share in recoveries equally on an enforcement. These provisions tend to be tailor-made for each case and, under English law at least, the mechanics by which pro rata sharing is achieved can be problematic.[23] If one layer of finance is to be subordinated to another, the intercreditor agreement will usually set out the terms of the subordination. Some rather more specific intercreditor issues arise with export credit agencies and EIB and these are discussed in section 8.6.

---

[23] For example, if pro rata sharing is achieved by an assignment of claims, this may constitute trafficking in (a bankrupt's) claims and be void as contrary to public policy.

Chapter 6

Security and Related Issues

6.1 THE PURPOSE OF SECURITY

The common view of security is that lenders take security over an asset in order to sell it if their loan is in default and to apply the proceeds against amounts outstanding under the loan. This is the "aggressive" nature of security — lenders are given rights entitling them to take a valuable asset away from their borrower and to dispose of it for their benefit. In order for this view to coincide with reality, the asset in question should be relatively freely marketable and have a fairly ascertainable value and the lenders should be free to exercise their rights without the need for third party consents.

Whilst these factors may be present in a project financing (as they may well be in a simple property development financing), they more frequently are not. Often the market is extremely limited (not everyone wants to buy a power plant in a developing country), ascribing a value to a project can be extremely haphazard (particularly if it is in a semi-complete state) and third party (particularly governmental) consents are often required to any form of enforcement action.

So why bother with security in project financing? The answer is that there are at least two other reasons for taking security which are highly relevant. These are:

(a) *security serves a "defensive" as well as an offensive purpose* — if a creditor has security over an asset, he ranks ahead of the general unsecured creditors and the ability of the unsecured creditors to interfere in the relationship between the debtor and the secured creditor is thereby limited; and

(b) *security may (depending on the legal systems concerned) entitle lenders to use an asset as opposed to merely selling it.*

149

The idea behind the defensive purpose of security is that the unsecured creditors would have little to gain by pursuing potentially disruptive action against the debtor (such as seeking to have it wound up) and that, even if the unsecured creditors did take such action, the secured creditors would to a large extent be insulated from its effects. The other purpose identified above (the "management" purpose) is really to give the lenders the option of taking over a project (and, if necessary, completing it) themselves.

The management purpose of security is easier to achieve in some jurisdictions than in others. English law has long allowed secured lenders to appoint a receiver and manager over a company's business and assets who will run the business with a view to repaying any amounts due to the lenders. The concept of receivership under English law is a well developed one and it is possible to advise both lender and borrower with some degree of certainty. Other jurisdictions, however, do not permit a creditor to run a debtor's business, either because this is simply a form of enforcement remedy which does not exist in that jurisdiction (as is the case with many continental legal systems) or because the jurisdiction in question has developed a bankruptcy procedure which actually prohibits secured creditors running a debtor's business effectively for their own account (as is the case with "Chapter 11" proceedings in the United States of America). If it is not possible to exercise management control over a project company through the enforcement remedies attaching to the security the company itself gives, it may be possible for lenders to obtain this control by taking security over the shares in the project company. This would theoretically entitle them to assume the rights of the shareholders on a default and replace the project company's management (although it must be said that, in some jurisdictions, the only remedy afforded to a pledgee of shares is judicial sale). Taking control of the project company through security over shares will usually result in the lenders assuming rather more directly the risks discussed in Section 6.5 below and careful advice should be taken in the relevant jurisdiction. The same comment applies to the other device usually discussed as a possible way of giving the banks control over a project, namely the issue to them of a "golden share". A golden share would typically give the banks the ability to replace the project company's board on an event of default or acceleration.

It should be borne in mind that, whilst security over the shares in a project company may be capable of delivering control of the company and hence of the project to the lenders, it will not afford them any priority over the project company's other creditors (but only over those of the charging shareholders).

6.2 THE FEATHERWEIGHT FLOATER

One note of caution needs to be sounded in relation to the comments in this Chapter about the capitalist nature of English security law. The Insolvency Act 1985 (later to become the Insolvency Act 1986) marked a watershed in the legislature's attitude towards secured creditors. The Act provided for the first time for an insolvency official (an administrator) to be appointed who was neither a liquidator (charged with winding up a business) nor a receiver (charged with realising security for the benefit of the secured creditors who appointed him). An administrator can be appointed by the court on the application of any creditor (not just a secured creditor),[1] owes duties to all of a company's creditors (not just its secured creditors),[2] manages the affairs and business of a company[3] and has to be appointed for one of four specified purposes, one of which is the survival of the company and the whole or any part of its undertaking as a going concern.[4] Furthermore, if an administrator is appointed, any receiver who has already been appointed is either bound to or can be made to vacate office.[5] The idea is that, if the administrator is charged with pulling the company round, he must have full management control over the company's assets and the continuance in office of any competing receiver is inconsistent with this. Once appointed, an administrator can dispose of property subject to a floating charge as if it were not subject to such charge and, with the consent of the court, can also dispose of property subject to a fixed charge (the original chargee maintaining his priority in relation to the disposal proceeds, however).[6] The banks' general complaint is that the appointment of an administrator robs them of the ability to influence or control the timing of any realisation. The making of an application for an administration order is therefore a potent weapon for the unsecured creditor (often a trade creditor) in his battle against the secured creditor (usually a financial creditor); the secured creditor no longer necessarily reigns supreme.

As has already been mentioned,[7] the only way that a secured creditor can block the appointment of an administrator is to appoint

---

[1] s.9(1) of the Insolvency Act 1986.
[2] Any creditor can invoke the statutory right of challenge of the way the administrator is managing the company's affairs, for example: see s.27(1) of the Insolvency Act 1986.
[3] s.8(2) of the Insolvency Act 1986.
[4] *ibid.*, s.8(3)(a).
[5] *ibid.*, s.11(1) and (2).
[6] *ibid.*, s.15.
[7] See footnote 4 to Chapter 5.

his own administrative receiver and to do this he has to have: (i) a floating charge; and (ii) security over the whole or substantially the whole of the company's property. These requirements can prove irksome to a borrower with assets other than simply those included in a project and which he may also wish to develop by means of project finance. The "featherweight floater" is designed to meet such a borrower's concerns by giving a bank providing project finance in relation to a project (the "first bank") a floating charge over all of the borrower's assets but then allowing the borrower to do what it likes with those of its assets which are not included in the project in question. The borrower may even give security over such other assets to another bank (a "subsequent bank"). Because these other assets may include assets which will be the subject of other project financings, the floating charge documentation usually provides, in order to facilitate the putting into place of any such project financing, that the first bank has to enter into a deed of priorities with any subsequent bank who provides such project financing. Such a deed of priorities will make it clear that the first bank's interests in the other assets are, with one exception, totally subordinate to those of the subsequent bank in relation to such project financing. The exception is that the first bank may appoint an administrative receiver to block the appointment of an administrator.

The documentation issues that arise out of the featherweight floater can best be explained by looking at some sample wording. If a featherweight floater were included in a general security document which also gave a bank security specifically over the project that it was financing, a clause along the following lines might be included to give effect to the featherweight floater concept. Cross-references to this clause would obviously have to be made throughout the security document where appropriate.

"Featherweight Floating Charge

In relation to the security created by way of floating charge by or pursuant to this Deed over assets ("Unrelated Assets") which do not comprise Project Assets:

(a) such security shall only be enforceable immediately upon the date of a petition being presented to the court under section 9 of the Insolvency Act 1986 for the making of an administration order in relation to the Borrower under section 8 of that Act;

(b) such floating charge may only be enforced by the appointment of a receiver;

152

(c) such floating charge shall only crystallise upon the presentation of such a petition;

(d) the Finance Parties shall not otherwise be entitled to change the nature of their security over the Unrelated Assets into a fixed security;

(e) any security created by the Borrower (now or in the future) over the Unrelated Assets in favour of third parties shall rank ahead of any security over the Unrelated Assets created in favour of the Finance Parties (but without prejudice to paragraphs (a)-(c) above);

(f) the Finance Parties shall, at the request and cost of the Borrower, enter into a deed of priorities with any such third parties in order to give effect to paragraph (e) above; and

(g) if a Receiver or any Finance Party receives any money or other benefit on an enforcement of this Deed insofar as it relates to an Unrelated Asset, it shall account for the same to the holder of any other Security Interest over such Unrelated Asset or (if there is no such holder) hold the same on trust for the Borrower."

By way of explanation of the above:

Paragraph (a): there is no need for the featherweight floater to be enforceable in any other circumstances. Indeed, the rationale behind the concept is that it should not be enforceable in any other circumstances (such as upon the occurrence of an event of default or acceleration).

Paragraph (b): this is the only remedy the holder of a featherweight floater needs or is entitled to have. It would be totally inconsistent with the rationale behind the concept for him to be able to exercise any of the other enforcement remedies (sale, possession or foreclosure).

Paragraph (c): a floating charge will, under general law, crystallise (*i.e.* be converted into a fixed charge) upon the chargor going into liquidation or receivership or upon the cessation of the chargor's business. It seems that the chargor and chargee can also agree — as a matter of contract between themselves — that a floating charge will crystallise on the occurrence of other events (*e.g.* events of default).[8] The effect of crystallisation of a floating charge is that the chargor can no longer deal with the assets the subject of the floating charge in the ordinary course of business (one of the hallmarks of such a charge). Crystallisation in circumstances other than the presentation of a petition for the making of an administration order would rob the chargor of his ability freely to deal in Unrelated Assets.

Paragraph (d): this largely supplements *(c)* and is aimed at limiting, for example, the scope of further assurance clauses.

Paragraph (e): any security over the Unrelated Assets ranks ahead of the featherweight floater.

Paragraph (f): this has been mentioned above. For certainty, the form of such a deed of priorities is sometimes negotiated in advance.

Paragraph (g): this paragraph deals with what happens if an administrative receiver appointed to block an administrator actually enforces the featherweight floater in relation to an Unrelated Asset. If such Unrelated Asset has been charged to a third party, the receiver must account to such third party for any amount recovered from such asset. If it has not been so charged, he must hold any such amount on trust for the chargor.

The banks' concerns about the appointment of an administrator (and hence the need for a featherweight floater) need to be put into context following the observations made by the Court of Appeal in *Re Atlantic Computer Systems plc.*[9] In that case, the court reluctantly agreed to give guidance on the principles to be applied on applications for the grant of leave under section 11(3) of the Insolvency Act 1986 (the section which states that, whilst an administration order is in force, no steps can be taken to enforce any security over the property of the company in question without either the administrator's consent or the leave of the court). The court's observations and guidance are probably *obiter*, although the case was decided in a manner consistent with the guidance and, even if *obiter*, such a deliberate pronouncement by the Court of Appeal obviously carries great weight.

The following are the observations made in *Re Atlantic Computer Systems plc*[10] which are the most relevant in the present context. The case was to do with equipment leasing but the observations are

---

[8] *Re Brightlife Ltd* [1986] 3 All E.R. 673. The decision in the case about the ranking of preferential creditors' claims (they were postponed behind a crystallised floating charge) no longer applies because such claims now take priority over a charge which, "as created", is a floating charge: Insolvency Act 1986, s.40. That part of the case dealing with crystallisation by notice still applies, however.

[9] [1992] 1 All E.R. 476.

[10] At pp. 500–503.

capable of — and were clearly intended to — apply to straightforward security as well and so the observations are formulated here in the language of security rather than that of leasing.[11]

(i) If granting leave to enforce security is unlikely to impede the purpose for which the administration order was made, leave should normally be given. Otherwise, the court will have to balance the legitimate interests of the secured creditor in question with the legitimate interests of the other creditors of the company.

(ii) The court will, it seems, grant leave where not to do so would be inequitable. It will normally be a sufficient ground for the grant of leave if significant loss would be caused to the secured creditor by a refusal but the court will still conduct its balancing exercise and will refuse leave if substantially greater loss would be caused to others by the grant of leave or if their loss would be out of all proportion to the benefit conferred on the secured creditor. In conducting its balancing exercise, the court will also have regard to the probability of a party incurring the perceived loss. In the case of an application by a secured creditor, the court would have regard to whether or not the creditor was fully secured since, if he was, delay in enforcement would be likely to be less prejudicial than in cases where his security was insufficient.[12]

(iii) The court may grant leave unless the administrator takes certain steps. This is, of course, equivalent to refusing leave but imposing terms and the court expected that this type of order would be made frequently. The example Nicholls L.J. gave in his judgment was that the permanent loss to a lessor flowing from his inability to repossess his property should be small if the administrator is required to pay the rental payments.

Nicholls L.J. also referred to and adopted certain comments made by Sir Nicholas Browne-Wilkinson V-C in *Bristol Airport plc v. Powdrill*.[13] The relevant part of Nicholls L.J.'s judgment reads:

---

[11] It is also important to appreciate that we are here dealing with fixed security. S.15(1) of the Insolvency Act 1986 allows an administrator to dispose of any property which is subject to a floating charge as if that property were not subject to such charge. By s.15(4) of that Act, the chargee acquires the same priority in respect of the assets representing any such property so disposed of (*e.g.* cash sale proceeds) as he would have had in respect of the original property. An administrator can therefore effectively overreach the interests of the holder of a floating charge, but he cannot do this on his own authority in relation to the holder of any other security (he will need a court order: see s.15(2), (3) and (5) of the Insolvency Act 1986).

[12] Presumably because of s.15(4) and (5) of the Insolvency Act 1986.

[13] [1990] 2 All E.R. 493, 507

".. . so far as possible, the administration procedure should not be used to prejudice those who were secured creditors when the administration order was made in lieu of a winding-up order . . . The underlying principle . . . is that an administration for the benefit of unsecured creditors should not be conducted at the expense of those who have proprietary rights which they are seeking to exercise, save to the extent that this may be unavoidable and even then this will usually be acceptable only to a strictly limited extent."

In view of the above comments, one could be forgiven for wondering why banks still have concerns over the appointment of an administrator. The point is to do with certainty, however. *Re Atlantic Computer Systems plc* is helpful insofar as it goes, but it does not provide the banks with certainty and predictability. They still have an understandable desire to know whether or not, in the last resort, they can rely on their security. Security is, after all, intended to make them secure.

6.3 COMPARATIVE ISSUES

English security law is extremely capitalist and flexible. Some of the more important features of English security law from the point of view of a project financier are as follows:

(a) it allows security to be taken over virtually all types of assets;

(b) it allows security to be taken over assets which do not yet exist ("future assets");

(c) it allows security to be taken relatively simply (by means of the floating charge) over all of a company's assets and yet allows the company to continue to deal with those assets in the ordinary course of business;

(d) security can be taken over virtually all classes of asset without taking possession of that asset (in other words, English law recognises non-possessory security interests);

(e) it allows enforcement (including by way of sale) to be effected without involving the courts;

(f) sale is not the only enforcement remedy — a secured lender can also operate an asset (either by taking possession of the asset himself or by appointing a receiver);

156

(g) certain types of security (fixed security) will rank ahead of preferential creditors;

(h) only minimal fees and duties are payable on the creation of security and only the normal transfer taxes (*e.g.* stamp duty) are payable on its enforcement; and

(i) the trust concept allows interests in security to be transferred relatively simply (and, in a secured syndicated loan, the security is usually vested in the agent bank as agent and trustee for itself and the other banks).

Unfortunately, not all jurisdictions are so accommodating. The following differences might emerge in the course of an examination into the type of security available under the laws of an overseas jurisdiction (cross-referring to the same paragraphs set out above):

(a) security may not be capable of being taken over certain types of asset (*e.g.* intellectual property rights);

(b) security may only be capable of being taken over a very restrictive category of future assets (for example, future receiveables arising under an existing contract)[14];

(c) there may be no concept similar to a floating charge;

(d) security may only be capable of being taken over assets which are not subject to a title registration system by transferring possession (although jurisdictions vary with regard to what constitutes possession for these purposes and sometimes only constructive possession (*e.g.* by attornment) may be required instead of physical possession);

(e) enforcement remedies may only be capable of being exercised through the courts;

(f) judicial sale may be the main (or only) enforcement remedy and the concept of a receiver (or a similar concept) may not exist;

(g) preferential creditors may rank ahead of all types of security;

(h) significant notarial fees, stamp duty and registration fees may be payable in respect of the taking of security (and, sometimes, even on its release); and

---

[14] An extreme example of a jurisdiction having difficulty with security over future assets is Portugal where, on one interpretation of the law, effective security cannot be given over insurance proceeds since they are contingent upon a claim being made and therefore constitute future assets (over which security cannot be granted) at financial close.

(i) the trust concept may be totally alien and, if the composition of a bank syndicate changes, new security may have to be taken.

Although this is a generalisation, it is normally possible in any jurisdiction (other than strict socialist ones) for security to be given over real estate, fixtures, present receiveables and shares in a company. Security over moveables is frequently a problem (usually even more so if the moveables in question are spares which are subject to a pooling arrangement) and the requirements for security over bank accounts usually have to be carefully explored.

Where the cost of taking security (in terms of notarial fees, stamp duty and registration fees) is high and the relevant fees and duties are assessed by reference to the amount of liabilities secured, it may be possible to contain the cost by persuading the banks to limit the amount of liabilities they secure on each relevant asset. Take an example where certain banks lend U.S.$350,000,000 to a project company involved in a power project, the only security available to them is over the real estate and the turbines, such security has to be taken in separate documents and each document is stampable at 0.5 per cent of the amount secured. There is little point in securing the full U.S.$350,000,000 (plus interest) on the turbines since the turbines will not realise that much. In these circumstances, the banks should be prepared to limit their claims to an amount which approximates to the realisable value of the turbines, although care will have to be taken over whether or not the turbines are an appreciating or depreciating asset. If they appreciate in value over time, the banks may wish to increase the amount secured to allow for this.

Some jurisdictions actually require security to be taken for a finite, stated amount as a general principle, unrelated to the issue of stamp duty or fees. In such a jurisdiction, it will not be possible to take "all moneys" security and the banks will have to try to calculate the maximum amount of their claims. This will usually involve them having to decide upon a maximum amount of interest that they wish to have secured on the asset in question. If their interest is floating rate, they will have to form a view on how high those rates are likely to rise. This type of jurisdiction also sometimes requires the secured amounts to be expressed in the domestic currency irrespective of the fact that the banks may actually be lending in a eurocurrency. Here the banks will be exposed to the risk of adverse exchange rate movements. It may be possible to provide them with some degree of protection if the amount secured can be stated to be escalated in accordance with an index which tracks domestic inflation, but this is not always permitted.

158

Some jurisdictions' security laws can also contain some unpleasant surprises for the unsuspecting in the way that they treat creditors with a high level of security over a debtor's assets. Paragraph 419 of the German Civil Code provides, for example, that, if a person "takes over another's entire property", that other's creditors may enforce their claims against both parties. This may apparently have the effect in certain circumstances of making a bank which took security over all of a debtor's assets liable for all of his debts.[15] Some jurisdictions (including Germany) also have rules which prohibit creditors being excessively secured (*i.e.* the value of their security being disproportionately high compared with the amount of their claim).

6.4 DIRECT AGREEMENTS AND COLLATERAL WARRANTIES

(a) *Direct agreements.* Direct agreements are agreements entered into between the project company, the banks financing a project and the parties to the project's key underlying commercial contracts. The key contracts for these purposes would typically include the concession agreement (if any), the main construction contract, any operation and maintenance agreement, any long-term supply contract and any long-term sales contract. Direct agreements are also sometimes sought from the authorities issuing consents necessary for the project.

The objective of a direct agreement is basically to enable the banks to "step into the shoes" of the project company if it defaults in its loan obligations. The extent to which direct agreements are required in any particular project financing will be dictated by the terms of the underlying contracts, the extent to which the banks' security carries with it management powers (see sections 6.1 and 6.3 above) and the scope of the proposed security package. Because direct agreements draw third parties into a project's financing arrangements, they are often heavily (and fiercely) negotiated. A third party long-term supplier of coal to a power project may not take kindly, for example, to a request that he should forego (at least to some extent) rights of termination that he considers perfectly

---

[15] By way of explanation, one way of taking security over an asset under German law ("Sicherungsübereignung") involves the (notional) transfer of title to that asset to the creditor.

normal and which, paradoxically, he would probably be able to retain for purchasers with a far better credit standing than a sole purpose project company. However, third parties can sometimes be pleasantly surprised by the extent to which they are able to turn direct agreements to their advantage and clearly set out the conditions on which they would be prepared to allow the lenders to step into the project company's shoes. With careful negotiation, a form of direct agreement acceptable to all parties can usually be agreed.

Banks would usually expect a direct agreement relating to a commercial contract to contain the following:

(i) consent from the third party to the project company charging or assigning by way of security the project company's rights under the relevant contract (to the extent such consent was required);

(ii) an undertaking from the third party that it would not exercise any right it had to terminate the contract without first giving the banks a specific number of days' prior written notice;

(iii) an agreement from the third party that, if it gave the banks notice of the type referred to in (ii) above and the lenders in turn gave it a counternotice, then the third party would either allow the banks (or a receiver or similar agent appointed by them) to assume the project company's rights and obligations under the contract for a specified period of time or allow the transfer of the contract to a separate company (a "work-out" vehicle) established by the banks for this purpose[16]; and

(iv) if the third party had the right to terminate the contract upon the enforcement of any security granted by the project company, an agreement that the third party would not do so in the case of an enforcement by the banks of their security so long as such enforcement was in accordance with the terms of the direct agreement (see below).

As far as banks are concerned, a direct agreement can therefore be said to perform both a defensive and an aggressive function. It performs a defensive function in that it protects the banks against a

---

[16] As noted in section 5.8 above, banks argue that, in order for these arrangements to protect them properly, the delivery to them of a notice under (ii) above should by itself constitute an event of default.

precipitous termination of a project contract by the other contracting party and it performs an aggressive function in that it allows the banks to seize control of the project company's rights under the project contract upon a general enforcement of their security.

It should also be noted that the typical direct agreement will refer to a novation of the project contract in two different types of circumstances. The first is that envisaged in (iii) above: the project contract is to be novated to a work-out vehicle, really as a holding measure. The second is that the project contract is to be novated to a trade buyer, someone who wishes to buy the project outright from the banks on an enforcement. Failure to appreciate the above can lead to confusion. Although use of the terms is by no means widespread, a person to whom the project contract is novated as a holding measure is sometimes referred to as an additional obligor,[17] while a person to whom the project contract is novated as part of a trade sale is sometimes referred to as a "substitute obligor".

If the person granting the concession retains the right to intervene and run the project *in extremis*, the banks' direct agreement with him should clarify the relationship between his intervention rights and the banks' step-in rights. The logical position is that, if the person granting the concession intervenes before the banks step in, they should not object so long as he accounts for the repayment of and the payment of interest on the loans out of the project's cash flows[18] and, if the banks step in before he intervenes, he should not object because the banks should be subject to his intervention powers by virtue of their having stepped into the concession agreement. If the person granting the concession has also bolstered up his intervention powers by having direct agreements with the other contracting parties (such as the contractor), it should probably be made clear that a step-in or intervention by him will prevail over any step-in effected or purported to be effected by or on behalf of the banks.

Examples of checks and balances often sought by third parties on the other end of a direct agreement are a right to buy the banks' loans from them so that the third party can take effective control of the situation on a default, pre-emption rights on a sale of the project, a requirement for any work-out vehicle to have the necessary technical expertise and an acceptable capital structure and funding arrangements, a limit on the period during which the banks

---

[17] See the references below to step-out and co-obligors.
[18] The banks would in such a case be taking a risk on the ability of the person granting the concession to run the relevant project.

can control the project[19] and (because of the disruption to the project that would otherwise be caused) an agreement that the banks can only "step in" once. Banks dislike pre-emption rights because it may be difficult to persuade third parties to make sensible bids for the project if they know that their bids may be defeated through the use of pre-emption rights. One possible solution is to require the person invoking the pre-emption rights (*e.g.* the host government) not only to match the best terms offered by third parties but also to pay for the bid preparation costs of the third party who would have purchased the project if the pre-emption rights had not been invoked. Host governments and other people granting concessions have also in the past found direct agreements that the banks have wished to enter into with them a useful means of trying to get the banks to attempt to save a project in distress before they have to. This is done by agreeing to pay a slightly higher level of termination compensation if the banks step in than would have been payable if the banks had not. A minimum step in period is normally required for the banks to earn the right to a higher compensation payment in order to protect the host government against manipulation (*i.e.* the banks stepping in and then immediately stepping out). The idea is that the banks must make a good faith attempt to rescue the project. The higher compensation will therefore obviously not be paid if the concession agreement is terminated for breach during the step-in period.

Some direct agreements proposed by the contracting counterparties (rather than the banks) require the banks to guarantee (through the issue of a "step-in undertaking") the obligations of a work-out vehicle to whom the relevant contract is novated or of the project company in receivership. This requirement is of dubious legitimacy: if the banks agree to such an undertaking, the relevant contractual counterparty will actually have a better credit risk (the banks) when the project is struggling than he would have had if the project had not encountered difficulties (the project company is, after all, a highly-geared sole purpose entity). A government's response to this argument is usually that, while the banks maintain that they are assisting the government by moving in to save an otherwise doomed project, in fact what they are doing is blocking the ability of the government to move in and save the project itself.

---

[19] This is usually expressed as a limit on the duration of the "step-in period" and is usually only appropriate for the key project contracts (*e.g.* the concession agreement or the power purchase agreement). It can be as short as two years and as long as five. Banks will argue that there should be no such limit: they should be able to run the project until their loans are repaid. Governments and power purchasers will retort that they do not want banks running their infrastructure or power plants.

If the government is to be forestalled in this way, the banks must provide the undertaking.

Banks, by contrast, seek to limit their liability on a step-in. They will frequently insist that, if they step-in, they (or their receiver or work-out vehicle) should only be responsible for those outstanding liabilities of the project company of which they are expressly notified by the contracting party. Failing this, they will seek to negotiate a cap on the amount of such pre-existing liabilities. They may also seek to negotiate a general cap on their liability (or the liability of their receiver or work-out vehicle) on a step-in, although this is often difficult to achieve.

Direct agreements can be shamefully long. The essential clauses for a direct agreement relating to a commercial contract can probably be reduced to the following, however:

"(a) The Agent [Bank] may, at any time, notify the Contracting Party that the New Entity shall be and be deemed to be a party to the Relevant Contract in place of the Borrower.

(b) The Agent (or the New Entity) may at any time thereafter, by a further written notice to the Contracting Party, require the Contracting Party no longer to treat the New Entity as the party to the Relevant Contract and the New Entity shall be released from all future obligations under the Relevant Contract from the date specified in such notice (being no earlier than the date of such notice).

(c) The Contracting Party agrees that, if it has the right to terminate the Relevant Contract and is intending to exercise such right, it will give the Agent at least [90] days' notice of its intention.

(d) During the period referred to in paragraph (c) above, the Contracting Party shall continue to comply with all its obligations under the Relevant Contract and shall not terminate the same. Once the New Entity has been sub-stituted for the Borrower in accordance with the above, the Contracting Party shall afford the New Entity [a reasonable time] [[ ] days] in which to remedy any outstanding breach and shall allow the New Entity to transfer its rights under the Relevant Contract to any purchaser of the Project Assets."

The "New Entity" in the above wording is the work-out vehicle.

The above wording is suitable for a jurisdiction which does not have a remedy similar to receivership. It could also be used, with a

163

little adaptation, for a jurisdiction which did have such a remedy. Paragraph (b) would have to include a reference to any receiver appointed by the banks, for example. Sometimes the direct agreement is used as a convenient document in which to place undertakings between the relevant contractual counterparty and the banks. For example, the counterparty may have licensed the project company to use certain intellectual property rights. The direct agreement can extend that licence to the banks.

While paragraph (a) in the above wording states that the banks can exercise their rights to step in at any time, the project company will obviously want the banks to agree in the credit agreement that they can only do so following an event of default or acceleration. Paragraph (a) states that the right is exerciseable at any time so that the contracting party is not required to enquire as to whether or not an event of default or acceleration has occurred. Paragraph (b) in the above wording is the important right for the banks to "step out". What they will be anxious to avoid is that they are forced to inherit all of the project company's obligations under the contract in question, including its long-term obligations in relation to abandonment costs. Of course, the contracting party may insist that this is the price for him agreeing to the banks having step-in rights. The usual riposte to this is that even a temporary step-in must be of benefit to the contracting party because, without it, he will only be an unsecured creditor for any amounts he is owed and will have lost the ability to earn future amounts under the contract whereas, if the banks step in, not only will they (or an entity controlled by them) pay any amounts due and owing to the contracting party under the contract, they (or such entity) will also be liable for amounts becoming due during the period of the step-in. Furthermore, if the banks did not step in, the project company would probably not have been able to meet those obligations (such as abandonment costs) in any event (because the assumption is that the banks will be stepping in when the project company is insolvent). In the context of an English law receivership, a receiver will be personally liable on any pre-existing contracts which he adopts. It used to be thought that merely continuing to comply with the company's continuing obligations under a contract did not constitute adoption, but this proposition was soundly quashed by *Powdrill v. Watson*[20] where the House of Lords held that, if an administrator or receiver simply continued with an employee's contract of employment for more than 14 days, they adopted that contract.

---

[20] [1995] 2 All E.R. 65 (the *Paramount* case).

Note that, in paragraph (d), the contracting party is bound to continue performing his own obligations during the so-called "suspension period", the period during which he may not terminate the contract. Contracting parties should insist that this should only be if the project company (or the banks on behalf of the project company) pay for any goods or services supplied by the contracting parties as a result. It is clearly inequitable for a contracting party to be expected to supply fuel for free during the suspension period, for example.

If, in the case of a jurisdiction with no receivership remedy, the banks can get comfortable with the possible liabilities that might result from an enforcement of any security they may have over the project company's shares and can take over control of a project in this manner, this is almost certainly a better alternative to either stepping in directly themselves or trying to transfer the project to a work-out vehicle. The former course of action would be fraught with potential direct liability for the banks and the latter may be more of a theoretical than a real right because of the sheer volume of legal work that may be involved in essentially transferring a business from one company to another. New consents may need to be obtained, for example, and a transfer of a business may attract stamp duty or have other tax implications. Furthermore, some jurisdictions (and England is probably no exception) have a rule against "self-dealing", *i.e.* a mortgagee selling the mortgaged asset to himself or to a person connected with him.[21] In addition, in a civil law jurisdiction with limited security available over contractual rights and even more limited enforcement remedies, it may be difficult to establish the basis of the banks' rights to bring about the novation of a project contract. If the basis is simply a contractual agreement with the project company coupled with agency, this may be vulnerable if the project company is insolvent.

Banks will normally seek to have a direct agreement with a licensing authority that contains either a confirmation that that authority will not revoke a particular licence by virtue of a step-in or an undertaking to grant a new licence, on no less favourable terms, to a work-out vehicle. The licensing authorities usually consider this an unwarranted fetter on their statutory powers but a compromise can usually be achieved whereby the authority agrees not to cancel the existing licence for a limited period of time (say three months) or to grant the work-out vehicle a temporary licence. In both cases,

---

[21] The rule is basically intended to protect against mortgaged assets being sold at an undervalue and thereby constituting unfair foreclosure. The English rule does not appear to be an absolute one but the mortgagee will have to prove that the consideration for the transfer of the asset to the connected person was (essentially) a fair one: *Tse Kwong Lam v. Wong Chit Sen and others* [1983] BCLC 88.

the authority will need to be satisfied that the project company or the work-out vehicle (as the case may be) will have the necessary technical and financial resources to continue to run the project for the period of the extension of the original licence or for the duration of the temporary licence. The idea is that the banks are given a limited period of time in which to organise a proper application to the relevant authority for a full licence and are permitted to run the project in the meantime.[22]

Banks have in the past also sought direct agreements from a project company's shareholders containing a commitment from them to subscribe for any deferred or contingent equity in accordance with the terms of the shareholders agreement. This is an attempt to establish a direct contractual link between the shareholders and the banks and can meet with fierce resistance. To some degree, however, the banks may have legitimate concerns as an assignment (if this is permitted) of the project company's rights to call in any deferred or contingent equity may be flawed. It may subject them to certain rights of set-off that the shareholders may have against the project company, for example.

A note of caution needs to be sounded in relation to stepping into a project through the medium of a receiver. An English law security document will usually provide that any receiver is the agent of the company, not of the banks, in order to deflect liability for the receiver's actions away from the banks. The receiver's principal is the company and it is the company to whom third parties who suffer injury, loss or damage at his hands should look. If the banks control the manner in which a receiver seeks to work out their debts, they will run the risk that, as against third parties, they become the receiver's principal.

From the borrower's perspective, direct agreements merely represent another form of security. Borrowers are therefore often keen to ensure that they still have the equivalent of an equity of redemption. In other words, the fact that the banks take control of a project through the medium of direct agreements should not mean (if the banks do not sell the project or the project company) that a borrower loses his contractual rights forever. There are arguments for and against this position but, if it is accepted that the project contracts should in effect be returned to the original borrower in these circumstances after the banks have stepped in and repaid

---

[22] Direct agreements and step-in rights in regulated industries can be fraught with difficulty. For example, the banks' right to novate a U.K. rail franchise will probably be a track access option under s. 17(6) of the Railways Act 1993 and hence a regulated agreement. If the Rail Regulator's consent is not obtained, the banks' right would be unenforceable: see s.18(1) of the Railways Act 1993.

their loans, the question arises of how this can be achieved. The problem is, of course, that the project contracts may have been transferred away from the borrower and into the banks' work-out vehicle. Providing for a simple retransfer will work legally but may highlight the issue for the other contracting parties. The usual way for this issue to be resolved in practice is to provide for the work-out vehicle to become a *co-obligor* with the borrower under the various project contracts, for the contracting parties only to deal with and look to that vehicle during the period of a step-in and for the vehicle simply to retire from the contracts once the loans have been repaid. The co-obligor concept is also a useful device with which to ensure that the banks or a work-out vehicle can effectively step out of a project contract into which they have been novated. If they were the only other counterparty to the contract, their stepping out of the contract might be dependent either on finding another person to assume their rights and obligations or on a release from the contracting party. If they are co-obligors, they can (so long as this is pre-agreed in the direct agreement) simply retire from the contract and throw the obligations back onto the project company.[23]

(b) *Collateral warranties.* Collateral warranties are most frequently found in property development financings. The purpose of a collateral warranty is to have a party who contracts with a project company (for example, a contractor or a professional adviser such as an architect or electrical and mechanical engineer) give certain undertakings and acknowledgements direct to the project company's banks. To some extent, collateral warranties will cover the same ground as direct agreements but they will also contain:

   (i) an acknowledgement that the third party owes a duty of care to the lenders;
  (ii) (in the case of a contractor) a warranty that its work will be fit for the purpose for which it was carried out and comply with all relevant statutory requirements;
 (iii) an undertaking not to use (or recommend the use of) certain "deleterious materials" in construction work;
  (iv) provisions entitling the banks to have access to any relevant plans and specifications on an enforcement; and
   (v) a representation as to the level of the third party's insurance and an undertaking to continue a minimum

---

[23] If the co-obligor device is accepted, however, it is important to ensure that a continuing insolvency of the borrower cannot be used as a reason for terminating the relevant contract as against the banks or the work-out vehicle.

amount of cover for a specified period (usually the relevant limitation period).

Some of the professional bodies in the United Kingdom have now published standard forms of collateral warranties for their members in an attempt to give the practice of obtaining collateral warranties some degree of uniformity. Collateral warranties are another Anglo-Saxon concept and practice and lawyers will be met with blank faces asking for them from, say, a German contractor.

6.5   ENFORCEMENT AND LENDER LIABILITY

There are broadly speaking two general types of liability that lenders may incur when enforcing security given by a project company: first, they may incur liability to the project company and any guarantors of its debts (because, for example, they sell the project company's assets below value) and, secondly, they may incur liability to third parties *either* because of contracts entered into by the project company or in the course of enforcement *or* because of acts done by the lenders (or their agents) in the course of enforcement.

English law recognises that secured creditors owe a debtor and any of his guarantors[24] duties on the enforcement of security. The most notable example is perhaps the position that English law has taken over the exercise by a secured creditor of his right of sale. As we have seen (in Section 6.3), a secured creditor can, under English law, sell an asset over which he has security without having to obtain a court order. Nevertheless, the courts have held that, whilst a secured creditor is generally under no duty as to when he exercises his power of sale, he must sell at a "proper price" or at the "true market value" when he does exercise this power.[25] In addition, English law holds a secured creditor who enforces his security over an asset by taking possession of that asset liable to the debtor for any damage to that asset caused by the creditor's gross or wilful negligence whilst in possession. These duties cannot be wholly avoided by enforcing through the appointment of a receiver as a receiver owes similar duties to the debtor. It is also doubtful whether any of these duties are capable of being excluded.

As far as liability to third parties in contract is concerned, this can arise under English law in a number of ways. As we have seen in

---

[24] See *Standard Chartered Bank Ltd v. Walker* [1982] 3 All E.R. 938.
[25] See *Cuckmere Brick Co. Ltd v. Mutual Finance Ltd* [1971] 2 All E.R. 633.

the context of "stepping out" (in section 6.4), a receiver will be personally liable for any contracts which he adopts and a direct agreement may only permit the appointment of a receiver over a particular contract if he expressly agrees to be bound by the terms of that contract (including the obligations). A receiver will, not surprisingly, usually ask the lenders appointing him for an indemnity against any personal liability he incurs as a result of his appointment.

As far as liability to third parties at large is concerned, this will usually arise by virtue of the lenders, a receiver appointed by them or their respective agents having control over and/or possession of a company's assets. Under English law, lenders may also incur liability as "shadow directors".[26] Whilst it is considered unlikely that the risk of shadow director liability would arise on an enforcement using a traditional method of enforcement (such as an exercise of the power of sale or the appointment of a receiver), it is a much greater risk where the lenders use a work-out vehicle (see section 6.4 above).

Probably the type of liability to third parties at large which most concerns lenders at present is liability for environmental pollution and clean-up costs. This is discussed in more detail in Chapter 9.

6.6   NORTH SEA SECURITY

Issues arising when taking security over a project company's interest in an oil or gas field in the North Sea deserve separate treatment since slightly different issues arise. These issues are best understood in the context of the contractual framework that exists in the North Sea and discussion of them has therefore been postponed to Chapter 10.

6.7   SPONSOR SUPPORT

(a) *Completion guarantees.* To understand the limitations of completion guarantees, it is necessary to understand the distinction

---

[26] By s.741(2) of the Companies Act 1985, a "shadow director" is "a person in accordance with whose directions or instructions the directors of [a] company are accustomed to act". Shadow directors only incur liability as such where the Companies Acts expressly state. For a fairly recent pronouncement on what is in practice required for a person to be a shadow director, see *Re Hydrodam (Corby) Limited (in liquidation)*, The Times, February 19, 1994. In *Re PFTZM Ltd (in liquidation), Jourdain & Ors. v. Paul*, [1995] B.C.C. 280, the Companies Court declined to accept that lenders exercising tight controls over a borrower's cash when the borrower fell into financial difficulties consituted a *prima facie* case that the lenders were shadow directors.

between a claim for the payment of a debt and a claim for damages. A debt is an agreement to pay a definite sum of money either in return for the performance of a specified obligation or on a specified date or on the occurrence of a specified event or condition. A claim for damages is a claim for general compensation for the non-performance by a party of a contractual obligation. Someone claiming payment of a debt need only prove that he has performed the specified obligation or that the relevant date, event or condition has occurred. He does not have to prove that he has suffered any loss. By contrast, a person claiming damages has to prove that the breach of the contract by the other party has caused him loss, that that loss was reasonably foreseeable at the time the contract was entered into and that the person claiming damages took all reasonable steps to mitigate his loss.

The simplest form of a classic completion "guarantee" in the context of a project financing is an undertaking to ensure that completion of the project occurs by a specified date. There is usually a definition of completion — in property development financings it may simply be the issue by the contract administrator or project architect of his certificate of practical completion. It is highly unlikely that an English court would give an order for specific performance of such an undertaking; a breach of such an undertaking would give rise to a claim for the payment of damages rather than a claim for the payment of a debt. Anyone pursuing such a claim would have to overcome the causation, remoteness and mitigation hurdles mentioned above. The amount of damages payable to lenders with security over a semi-completed project is also difficult to assess because the security will probably have at least some value. In these circumstances, the measure of damages is unlikely to be the amount due and owing to the lenders from the project company.

The weakness of the remedies available for breach of a completion guarantee usually comes as a shock to lenders and their initial reaction is to try to find some way of improving their remedies. There are probably really only two ways to do this short of asking the sponsors actually to guarantee the loans until completion. First, the lenders can seek to obtain a debt claim against the person giving the completion guarantee (typically one of the sponsors) by requiring him to undertake to pay a fixed sum if completion does not occur by a specified date (but this may constitute a penalty and be unenforceable under English law). Secondly, they can insist that the sponsor in question provides them with a letter of credit or bond from a bank, the terms of which enable them to call on the letter of credit or bond if completion does not occur when it should. This second route is the more reliable legally, but it comes at a price — someone will have to pay the issuing bank's fees (although such fees are frequently passed onto the project company and treated as part of the general financing cost).

If the sponsors do agree to guarantee the loans until completion and often in the case of any other form of completion support, a borrower should be able to negotiate a significant softening of the events of default in his project credit agreement which relate to the project's construction — why should the insolvency of a third party contractor in the construction phase be a problem if the sponsors are guaranteeing that completion will occur on or before a specified date? Depending on the strength of the sponsor support, a borrower may even be able to achieve the position that the only event of default relating to the construction of the project is that completion does occur by a long-stop date. Even then, the sponsors may be able to negotiate a position whereby the banks do not accelerate the loans so long as the sponsors continue to pay debt service as and when it falls due.

(b) *Other forms of support.* Other possible forms of sponsor support (ignoring the issue of normal guarantees or the provision of bank guarantees) include the following:

    (i) *Interest guarantees* — as the name suggests, this is a guarantee of simply the interest accruing on a loan and not of the principal. It is, however, disingenuous to suppose that there is any difference between this and a full guarantee in practice since the only way that a person issuing an interest guarantee can stem a continual haemorrhage of his cash resources should the borrower get into financial difficulties and the interest guarantee be called is for the guarantor to repay the principal of the loan in order to stop interest accruing.

    (ii) *Shortfall guarantees* — these are guarantees of any amounts that may remain outstanding after the banks have enforced all of their other security. The risks for the guarantor are that the enforcement might take a considerable amount of time (thereby increasing his liability in respect of interest) and that the banks enforce in a less responsible way they might otherwise because they know that any shortfall will be covered.[27]

    (iii) *Cash injection undertakings* — these are undertakings to inject capital into the project company in certain

---

[27] See in this respect section 6.5.

circumstances (usually the occurrence of cost over-runs). The money is usually to be made available by way of additional share capital or, more frequently (because of the greater flexibility it allows), by way of a subordinated loan. Loans can be subordinated in a number of different ways and it is important that the parties agree on the appropriate level of subordination for their particular project — for example, are the subordinated lenders to be allowed to receive interest payments on the subordinated loan so long as the senior loans are not in default or is the subordinated loan to be treated as quasi-equity so that the subordinated lenders receive no payments at all whilst any of the senior loans are outstanding?

(iv) *Price underpinning* — the sponsors may agree to "guarantee" a minimum or "floor" price for the project company's products. A highly sophisticated example of this is a "contract for differences" entered into by a regional electricity company in a United Kingdom power generation project.[28]

(v) *Comfort letters* — the sponsors may agree to give a "comfort letter" to the lenders. The sponsors will usually understand by this a letter which is not legally binding but the lenders may have a different view. In order to avoid misunderstandings and costly litigation later, it is important for all of the parties to be clear on the extent to which a comfort letter is intended to be legally binding from the outset. Comfort letters will typically address continued ownership of the project company by the relevant sponsors and the provision of personnel and technical resources to the project company. They may also include a statement of a sponsor's present intention were an event of default to occur in the future under the project credit agreement.

---

[28] See section 10.3(b).

Chapter 7

Insurance Issues

7.1 THE LENDERS' PERSPECTIVE

Insurance is unfortunately an area of project finance which rarely receives the attention it really deserves. Agreeing the insurance arrangements with the lenders (who have a legitimate interest in the insurances taken out in relation to a project) is often left until late in the day. It should not be, because perfecting the lenders' security interests in insurances can be complex and time consuming, especially where the project company is a member of a consortium involved in developing a particular project (as is frequently the case in North Sea and other energy projects).

The lenders' interests are twofold: first, to ensure that they are satisfied with the scope of the proposed insurance cover (the risks covered, the exclusions, the amounts of cover and the deductibles) and, secondly, to ensure that their interests in the insurances are adequately protected. In addition to insurance against physical damage and third party liability, lenders may wish the project company to take out pollution insurance and delay in start-up and/ or business interruption insurance (these last two categories of insurance being insurance against loss of revenue). Although many insurances can only be placed on an annual basis, lenders will want to be satisfied that adequate insurance cover will continue to be taken out for the life of their loans. There is clearly a performance risk in relation to the project company continuing to renew its insurances but insurances are often initially effected by contractors in construction projects and, where the project company is a member of a consortium, the project's main insurances may be effected by a single member of the consortium (such as an operator in a North Sea development) with each consortium member taking out "top-up" cover to the extent it felt that the main cover was inadequate. (Both of these approaches may result in lower pre-miums being paid.) Where insurances for a project are effected by a

173

third party in this way, the lenders will frequently request some form of direct contractual undertaking from the third party in relation to the insurances. (It must be said, however, that this is not the practice in the North Sea, although it appears that (for cost and control reasons) there is a movement away from having operators place the entire insurance package). Brokers are in any event usually asked to enter into fairly standard undertakings whereby they undertake, for example, to notify the lenders direct of any proposed cancellation of cover and of any proposed amendment to the terms of any policy (see below).

As far as perfecting security interests in insurances is concerned, lenders may seek to become co-insureds on the relevant policies (and to become direct beneficiaries of separate and independent policies) or they may simply accept that their interests in the policies should be noted (with or without "loss payable" clauses being attached to the policies). Loss payable clauses are directions to the insurers to pay all insurance moneys below a certain level to the project company and above that level to the lenders. Loss payable clauses in relation to third party liability insurances have to be fairly carefully drafted because in some jurisdictions lenders are not entitled to intercept insurance moneys payable to injured third parties. This matter is dealt with under English law by section 1 of the Third Parties (Rights Against Insurers) Act 1930. That section provides that, if a company which is insured against liabilities to third parties goes into liquidation, then that company's rights against the insurer are transferred to any third party to whom the company incurred a liability. Any attempt to provide otherwise in a contract of insurance will be of no effect.

Banks now usually insist on being co-insureds on the relevant policies taken out in connection with a project and on appropriate loss payable clauses being attached (with the insurers being directed to pay physical damage insurance proceeds to the agent bank for payment into a compensation account (see section 5.5(c)).

7.2 THE NON-VITIATION ISSUE

Banks insist on being co-insureds because this gives them a direct contractual claim on the insurers. Merely noting the banks' interest will at best mean that the insurers cannot obtain good discharge by paying the insured (*i.e.* the project company) and at worst mean that the insurers must enquire as to the nature of the banks' interests before paying away insurance proceeds. There is, however, an important distinction between a co-insured and a joint insured. In order to be joint insureds, the insureds must have the same interest in the insured property (the best example is the interest of a husband and wife in a jointly-owned matrimonial home). By contrast, co-insureds have different insurable interests in the insured property (and a mortgagor and a mortgagee are good examples of co-insureds). Unfortunately, the insurance market uses both terms almost interchangeably and this has led to a great deal of confusion. The distinction is critical in the context of the insurers' rights to avoid a policy (whether for breach of a condition, for non-disclosure of a material fact or otherwise). Where the insureds are joint insureds, non-disclosure by one insured will entitle the insurers to avoid (or vitiate) the policy against both insureds. But, where the insureds are co-insureds, non-disclosure by one insured will *not* entitle the insurers to avoid (or vitiate) the policy as against the other insured. This distinction was recently re-emphasised in *Maxwell Communication Corporation PLC (in administration) and others v. New Hampshire Insurance Company*,[1] but there is a line of authority going back many years which supports the proposition. Indeed, Staughton L.J. cited the following statement from Sir Wilfred Greene MR in *General Accident Fire and Life Assurance Corporation v. Midland Bank Limited*[2] when giving his judgment in the *Maxwell* case[3]:

"That there can be a joint insurance by persons having a joint interest is, of course, manifest. If A and B are joint owners of property . . . an undertaking to indemnify them jointly is a true contract of indemnity in respect of a joint loss which they have jointly suffered. Again, there can be no objection to combining in one insurance a number of persons having different interests in the subject-matter of the insurance, but I find myself unable to see how an insurance of that character can be called a joint insurance. In such a case, the interest of each of the insured is different. The amount of his loss, if the subject-matter of the insurance is destroyed or damaged, depends on the nature of his interest, and the covenant of indemnity which the policy gives must, in such a case, necessarily operate as a covenant to indemnify in respect of each individual different loss which the various persons named may suffer. In such a case there is no joint element at all."

---

[1] Court of Appeal; judgment delivered September 6, 1996.
[2] [1940] 2 K.B. 388.
[3] [1940] 2 K.B. 388, 404.

A policy where the various insureds have a different interest in the insured property is called a composite policy. Having held the policy in the *Maxwell* case to be a composite policy, Staughton LJ then went on to cite a passage from Lord Sumner's judgement in *P. Samuel & Co. Ltd v. Dumas*,[4] a case where a ship was insured for the benefit of both the shipowner and the holders of a mortgage over the ship[5]:

> "Fraud is not something absolute, existing in vacuo; it is a fraud upon someone. A man who tries to cheat his underwriters fails if they find him out, but how does his wrong against them invest them with new rights against innocent strangers to it?"

Staughton L.J. then stated that, although that case was a case of wilful misconduct, not of non-disclosure, the principle was the same: if, on its true construction, a policy of insurance with a number of insureds was a composite policy,[6] an innocent party could still recover.

Until recently, insurers actually used to clarify the position of banks and co-insureds in policies by including an endorsement known as the "non-vitiation endorsement". A typical form of this endorsement was as follows:

> "The liability of the insurers under this policy to any one of the insureds shall not be conditional upon the due observance and fulfilment by any other insured of the terms and conditions of this policy or of any duties (including duties of disclosure) imposed on such other insured in relation to this policy and such liability shall not be affected by any failure in such observance or fulfilment by any such other insureds."

This endorsement was usually included as a matter of course with no extra premium being charged.

However, the position at general law in relation to composite policies and the position set out in the old form of non-vitiation endorsement was slowly perceived by insurers to be unfair to them. It is not for nothing that contracts of insurance are contracts *uberrimae fidei*, contracts of the utmost good faith. Insurers assess a risk and charge a premium based on the facts as disclosed to them:

---

[4] [1924] AC 431.
[5] [1924] AC 431, 469.
[6] It is worth noting that the Court of Appeal came to this conclusion in the *Maxwell* case notwithstanding the fact that the relevant policy contained a clause headed "Joint Insured". The court sought to ascertain the true intention of the parties through a proper construction of the words of the policy.

if a party fails to disclose a material fact, then, had they known that fact, the insurers may not have underwritten the risk in question at all or may alternatively have charged a higher premium. This whole notion — the very basis on which insurers write insurance contracts — is undermined if, because of the existence of an innocent co-insured, the insurers have to pay out under a policy notwithstanding a material non-disclosure or breach. The banks' position, however, is that they are lending against an asset or the insurance proceeds that will be payable if that asset is destroyed: the prospect of the insurance proceeds not being paid merely by virtue of a non-disclosure by another insured (*e.g.* the project company, the contractor or any of his sub-contractors) is simply not acceptable.[7] The banks maintain that to avoid a policy as against them for another insured's non-disclosure or breach corrupts the basis of project financings: such financings are, after all, loans to projects not loans to companies with balance sheets. The truth is, of course, that there is a clash of equities.

Quite possibly because of the distressed state of the insurance market in the early 1990s following a disastrous run of claims brought about by hurricanes, earthquakes and other disasters, the insurance market began to turn against the inclusion of non-vitiation endorsements. The early resistance from the insurance market took the form of including non-vitiation endorsements which would only apply in the case of an innocent non-disclosure or innocent breach by another insured. However, although the form of the endorsement itself was qualified, insurers frequently overlooked the need to address the underlying position with regard to composite policies under the general law. By 1996, however, the insurers in the London markets and in many European reinsurance centres had caught up and insurance policies were actively seeking to exclude the possibility that they could be kept on foot for the benefit of the banks notwithstanding a breach or a material non-disclosure of any nature by another insured. Non-vitiation cover for projects eventually became so scarce that a specific policy was introduced into the project finance insurance market (the lenders' non-vitiation scheme) specifically to cover lenders against the risk that a project's primary insurances are avoided for non-disclosure or breach.[8] Two crucial features of this scheme are that:

(a) the insurers charge a premium for it; and

---

[7] If an insurance policy is avoided for non-disclosure of a material fact, it is avoided *ab initio*. Not only do all insurance premia have to be returned (by the insurers), but so do any insurance recoveries (by the project company).

[8] It is curious to note, however, that this type of policy, the mortgagee's protection policy, has been available to banks for many years in ship financings.

(b) the insureds (the banks) can only receive payment under it if the loss in question was insured and the primary insurers were entitled not to pay out under the primary insurances as a result of a non-disclosure. This may take some time to establish.

The delay in pay-out makes the lenders' non-vitiation scheme not particularly attractive to banks and this fact, complied with a limited capacity on the part of the insurers and a direct disclosure obligation on the banks, has led to the scheme only being used to date in a modest number of projects.[9]

At the end of the day, the non-vitiation issue may simply come down to an issue of premium: if insurers are paid additional premium, they may be prepared to take on what they perceive as additional risk.[10] Unless and until this is accepted, the following is a list of various ways to address the banks' concerns on the issue:

(i) Obtain a full non-vitiation endorsement. As noted above, this seems unlikely to be achievable in the London market given its current attitude, but other insurance markets (most notably the United States insurance market) may well be prepared to provide full non-vitiation cover.

(ii) Get the project company's insurers to agree, before writing the policy in question (*e.g.* the contractor's all risk policy), that they are satisfied that full disclosure of all material facts has been made to them and have a statement from them to this effect as a condition precedent in the project credit agreement. The limitations of this possible solution are first that it will not help to the extent that the relevant cover needs to be renewed during the life of the banks' loans[11] and secondly that it will not help if any of the

---

[9] At the time of writing, the insurers behind the lenders' non-vitiation scheme saw it working in conjunction with a clause — the "Multiple Insureds Clause" — which they had developed for inclusion into composite policies (*e.g.* construction all risks policies taken out for the benefit of the employer and the contractor). That clause seeks to set out the conditions on which the insurers would be prepared to accept separate liability to each individual insured (but not banks) and to provide certainty. The only way the banks are able to benefit from the use of the clause is to take an assignment of their borrower's interest under it. Although the clause protects the borrower against non-disclosure by another insured (*e.g.* the contractor), it will not protect the banks against a non-disclosure by the borrower (hence the ostensible need for the lenders' non-vitiation scheme). The terms of the clause in its originally published form were also much more restrictive than the common law rules.

[10] This seems to be the position that the Association of British Insurers are tentatively moving towards. There is in any event evidence that the non-vitiation issue is only of major concern to the construction period insurers: non-vitiation cover at present still appears to be fairly readily obtainable for the operating period.

[11] Terrorism cover, for example, needs to be renewed annually.

insureds is under a continuing duty to disclose material facts during the course of the insurance. The law is unclear on whether or not such a continuing duty exists.

(iii) Protect the banks through taking out a policy under the lenders' non-vitiation scheme. The brokers for the banks' policy should be separate from those for the primary policies since there might otherwise be a risk that an act or omission by the broker which was imputed to his principals under the primary policies and which vitiated those policies was also imputed to the banks and hence vitiated their policy.

(iv) Protect the banks by taking out a parallel policy to the main policy but with the banks as the only insureds. A major condition imposed by the insurers providing such parallel policy may well be that the main insurers cannot be told of the existence of the parallel policy. A major drawback of the parallel policy is that the onus of providing full disclosure of all material facts now falls on the banks (as the only insured parties). A substantial part of the information that the banks provide the insurers is likely to come from the project company and sometimes the banks will simply pass on the information pack prepared by the project company for its primary insurances. If the information pack omits a material fact, this omission will simply be adopted by the banks and made by them under their parallel policy.

(v) Obtain an indemnity from each of the other insured parties (*e.g.* the contractor) to the effect that, if such other insured causes the insurance policy to be avoided, it will indemnify the project company or the banks against any loss they suffer as a result. Whether the banks accept this solution will usually depend on the creditworthiness of the other insured parties.

(vi) Obtain an indemnity from the project company's shareholders against any loss the banks suffer as a result of an insurance policy being avoided. This is unlikely to be acceptable to the shareholders in the context of a limited recourse project financing.

7.3 TYPICAL INSURANCE PROVISIONS IN A PROJECT CREDIT AGREEMENT

While practice does vary, the provisions in a project credit agreement dealing with taking out and maintaining insurance tend either

179

to be in a relatively short form or to be fairly extensive. Whether the long or short form is opted for seems to be dictated by matters such as the perceived importance of insurance in the project, the complexity of the insurance package, how tailor-made or standard that package is and cost (including the cost of lawyers preparing and negotiating the longer form). In a North Sea project, where the insurance package is relatively straightforward and well-known, a short form insurance clause might look like this:

"The Borrower will, in relation to the Borrower's Interest and Borrower's Petroleum, maintain with insurance companies of repute insurance cover against such risks and on such terms (including amounts and deductibles) as would customarily be taken out by other licensees in the United Kingdom sector of the North Sea of a similar financial standing involved in similar projects."

This approach obviously requires there to be other licensees of a similar financial standing involved in similar projects. It may work for the North Sea where there are usually a number of projects of differing sizes underway at any time, but it will not work for the truly "once-off" project.

The more extensive provisions that would be found in a project credit agreement are as follows:

(a) *An undertaking to effect the required coverages.* The banks' specific requirements in relation to the project would be separately listed for the construction and operational phases. (This is because different insurers provide cover for each of the construction and operational phases.) The problem of ensuring that there is no insurance gap (in terms of time) is usually solved by simply providing that the operational insurances commence on the termination of the construction insurances. The coverages that would be specifically addressed would be physical damage insurance, third party liability insurance, delay in start-up and/or business interruption insurance and pollution insurance. The insured amounts that the banks require and the maximum deductibles that they are prepared to allow would be specified for the construction phase but it might not prove possible to do this for the operational phase (completion may be too far in the distant future) and, if this is the case, the agent bank will normally be given discretion to determine the required amounts and permitted deductibles for that phase. This obviously exposes the borrower to the risk that the banks impose unrealistic or extremely expensive levels of cover (it is often

180

said that any form of cover is available at a price) and the borrower should guard against this.

There is also usually a fairly bland undertaking for the borrower in addition to effect any extra insurances required by law (such as workmen's compensation insurance).

Delay in start-up and business interruption cover[12] are now generally only available for loss of revenue which stems from physical damage to the insured property caused by an insured risk. The reason for this is that such cover is usually provided by the same insurers as those who provide the physical damage cover and they are able to control how much they have to pay out under the loss of revenue cover by controlling the rate at which the damaged property is reinstated or repaired. So, if a turbine in a power plant is damaged by an insured event, the insurers may decide to fly it back to the manufacturer for repairs rather than sending it back by ship in order to shorten the period of lost revenues. Insurance cover against loss of revenue which is not consequent upon physical damage is an extreme rarity.

Delay in start-up and business interruption cover are in any event very expensive forms of coverage. The cost can obviously be mitigated by adjusting the deductibles and the insured amounts. The deductibles are generally so-called "time deductibles"; in other words, the project company must bear the first 30 days (say) of lost revenue itself. The insured amount will vary from project to project, but banks usually insist on an insured amount which, subject to the deductibles, will cover all the project company's principal fixed costs for a period (180 days, for example). The fixed costs will include interest on the banks' loans and sometimes a specified number of principal instalments as well. They may also include amounts such as a gas take-or-pay liability (although the project company should usually get relief from such liability in a gas sales agreement through *force majeure* (see section 3.10)). The period of time for which the banks may require cover for lost revenue is often determined by the length of time it would take to repair or replace the damaged property. Delay in start-up and business interruption insurance will generally not pay out if repair or reinstatement is not to take place.

---

[12] The convention is that "delay in start-up" is the name given to insurance cover against loss of revenues prior to completion of a project and "business interruption" is the name given to such cover after completion. The relationship between delay in start-up cover and a contractor's liability to pay liquidated damages for delay is often misunderstood. There should usually be no overlap since the reason why any delay in start-up insurance proceeds are payable should usually be the occurrence of a *force majeure* event and *force majeure* usually relieves a contractor of his obligation to pay liquidated damages for delay.

(b) *A mechanism to increase the insured amounts.* It is rare for an insurance package to be put in place covering the entire life of a project or of the loans. Policies are often renewable annually and, if this is the case, the banks will insist on an agreed mechanism whereby the amounts insured (for physical damage at least) can be increased. There are various alternatives, ranging from simple index-linking to a procedure whereby the borrower and the agent bank seek to agree on new values in the first instance, with resort being had to an expert in the event of disagreement. The insured amounts for physical damage can either be full replacement values or *first loss sums*. Where an asset is insured on a first loss basis, the sum insured is not the cost of rebuilding the entire asset but the cost of repairing the maximum amount of damage that is estimated to be possible on any one occurrence. An example often given is an exceptionally long pipeline where it is difficult to conceive of an accident which would write off the pipeline along its entire length. Insurance for such a pipeline on a first loss basis might, for example, take the cost of replacing the major compression system as the sum to be insured. In addition, as noted above,[13] there is a distinction between insuring assets for their replacement value or on an indemnity (or "actual cash value") basis. The former basis is intended to provide "new for old", *i.e.* it is intended to pay for the costs of rebuilding the asset destroyed. The latter basis is intended simply to compensate the insured for the loss of the asset in question, *i.e.* the value of, for example, a 10 year old power station.

(c) *Undertakings relating to the quality of the insurances.* These undertakings would include an undertaking to effect insurances through a broker and with insurers approved by the banks and in terms acceptable to the banks. The banks' requirements with regard to a policy's terms will include the relatively mundane (*e.g.* the exclusions that will be permitted) but will now also usually address more complex issues such as the non-vitiation issue.

The project company will usually be required to procure that the insurers inform the agent bank direct of any changes to the terms of the policies in question (the project company will usually fulfil its obligations in this regard through the use of broker's undertakings (see (d) below)). Such changes might come about on an annual renewal date or at any time if the terms of the original policy allowed unilateral variation. The insurers will also usually be required to give the agent bank 30 days' notice of cancellation of a policy (so that, for example, if cancellation will occur because of

---

[13] section 5.8(e).

non-payment of a premium, the banks can pay the same and keep the policy alive).

(d) *An undertaking to procure that the broker effecting the insurances gives the banks a letter of undertaking.* A typical broker's letter of undertaking will require the broker to:

(i) Arrange for "loss payable clauses" in an agreed form to be included in any policies that are issued. As noted previously, loss payable clauses in relation to physical damage policies specify that recoveries up to a certain threshold amount should be paid to the borrower, but that recoveries above that amount should be paid to the agent bank. Loss payable clauses in relation to third party liability usually specify that recoveries should be paid to the agent bank except where the borrower has already discharged his liability to the third party who suffered the relevant loss, damage or injury (when the recoveries should be paid to the borrower) or where the insurer proposes paying such third party direct (when the recoveries should be so paid).

(ii) Arrange for a notice of assignment (*i.e.* the banks' security assignment) to be endorsed on each policy when it is issued. Notice to the debtor (in this case the insurer) is required in order for an assignment to constitute a legal (as opposed to an equitable) assignment[14] and the giving of notice tends to establish and preserve priorities.[15] A practice has arisen for these notices to be joint notices, *i.e.* notices signed by both the assignor (the borrower) and the assignee (the agent bank). In some jurisdictions, however, joint notice (or acknowledgement of receipt of a notice) may actually be a requirement for a valid assignment.

(iii) Hold the insurance slips and policies when issued to the banks' order (but without prejudice to the provisions of the loss payable clauses (see (i) above)).

(iv) Advise the agent bank of any non-payment of premia, of any material changes to the terms of the insurances and of any circumstances which arise which might result in any insurance being avoided.

---

[14] s.136 of the Law of Property Act 1925.
[15] See *Dearle v. Hall* (1828) 3 Russ 1.

(e) *An undertaking to pay all premia when due and to provide the agent bank with evidence of payment.*

(f) *A "self-help" remedy.* This is what it sounds. If the borrower defaults in any of his insurance obligations, the banks can perform those obligations in his name and at his expense.

7.4 MANDATORY LOCAL INSURANCE; REINSURANCE

A problem that often arises in projects in the emerging markets is that the host government has a rule (designed to encourage the growth of a local insurance industry) that all insurances have to be written locally. The local insurers will obviously reinsure (they would probably not otherwise be able to meet a major claim) but this will be of scant comfort to the sponsors, the project company and the banks if they are concerned about the local insurers' creditworthiness since the project company will by definition only have a claim against the local insurers.[16]

The following are examples of ways to overcome problems posed by a requirement for mandatory local insurance:

(a) *Require the local insurers to give the project company a security assignment of the relevant reinsurance policies.* This is not always possible, not least because the local insurers may be subject to negative pledges. Such an assignment might also in and of itself constitute a breach of a local legal requirement for local insurance. The risk of this being the case will be greater in jurisdictions (such as Turkey) which do not recognise the concept of security assignments of contractual rights, only absolute assignments.

(b) *Require the local insurers and the reinsurers to enter into contractual cut-through arrangements.* These arrangements are usually tripartite arrangements between the local insurers, the reinsurers and the project company. They provide that, in the case of a claim, the project company may call upon the reinsurers to pay it direct. The banks would usually take a security interest in the project company's rights under the arrangements. The problems with contractual cut-through arrangements are:

---

[16] Note that some jurisdictions require a minimum percentage of the risks (*e.g.* 5 per cent) to be retained by their local insurers (in order to maximise the local insurers' premium income). At least one jurisdiction (the Republic of Croatia) has now even legislated that some of the reinsurance must be effected in the local market.

    (i) they may also in and of themselves constitute a breach of a local legal requirement for local insurance;

    (ii) they are contractual and may therefore be treated as a voidable preference on a bankruptcy of a local insurer (or be capable of being avoided on such a bankruptcy on other grounds); and

    (iii) (from the reinsurers' point of view) they may, because of (ii) above, expose the reinsurers to the risk of double payment, once to the project company and once to the local insurer's liquidator.

(c) *Have the sponsors form their own captive insurance company in the jurisdiction in question.* Although this company would still have to reinsure, the sponsors could ensure that the only insurance business that it carried out was in relation to the project in question and that the proceeds of the reinsurance should therefore always be available to meet any claim that the project company had. Although this solution would involve the sponsors becoming familiar with the local jurisdiction's laws relating to the establishment and operation of insurance businesses, it is not as far-fetched a solution as it at first sight might appear — various major oil companies set up a captive Bermudian insurance company (Oil Insurance Limited) because of a lack of capacity in the insurance markets for various aspects of their business (notably pollution).

The documentation relating to reinsurance policies varies. It can be very simple and (as is often the case in the London reinsurance market) simply state that the reinsurers will "follow the fortunes of" the primary insurers. In such a case, although the dominant policy terms are those of the primary insurances, it is wrong to assume that the dominant insurers are the primary insurers since the reinsurers are likely to have had a great influence on the terms of the primary policies. Alternatively, the reinsurance policies may be detailed policies in their own right, very similar to the primary polices. Again, however, it is important to appreciate that the dominant insurers are likely to be the reinsurers and that the primary insurers will therefore have different terms and conditions to those of the reinsurance at their peril. This philosophy clearly dictates that the governing law of the reinsurance policies and of the primary insurance policies should be the same. This is, however, not always possible where there is a requirement for mandatory local insurance since there might also be a legal or practical requirement for the primary policies to be governed by local law.

It is also important to appreciate that, as they ultimately bear the risk, reinsurers will frequently control the primary insurers' conduct of claims.

7.5 MISCELLANEOUS INSURANCE ISSUES

The issue relating to the mandatory prepayment of insurance proceeds for physical damage has been discussed above (in section 5.8), as has the possible inclusion of an event of default relating to the non-availability of required insurance coverage.

Chapter 8

Export Credit and Multilateral Agencies

8.1 COMMERCIAL AND POLITICAL RISK

Key to an understanding of the role of export credit and multi-lateral agencies in any project financing is the distinction between commercial and political risk. If a project company cannot pay interest on its loans or pay dividends because the project is not performing as well as expected or because an offtaker has gone bankrupt, this is commercial risk. If, however, the project company cannot pay interest on its loans or pay dividends because the host government imposes restrictions on the remittance abroad of foreign currency or because of a collapse of the host country's banking system caused by civil war or other hostilities, this is political risk. Commercial banks can assess and accept commercial risks but they have a much more limited capacity to accept political risks.

Export credit agencies ("ECAs") and multilateral agencies are political animals; an ECA is owned (or franchised) by a government and a multilateral agency is owned by a number of governments. This political pedigree enables ECAs and multilateral agencies to provide long-term loans at fixed interest rates to the world's less prosperous nations and to protect lenders and/or investors against the consequences of certain political risks. In the context of loans, ECAs and multilateral agencies will accept political risks either by making the loans to the project company themselves or by guaranteeing to commercial lenders the repayment of their loans (and the payment of interest on those loans) if the reason for non-payment is a political risk. Commercial lenders will usually have to satisfy an ECA providing them with a political risk guarantee that a political risk has occurred before such ECA pays a claim.

The classic political risks that ECAs and multilateral agencies will accept are:

    (a) *political violence, i.e.* war, military action (such as a *coup d'état*), revolution, civil disturbances, terrorism and sabotage;

187

(b) *expropriation*, including requisition, the freezing of assets, discriminatory taxation, the unjustified cancellation or non-renewal of consents (including import licences) or the imposition of a new requirement for a consent; and

(c) *transfer risk, i.e.* the inability of the project company to obtain required amounts of foreign currency and remit them off-shore due to the imposition of exchange controls or due to a moratorium or any similar action being declared or taken by the host government.

They may also insure against the risk that a government breaches specific undertakings. To the extent that those undertakings are guarantees of payment by a state-owned offtaker (*e.g.* a state electricity board), this will have the effect of converting all or a large part of the credit risk of a project to a credit risk on the institution(s) providing the political risk cover. ECAs may also be in a position to provide enhanced political risk cover for events such as change in law, change in taxation, interference in the project in question and the revocation of licences if they are able to obtain appropriate guarantees or assurances from the host government.

In the case of transfer risk, it is important to differentiate between the project company not being able to make a payment in foreign currency because it is bankrupt and does not have enough local currency with which to buy the required amounts of foreign currency (a commercial risk) and it not being able to make a payment in a foreign currency because all foreign currency reserves are held by its country's central bank and the central bank is bankrupt (a political risk). ECAs providing only political (and not commercial) risk cover to commercial banks will protect themselves against the possibility of paying out for what is in effect a commer-cial risk (bankruptcy of the project company) by requiring, as a condition of payment under their guarantee, that the project company has deposited local currency with the central bank in an amount which would have been sufficient to purchase the required amount of foreign currency had the central bank held sufficient foreign currency reserves.

When analysing the level of political risk in a country, it is important to ascertain whether or not there is an investment protection treaty with that country. These treaties follow a fairly standard pattern and will usually include provisions along the following lines[1]:

---

[1] See, by way of example, the Agreement for the Promotion and Protection of Investments between the U.K. Government and the Government of the Sultanate of Oman, November 25, 1995, Cm 3163.

188

   (i) neither country will discriminate against investments made in its country by nationals of the other country and each country will observe any obligation it has entered into in relation to such investments;

  (ii) neither country will subject investments or returns of the other country's nationals to treatment less favourable than that which it gives investments or returns of its own nationals (this is the so-called "most-favoured-nation" status);

 (iii) each country shall afford the other country's nationals the same treatment as it affords its own nationals in relation to compensation for losses to investments caused by national emergency, revolt, insurrection or riot;

 (iv) each country shall not nationalise investments made in it by nationals of the other country otherwise than for a public purpose, on a non-discriminatory basis and for adequate and effective compensation; and

  (v) each country will guarantee the unrestricted transfer of investments made by and returns due to nationals of the other country.

The treaties are not merely agreements between governments. They usually include a provision that each government will allow international arbitration of any dispute between it and a national of the other government in relation to the obligations of the first government under the treaty. It is, however, unclear what an individual's rights would be (if any) were such an arbitration to find against one of the governments.

8.2 EXPORT CREDIT AGENCIES

The oldest ECA is the Export Credits Guarantee Department of the United Kingdom ("ECGD") which was originally established pursuant to the Overseas Trade (Credits and Insurance) Act 1920. That Act gave powers to the Board of Trade, "for the purpose of re-establishing trade ... between the United Kingdom and any country", to (*inter alia*) grant credits to United Kingdom persons, where it appeared "advisable so to do by reason of circumstances arising out of the war", in connection with the export to specified countries of goods produced or manufactured in the United Kingdom.[2] The USA's ECA, the Export-Import Bank of the United States

---

[2] Overseas Trade (Credits and Insurance) Act 1920, s.1(1). ECGD currently derives its powers from the Export and Investment Guarantees Act 1991.

189

(commonly referred to as "USEXIM"), was established in 1934 (at the time of the Great Depression) and its purpose was to aid and facilitate in financing United States exports to increase or sustain jobs in the United States.

The ECA's origins clearly lie in national movements to promote exports by subsidy and exporters who could avail themselves of support from their national ECA would clearly enjoy an advantage over exporters from countries without an ECA (or an equivalent programme). The world has now changed, however. Not only do almost all of the 29 member countries of the OECD and a large number of other countries have ECAs, but all bar six[3] of the OECD countries have agreed to co-ordinate and to a large extent standardise the financial support that their ECAs offer. The idea is to foster an orderly export credit market so that export orders are won not on the basis of who offers the most advantageous financial terms but on who provides the best goods and services for the lowest price. To this end, the relevant OECD countries participate in the "Arrangement on Guidelines for Officially Supported Export Credits" (the "Arrangement"). The original Arrangement was entered into in April 1978 and it has been amended and updated since.[4]

There are various advantages of including ECAs in a project's finance plan:

(a) the ECAs' repayment periods are often longer than those that would be available in the commercial bank market. This should increase the "debt capacity"[5] of a project and thereby increase shareholder returns;

(b) the ECAs will provide interest rate equalisation support to enable borrowers to benefit from long-term loans at fixed rates. ECA support can therefore play an important part in a project's interest rate hedging programme;

(c) the ECAs' political risk insurance (if available) may often be the key to whether a particular project goes ahead at all[6]; and

---

[3] The exceptions are the Czech Republic, Hungary Iceland, Mexico, Poland and Turkey.

[4] The current version is that published by the OECD in June 1992, incorporating all amendments to and including April 1992. The OECD is currently considering limited revisions in respect of project finance (e.g. to lengthen the six month grace period before repayments begin and to allow repayment on a more flexible basis than the current equal semi-annual instalment arrangements).

[5] i.e. the amount of debt as opposed to equity that can be used in financing a project.

[6] Lead arrangers of project loans where it is not possible to obtain ECA cover for all of the loans will often try to stipulate (e.g. through the prepayment provisions of the project credit agreement) that a fixed ratio of covered to uncovered loans must be maintained throughout the life of the facility.

(d) where an ECA will provide both political and commercial risk cover, banks can book the loans so covered as a credit risk on the government of the relevant country of the ECA and not a credit risk on the actual borrower or its country. This not only assists in obtaining internal credit approvals, it is also beneficial from a capital adequacy standpoint.[7]

One of the advantages of having multinational consortia bid for a project is the fact that each member of the consortium may be able to get its own ECA to support the project, thereby maximising the advantages that ECAs bring.[8] The competitiveness of a particular consortium's tender to a project company may well depend on the availability of support from a number of ECAs and this will in turn require that the consortium procure (or "source") the relevant goods and services from countries whose ECAs are involved. In such a case, the sufficiency of the project company's financing may well be dependent on the construction contractor sourcing his goods and services from the correct countries and, in order to keep costs low, the project company may not have contingency funding to cater for the possibility that the goods and services are sourced from elsewhere. There is therefore a risk that, if ECA support for the project company is arranged from Germany and the United Kingdom, for example, and the construction contractor decides to change his sourcing and procures a substantial piece of equipment from Brazil, the project company will — in the absence of any available bank funding — have insufficient finance available to pay for the equipment. Banks will often insist that, in such circumstances, the construction contractor will have to wait for his money. The following is a typical clause that is inserted into construction contracts to deal with the linkage between the ECA facilities and the construction contractor's entitlement to payment:

"8. ECA COVERAGE
8.1 Procurement of eligible materials for ECA coverage
The Contractor shall and shall procure that each Subcontractor and Supplier shall source all goods and services to be acquired or provided in carrying out the Work and shall carry out the Work in a manner which ensures that 85 per cent of the aggregate value

---

[7] A credit risk on an OECD ECA would at present be zero-weighted for capital adequacy purposes if the ECA was a government-owned or government-backed institution.
[8] Although it may also be possible to involve an ECA if there is a sub-contractor in its jurisdiction.

comprised in the Contract Price of materials supplied, work performed and associated services provided in carrying out the Work and which (on the basis of the ECAs' usual and customary requirements as at the date of this Construction Contract)[9] are eligible for financing by the utilisation of credit facilities provided by or having the benefit of political risk and/or commercial or comprehensive risk cover from each of the ECAs is not less than the amount set out below:

	Export Element (US$)	Local Element (US$)	Total (US$)
ECA 1	[ ]	[ ]	[ ]
ECA 2	[ ]	[ ]	[ ]
ECA 3	[ ]	[ ]	[ ]

8.2 Utilisation of ECA Credits

Without in any way limiting the obligations of the Contractor under Clause 8.1, the Contractor shall and shall procure that each Subcontractor and Supplier shall do all things necessary in good time which are requested by the relevant ECA in accordance with its standard practice or which the Employer notifies the Contractor it reasonably considers necessary and which are, in each case, within the control of the Contractor or a Subcontractor or Supplier (as the case may be) to permit the Employer to fully utilise the ECA Credits to the extent contemplated by Clause 8.1 including, without limitation:

(a) the submission or provision by the Contractor and any Subcontractor or Supplier to the Employer or any ECA of all documentation including but not limited to sourcing records, subcontracts, purchase orders, invoices, supplier certificates, guarantees, undertakings and shipping/freight documents and other information as may from time to time be reasonably requested by the Employer or required by any ECA in accordance with its standard practice;

(b) compliance with all drawdown and payment procedures required from time to time by any of the ECAs in order that utilisation may be made under any of the ECA Credits being provided or covered by such ECA and that such ECA's cover remains in full force and effect;

---

[9] Without the words in brackets, the Contractor would be exposed to the risk that he would not get paid (by virtue of Clause 8.3) if an ECA changed its eligibility criteria after the date of the construction contract.

(c) maintenance of all sourcing records necessary to satisfy the requirements of the ECAs;

(d) (to the extent that the same apply to or are required to be met by the Contractor or any Subcontractor or Supplier) the meeting of all conditions precedent, ongoing terms, conditions or requirements including the payment of any premia due to be paid to an ECA and any sourcing or related expenditure requirements of any of the ECAs such that the terms of any ECA Credit or the terms of cover provided by any ECA are complied with in all respects and that such cover remains in full force and effect; and

(e) the provision of all further reasonable assistance or support requested by the Employer in connection with the ECA Credits or their utilisation.

8.3 Effect of breach

If the Contractor breaches any of its obligations under Clauses 8.1 and 8.2 above and, as a result, the Employer suffers a shortfall in its available finance by virtue of any goods and services not being eligible for financing by the utilisation of the ECA credits:

(a) the Employer shall be entitled to withhold from the Contract Price an amount, equal to the finance or cover that would have been obtainable with the support of or from any ECA but for the Contractor's breach of its obligations in Clauses 8.1 and 8.2 until such time as the Employer in good faith determines that it has sufficient funds available to pay such amount taking into account its other payment obligations; and

(b) the Contractor shall indemnify and hold harmless the Employer from all losses and costs as may be reasonably incurred by the Employer resulting from such breach by the Contractor and its remedy."

To compound a contractor's problems in this area, he will also be expected by an ECA to enter into a "recourse" (or similar) agreement with it pursuant to which he will indemnify it for any loss it suffers as a result of any misrepresentation by him or as a result of the ECA making disbursements in respect of non-eligible goods. This agreement may also provide for the contractor to reimburse the ECA for a portion of any payment made by the ECA in respect of a default by the borrower at a time when the contractor's contract had been terminated as a result of a breach by the contractor.

The main provisions of the Arrangement relevant to a project financing are the following:

(i) There are maximum repayment terms. The precise term generally depends on how wealthy or poor the importing country is: for relatively rich "category 1" countries, the maximum term is eight and a half years and for the poorer "category 2" countries, the maximum term is 10 years.[10] There are special rules, however, for certain special sectors. For example, the maximum repayment term for power plants which are not nuclear plants is 12 years.[11]

(ii) Repayment of principal should normally be in equal and regular instalments which should be made not less frequently than every six months.[12] This obviously restricts the ability for juggling the repayment profile of a project's loans against an irregular or seasonal cash flow.

(iii) The first repayment of the export credit must be made not later than six months after what is termed the "starting point". The starting point is defined differently depending on the type of contract being financed. For a contract for the sale of capital goods which are useable in themselves (*e.g.* locomotives), it is the date the buyer takes physical possession of the goods in his country. For a contract for the sale of capital equipment for complete plant or factories where the supplier has no responsibility for commissioning, it is the date the buyer is to take physical possession of the equipment (excluding spare parts). For a construction contract where the supplier or contractor has no responsibility for commissioning, it is the date construction is completed. For any contract where the supplier or contractor is responsible for commissioning, it is the date when installation or construction has been completed together with preliminary tests to ensure that the equipment is ready for operation.[13] The latter definition will usually apply in the context of project financing (where a turnkey contractor will usually be responsible for commissioning) and, coupled with the previous requirement for equal instalments, it can sometimes

---

[10] Para. 4(a) of the Arrangement as amended.
[11] *ibid.,* para. 9(c). There are also special sector understandings for export credits for ships, nuclear power plants and civil aircraft (see Annexes II — IV of the Arrangement).
[12] Para. 4(b)(1) of the Arrangement.
[13] *ibid.,* paras. 4(b)(1) and 24(1).

cause a project difficulties immediately after commissioning when cash flows are only just beginning to build up. Where, as would be typical in a power project, there are a number of units to be constructed and each of them will be completed on a different date, there will be a choice for working out the first repayment date or dates. The starting point could be the mean commissioning date of all the units or the date of the commissioning of the last unit (although this would delay the first repayment date and so might be unacceptable). Alternatively, the loans could be divided up between each of the units with each tranche having a first repayment date linked to the commissioning of the unit in question.

(iv) There are minimum interest rates: ECAs should lend at the relevant commercial interest reference rate (or "CIRR").[14] There is a CIRR for each currency offered by the ECAs. It is a base rate plus 100 basis points (*i.e.* one per cent) and the base rate is set by reference to the yield on bonds of various currencies issued by the government of the currency in question (*i.e.* United States treasury bonds for United States dollars, United Kingdom gilts for sterling, etc.).[15]

Some ECAs lend direct and other prefer simply to guarantee the loans made by a commercial bank syndicate. An ECA lending large amounts direct would usually have a sub-participation (or funding) arrangement with a commercial bank syndicate behind the scenes. In either case, the commercial banks would fund themselves on a floating rate basis (*e.g.* LIBOR) and the ECA in question (or a related institution) would, if it was offering interest rate equalisation, commit to make the banks "top-up" payments (topping up the CIRR plus the margin received from the borrower to LIBOR plus a margin). An ECA offering interest rate equalisation would receive the surpluses arising if the interest rate situation was reversed.

(v) Interest should not be capitalised during the repayment term and should be payable not less frequently than every six months (the first actual payment of interest being not later than six months after the starting point (see above)).[16]

(vi) The purchaser of the exported goods and services (*i.e.* the project company) must make cash payments at or before the

---

[14] *ibid.*, para. 5(a) as amended.
[15] See note 2 to the Arrangement and Annex VIII to the Arrangement.
[16] Para. 4(b)(2) of the Arrangement.

starting point equal to 15 per cent of the export contract value.[17] The making of such cash payments is usually a condition precedent to loan disbursement.

Each ECA has different rules about the level of risk that it is prepared to accept and it is important to understand precisely what is on offer when structuring a financing involving ECAs. Some ECAs — most notably USEXIM — will not offer cover for commercial risks during the construction phase of a project financing (unless covered by a state guarantee)[18] and the level of cover offered in any given case (for political or commercial risks) will usually vary between 90 per cent and 100 per cent. For example, the German ECA (Hermes Kreditversicherungs A.G. ("Hermes")) will offer only up to 95 per cent cover post-completion for both political and commercial risks, whereas ECGD is prepared to offer up to 100 per cent.

The ECAs are prepared to finance a limited amount of local costs and/or goods and services exported from third countries. It is also important to understand the ECAs' rules in these areas when structuring a financing. The guiding principle is that ECAs must not finance, guarantee or insure more than 100 per cent of the value of goods and services exported.[19] Given the requirement for the overseas purchaser to make a cash payment of at least 15 per cent of the export contract value (see above), the ECAs' concession to finance local costs is obviously capped at the same 15 per cent. Some ECAs[20] will only cover third country supplies as an alternative to covering local costs although the ECA of any European Union Member State must cover subcontracts where the subcontractor is from another Member State so long as the aggregate amount of such subcontracts (together with any subcontracts with non-European Union third country suppliers) does not exceed 30 per cent (or higher percentages for smaller contracts).[21] There are otherwise wide variations with regard to the percentage of the main contract value that third country suppliers may represent either for the main contract itself still to be eligible for financing or for third country supplies (or a proportion of them) to be eligible for cover.[22]

USEXIM's position on third country supplies (or, to put it the other way, on required United States content) shows how an individual ECA's various rules interrelate:

---

[17] *ibid.*, para. 3.
[18] USEXIM expressly reaffirmed this position in February 1996 in order to negate rumours circulating at the time that they were preparing to change their policy in this area.
[19] Para. 6 of the Arrangement.
[20] *e.g.* COFACE, ECGD and SACE.
[21] See Council Decisions of December 31, 1973 (73/391/EEC) and July 27, 1976 (76/641/EEC).
[22] Ranging from 10 per cent in the case of Hermes to 70 per cent in the case of JEXIM.

(a) United States content must be at least 50 per cent of the total contract price;

(b) USEXIM's loan or guarantee may support up to 100 per cent of the United States content, but may not exceed 85 per cent of the total contract price (because of the requirement for a 15 per cent cash payment (see above));

(c) when the eligible foreign content is between 10 and 15 per cent, the total contract price less the 15 per cent cash payment is eligible for financing; and

(d) when the eligible foreign content is between 15 per cent and 50 per cent, only the United States content is eligible for financing.

The general principle that ECAs should offer broadly standardised financial support is bolstered by provisions in the Arrangement dealing with offering support on different terms ("departing from consensus") and other provisions dealing with agreeing common positions in relation to individual countries or types of transactions ("agreeing a common line"). If an ECA wishes to offer terms which do not conform to the Arrangement, it must give prior notice to the other ECAs, thereby giving them the opportunity to match its terms.[23] If any ECA wishes to propose a common line, it must give notice to all the other ECAs prior to the closing date for receipt of any bids (if applicable).[24] A common line proposal can be more or less onerous than the terms and conditions allowed under the Arrangement. If a common line is agreed (and disinterested ECAs are deemed to have accepted a proposal), it will supersede the rules set out in the Arrangement (but only for the project in question) and shall remain in force for an initial period of two years (subject to renewal). If, in relation to a project, any ECA intends to submit an offer which is more favourable than the common line applicable to that project, this will be treated as a derogation from consensus with the consequences set out above.

The cover that ECAs offer is not all-embracing. They will typically only guarantee repayment of principal and payment of interest and default interest at a specified rate. In addition, repayment of principal is only guaranteed on an unaccelerated basis, *i.e.* as and when repayment would have fallen due under the original credit

---

[23] Paras. 15 and 16 of the Arrangement. Of course, whether or not the right to match terms will in practice make a difference will depend upon whether any contractors from any other ECA countries are actually bidding.

[24] The common line rules and procedures are contained in Annex VI to the Arrangement.

agreement irrespective of any intervening acceleration of the loans. Costs such as breakage costs, fees and indemnity payments are usually not covered by ECAs. When an ECA is only providing political risk cover, there is also a question of causation to be resolved. Should the ECA pay under its guarantee when the occurrence of a political risk is only one of the possible causes for non-payment? ECAs sometimes try to provide in their documentation that they will only pay out if the political event is the "direct and sole" cause of the non-payment. This, it is submitted, is too strict: "direct and primary" represents a fairer balance between the parties.

The general attitude of ECAs to credit documentation varies. It is important to appreciate that some ECAs are relative newcomers to project finance and are at present still to some extent developing their own thoughts in the field. Some ECAs try to adhere fairly rigidly to their own standard forms but recent years have seen an increasing willingness on the part of some ECAs to be fairly flexible in their approach to the form that their documentation should take, particularly in large project financings. Whatever form of documentation is used will always provide for disbursement of funds against some form of evidence that the funds are to pay for goods manufactured or services performed by nationals of the relevant ECA's country (or for other eligible goods and services). The range of possible drawdown and payment mechanics is probably as follows:

   (i) a qualifying certificate ("QC") containing specified information in relation to the relevant goods and services and a representation as to their eligibility for funding is presented by the contractor to the agent bank and payment is triggered by that QC OR a drawdown notice (containing such information and representation) is presented by the borrower and payment is triggered by that drawdown notice (although this is probably limited to the reimbursement system referred to in (iii) below);

  (ii) in the case of payment being triggered by a QC, the QC is countersigned by the borrower OR it is not countersigned by the borrower[25]; and

 (iii) actual physical payment is made direct to the contractor OR it is made to the borrower for reimbursement upon proof

---

[25] Countersignature by the borrower protects the ECA because it minimises the possibility for the borrower to argue that the payment should not have been made. It means that the contractor needs the borrower's agreement before it can get paid. Some ECAs (*e.g.* COFACE, Hermes and SACE) appear to insist on the borrower's countersignature, but others appear happy to do without it.

that the borrower has paid the contractor in relation to the relevant goods and services.[26]

Various combinations of each permutation may also be possible, *e.g.* it would not be unusual for the disbursement mechanics to include the possibility of reimbursement to the borrower as well as payment to the contractor direct.

Although, as one would expect, the detailed terms of an ECA guarantee will be different depending on the ECA and the governing law, commercial risk guarantees issued by ECAs will invariably provide that the guaranteed banks must exercise their discretions under the relevant loan agreement as the guaranteeing ECA directs and both commercial and political risk guarantees will (as noted above) usually provide that the ECA will only make payments to the banks on an unaccelerated basis and that the ECA may at any time purchase the banks' interests in the underlying loans.

The governing law of the underlying credit documentation can sometimes be an issue when ECAs issue guarantees. Whilst it is more or less generally accepted that English and New York law are the two systems of law which international commercial banks prefer (and which they often insist on), complications can arise when the loan facilities for a project comprise a syndicate of international banks and one or more syndicates of banks located in the jurisdiction of one or more supporting ECAs. For example, a Franco-German construction consortium might put together a financing package for an overseas project which comprised loans (in relation to German goods and services) to be made available by the German partner's "house" German banks supported by the German ECA (Hermes Kreditversicherungs A.G. ("Hermes")), loans (in relation to French goods and services) to be made available by the French partner's "house" French banks supported by the French ECA (Compagnie Francaise d'Assurance pour le Commerce Extérieur ("COFACE")) and loans (in relation to that part of the price of German and French goods and services which the ECAs were not prepared to support, goods and services from other sources and working capital) to be made available by a syndicate of international banks based in London. In these circumstances (and particularly in view of the inevitable intercreditor agreement (see Section 8.6 below)), it would be eminently sensible to have all of the credit documentation governed by one law. Unfortunately, the likely outcome of the above example is that the international banks would

---

[26] By contrast to the previous footnote, this means that the borrower needs the contractor's agreement or co-operation before the borrower can get paid. The proof referred to is usually a receipt from the contractor.

insist on English law, COFACE would probably insist on French law[27] and Hermes would state that they would be prepared to operate under English law. The usual "damage limitation" exercise in this sort of situation is to have separate loan agreements, to try to have at least a common language for all of them (usually, for obvious reasons, English), to try to have common provisions (in particular, the warranties, undertakings and events of default) expressed in identical terms and to try to have any agreements which relate to all of the loan agreements (for example, the intercreditor agreement) governed by one law (usually English or New York law). This is not a situation unique to COFACE; USEXIM issues its guarantees under New York law and has a great (and understandable) preference for the loan agreements it is guaranteeing to be governed by New York law as well. This may cause problems if USEXIM's share of the overall loans is relatively small and other ECAs express a preference for English law.

Where all of the parties in a multi-sourced financing are prepared to have all of the credit documentation governed by one law, it is possible to have a documentary structure for the loans which consists of one agreement (a "co-financing agreement" or a "common terms agreement") which sets out all of the common provisions and a series of loan agreements in a sense subsidiary to that agreement which merely set out the funding mechanics for each different set of lenders (reflecting, for example, the different way in which interest may be calculated in different jurisdictions).

As far as intercreditor agreements are concerned in the context of ECA finance, most (if not all) ECAs accept the need for some form of intercreditor agreement between themselves and the commercial lenders to a project when the ECA finance is merely one part of a larger financing package. In fact, intercreditor agreements are often in the ECAs' interests since they will frequently lend on much longer maturities than commercial banks and probably need some form of protection against the banks taking a short term view.

Before leaving the topic of ECAs and the role they play in ameliorating political risk, it is worth noting in passing that ECAs also provide political risk cover for equity investments (*e.g.* ECGD's Overseas Investment Insurance Cover), some ECAs will offer "untied" cover (*i.e.* cover in relation to goods and services not supplied or provided from their own country) and there is a small (but growing) private political risk insurance market.

---

[27] COFACE's attitude may recently have softened, however.

8.3 MULTI-LATERAL AGENCIES: INTERNATIONAL FINANCE CORPORATION ("IFC") AND THE EUROPEAN BANK FOR RECONSTRUCTION AND DEVELOPMENT ("EBRD")

IFC is part of the World Bank group. Whereas the World Bank[28] itself is the entity which lends to sovereign states, IFC is its arm for supporting projects in the private sector. IFC's Articles[29] state that its purpose is to "further economic development by encouraging the growth of productive *private enterprise*[30] in member countries, particularly in the less developed areas". It is therefore IFC and not the World Bank that one tends to come across in true project financings.

IFC will typically participate in a project by taking a small equity participation and by making loans available pursuant to an Investment Agreement (although they can do either independently of the other). The Investment Agreement contains a loan structure which used to be particular to IFC and which is often referred to as the "A Loan/B Loan" structure. The A Loan is a loan advanced by IFC at its own risk, but the B Loan is a loan the funds for which are advanced by commercial banks and which is made at the risk of these commercial banks. Apparently, very few World Bank or IFC loans have not been repaid. Governments tend to try to repay World Bank and IFC loans even in times of severe economic hardship in order to avoid being denied further World Bank or IFC funds in the future. World Bank and IFC loans also enjoy a preferential position on the rescheduling of a country's debt. To the extent that the B Loan is lent by IFC, the B Loan should also benefit from this protection. This is the major advantage of IFC transactions for commercial banks and is usually referred to as the "IFC umbrella".

The relationship between IFC and each commercial bank in relation to the B Loan is set out in a Participation Agreement and IFC typically retains a high degree of control.[31] A separate inter-creditor agreement is usually only found where there are other lenders involved or security sharing arrangements are required.

---

[28] The proper name for which is the International Bank for Reconstruction and Development. The World Bank was established in 1944 pursuant to the Bretton Woods Agreement and IFC was established in 1956.

[29] Art. 1 of its Articles of Agreement.

[30] Emphasis added.

[31] Lenders normally accept this because of the political pressure it is perceived that IFC can exert on a default.

IFC has standard forms for the Investment Agreement and the Participation Agreement. One of the features of the standard documentation which is at first sight puzzling to borrowers is that, although IFC is ostensibly the lender of the B Loan, it only commits to lend to the borrower those amounts made available to it by the commercial banks pursuant to the Participation Agreement(s) and it does not accept an obligation to require the commercial banks to make amounts available to it as and when the borrower presents drawdown requests. A borrower therefore has no legal right to ensure that it receives the B Loan because it has no right to force, or to require IFC to force, the commercial banks to make amounts available to IFC in the first place.[32]

EBRD was established in 1990 pursuant to an international agreement signed by its member states. That agreement states [33] that EBRD's purpose is to "foster the transition towards open market oriented economies and to promote private and entrepreneurial initiative in the Central and Eastern European countries committed to and applying the principles of multi-party democracy, pluralism and market economics". EBRD is included in this section with IFC because there is also perceived to be an "EBRD umbrella" and EBRD has to date essentially modelled its own standard form documentation on that of IFC. EBRD is required by its constituting agreement to "apply sound banking principles to all its operations", something which earned it considerable criticism in its early days. The question usually asked — with some force given the relatively modest loans and investments in Eastern Europe that EBRD initially made — was that, if EBRD was simply to behave like any commercial bank, how could it realistically perform its perceived role of "kick-starting" the East European economies?

Whatever their respective constitutional positions, however, and whatever the political impetus behind them, it is a mistake to believe that IFC's or EBRD's involvement in a project means easy money. In practice, their officials can strike just as hard a bargain as any commercial bank.

---

[32] There is a concern that, if IFC is too transparent a conduit for the commercial banks' money, the banks and not it may be the beneficial owners of the interest payments, with the result that whether or not amounts had to be withheld on interest payments would fall to be dealt with by the host government's general withholding tax rules for interest paid to offshore banks and any applicable double taxation treaties and would not fall within any exemption in IFC's favour. This issue of who is the beneficial owner of interest payments is a general concern where a lender of record is in fact put in funds by another lender under a participation agreement.

[33] In Art. I.

8.4   THE EUROPEAN INVESTMENT BANK (THE "EIB")

The EIB is essentially the European Community's bank. It was set up in 1958 under Article 129 of the Treaty of Rome.[34] Its constitutional document is annexed to the EC Treaty and under the Treaty the role of the EIB is to "contribute . . . to the balanced and steady development of the common market in the interest of the Community" facilitating the financing of specified classes of project.[35]

The big advantage that the EIB can bring to a project is long-term fixed rate funding.[36] It can do this because it uses its credit standing to raise long-term fixed rate funds in its own name in the international bond markets[37] which it then on-lends to borrowers at a modest margin intended to cover its own costs and the creation of statutory reserves.[38] Although the obvious attraction of the EIB in the context of project finance is its fixed rate funding,[39] it can lend on a traditional floating rate basis as well as on a fixed rate basis and it has developed or is developing various interest rate options. Two examples of such options are what it calls *revisable fixed rate loans* and *variable convertible rate loans*. With revisable fixed rate loans, the interest rate is initially fixed for only part of the duration of the loan (for example, the first four years) and is fixed once again for a further period on the expiry of this initial period (and so on). The new fixed rate is proposed by the EIB and, if the borrower does not accept it, the EIB's documentation provides that the borrower must prepay the loans. With variable convertible rate loans, the interest rate is initially floating but the borrower has the option to convert all or part of the loans to a fixed interest rate at specified times.[40] The fixed rate will again be proposed by the EIB but, in this case, if the borrower does not accept it, the loans will remain on a floating rate basis.

---

[34] See now Arts. 198d ff. of the E.C. Treaty.

[35] The classes of project include projects for developing less-developed regions, projects for modernising undertakings and projects of common interest to several Member States (such as the Channel Tunnel) which are of such a size or nature that they cannot be entirely financed by other available means.

[36] The EIB will consider maturities in excess of 25 years for a TENs project.

[37] The EIB was the largest non-sovereign issuer of bonds in the world's capital markets in 1996. It has a AAA credit rating.

[38] The EIB is required to operate on a non-profit-making basis.

[39] Borrowing on a fixed rate basis from the EIB has been described as a natural low cost interest rate hedge. It can either reduce or remove altogether the need to hedge a project's interest rate exposure using instruments available from commercial banks (which is not without its difficulties: see section 5.7).

[40] On interest payment dates and up to four years prior to final maturity in the case of amortising loans (or up to three years prior to final maturity in the case of bullet repayment loans).

In some jurisdictions the EIB may lend to a local bank who will then lend the funds on to the borrower. More typically in project finance, however, the EIB will lend direct to the borrower and the EIB's loan documentation will then comprise either simply a Facility Agreement or a Facility Agreement and a series of Finance Contracts entered into pursuant to the Facility Agreement. In the latter case, the Facility Agreement sets out the basic terms of the EIB facility (amount, representations and warranties, undertakings and events of default) and the terms upon which the EIB will enter into Finance Contracts. A Finance Contract sets out the basic options open to a borrower in terms of interest rate (see above) and repayment terms (*e.g.* minimum grace period, annuity basis repayment or equal semi-annual instalments) for any tranche made available by the EIB under that Finance Contract. A typical procedure for the EIB making a tranche available under a Finance Contract is that the borrower requests the EIB to do so, specifying its preferred interest and repayment options, and, if (in the case of a request for fixed rate loans) the EIB is able to obtain matching funds on the fixed rate markets, the EIB sends the borrower a disbursement notice confirming the details of the proposed tranche. If the EIB is unable to issue a disbursement notice because funds in the relevant currency are not available to it, then the EIB may either make floating rate funds available or (in limited circumstances) issue guarantees (in the EIB's name) to enable the borrower to obtain long-term (although probably floating rate) funds in the commercial bank market on the strength of those guarantees. If the borrower prepays all or any part of a fixed rate tranche once it has been made available, it has to pay the EIB an indemnity amount.

The EIB will not generally accept completion risk in a project financing and the system that has been devised to enable stand-alone projects nevertheless to benefit from its funding advantages is to assemble a syndicate of commercial banks who are prepared to take completion risk and to have them issue bank guarantees or standby letters of credit[41] to the EIB to cover the EIB's loans during the construction period.[42] Where the EIB is to be the beneficiary of such instruments, it will include in its Facility Agreement a requirement that all such instruments be issued at all times by

---

[41] Standby letters of credit are, for the most part, the same as bank guarantees (payment is made against a document which simply specifies that there has been a payment default under the loan in question). It is largely a question of nomenclature brought about by historic regulatory problems that U.S. banks had with the issue of bank guarantees.

[42] This is not, of course, strictly necessary where the EIB lends to a local bank because EIB's credit risk is naturally the local bank.

"Qualifying Institutions" which are banks whose long-term debt is rated higher than a certain threshold by the rating agencies or which are otherwise approved by the EIB.[43] If a bank loses its Qualifying Institution status then, if the bank guarantee or standby letter of credit which it provided is not replaced by an identical instrument from a new bank which is a Qualifying Institution, the EIB will typically reserve the right to call on the instrument issued by the affected bank and to use the resulting cash it receives as cash collateral for a commensurate part of its loans (although the documentation is not always clear as to how this is done). When acting for the borrower or the syndicate, it is important to ensure in the documentation that any affected bank whose instrument is called in this way does not acquire particularly preferential treatment, whilst recognising that it has had to borrow funds on the interbank market to fund payment of the amount demanded. From the borrower's point of view undue preferential treatment could put a strain on the project's cash flows and from the point of view of the remaining banks undue preferential treatment would offend against the principle that all banks within a syndicate should be treated equally. One way of achieving some sort of balance would be to provide not that the affected bank was entitled to immediate reimbursement of the money it paid out but that its payment under the bank guarantee or standby letter of credit it issued constituted a loan which amortised as the remaining banks' exposure amortised. It might also be possible to go further and provide that the amount by which the (floating rate) interest on that loan exceeds the fixed rate that would have been payable to the EIB plus the guarantee fee that would have continued to have been payable to the affected bank is deferred in payment until all amounts due to the other banks have been paid in full.

The EIB is prepared to take project risk after completion. In some cases in the past it was prepared to release on completion all of the bank guarantees and letters of credit provided to it provided that certain (cover ratio) tests were met. Nowadays, however, it tends only to release its bank guarantees and letters of credit on a gradual phased basis, subject to continued compliance with specified (cover ratio) tests (and, even then, it will not necessarily release all of its bank guarantees and letters of credit). (This does not necessarily reflect a change in policy but probably more a different assessment

---

[43] The second limb of this test is to cater for banks whose debt is not rated (as will often be the case for domestic banks providing bank guarantees in some of the smaller European Union currencies) and to give the EIB some latitude should only a marginal down-grading occur.

of the risk involved in the project in question.) In the latter type of situation, the EIB is likely to have at any given time both guaranteed and unguaranteed loans outstanding and it should (broadly speaking) only be entitled to accelerate all or part of the guaranteed loans for problems related to the bank guarantees or their issuers and only be entitled to accelerate all or part of the unguaranteed loans for problems related to the project. The EIB's events of default should reflect this.

8.5   THE EUROPEAN INVESTMENT FUND (THE "EIF")

The EIF is a new financial institution set up to provide guarantees to support medium and long-term financing in two areas: Trans-European Networks (TENs) and Small and Medium sized Enterprises (SMEs). The impetus for the establishment of the EIF was given at the Edinburgh summit in December, 1992 when the Council of Ministers and the EIB were invited "to give urgent and sympathetic consideration to the establishment as quickly as possible of a European Investment Fund". The EIF was eventually established in June 1994. The EIF is an example of a public/private partnership. It is owned as to 40 per cent by the EIB, as to 30 per cent by the European Commission and as to 30 per cent by financial institutions from all 15 Member States (although not all of this last 30 per cent has yet been subscribed).

Article 2 of the EIF's statutes[44] provides that the EIF is to "contribute to the pursuit of Community objectives". Such contribution is to be by, amongst other things, supporting the development of the TENs in the areas of transport, telecommunications and energy infrastructure projects. The EIF's statutes authorise it to provide such support in two ways: first, by guaranteeing financings and, secondly, by taking equity participations. Its guarantees (or, at least, those under English law) are in a fairly customary and familiar form. The EIF will not normally guarantee more than 50 per cent of a project's investment cost. Based on the current authorised share capital of 2 billion ECU, the EIF's statutes foresee the EIF being able to provide guarantees up to 16 billion ECU.

8.6   INTERCREDITOR ISSUES INVOLVING ECAS AND THE EIB

ECAs which are taking commercial risk should clearly be treated on an equal footing with commercial lenders. How ECAs should be

---

[44] Published in [1994] O.J. L173/1.

treated in intercreditor arrangements when they are merely covering commercial lenders for political risk is a more difficult issue. The position of such ECAs on a default or an enforcement of security is probably relatively straightforward. If there is a payment default and the reason for the default is a political risk, then the banks will obviously be entitled to make a demand on the relevant political risk guarantee. On an enforcement, the ECAs should simply be able to share in recoveries pro rata in accordance with their outstanding exposure (which will generally be determined by reference to whether amounts have been paid out under the relevant political risk guarantee). It is less clear what votes, if any, an ECA covering only political risks should have when a decision has to be taken on whether or not to agree to a request from the borrower for the relaxation of a covenant or for the waiver of a default.

The starting position should be that voting on matters under the credit documentation affects credit risk; it is not relevant to political risk. If this proposition is accepted, it follows that the basic rule on voting should therefore be that the institution bearing the commercial (as opposed to political) risk should have the vote attaching to a loan participation. Subject to any relaxation that a ECA wishes to make for administrative reasons, banks participating in a facility which has the benefit of an ECA commercial risk guarantee will therefore have to vote as the ECA directs but the general rule for a loan which only has the benefit of an ECA's political risk guarantee is that the banks should be entitled to vote as they wish. The exception to this general rule is that an ECA guaranteeing only political risk should be entitled to a vote equal to the amount it has actually paid out under its guarantee (and the vote of the guaranteed banks should be correspondingly reduced).[45]

Another intercreditor issue between ECAs and commercial banks is trying to ensure that the ECA-backed loans (the "covered loans") and the banks' loans (the "uncovered loans") are drawn down by the borrower roughly pro rata (so that, if the borrower went into default, the ECAs' exposure would not be disproportionate to that of the banks (and vice versa)). It is usually not possible to achieve a perfect solution to this problem, not least because the covered loans will have to be drawn down as and when eligible goods and services

---

[45] There can be difficult discussions with ECAs providing only political risk cover, however, on the point as to whether or not they should be entitled to vote once a political risk has occurred and so it is inevitable that they will have to repay the banks. The issue is particularly acute in the drawdown phase when such an ECA would not (without a vote) be able to have any say on any proposed waiver of a condition precedent to drawdown. Such a waiver would, of course, increase its potential liability.

are delivered or performed. The minimum amount for a drawing under the ECA-backed loan documentation may also play a part: if the minimum amount is high, the borrower will have to pay the contractor's invoices from other funds (*e.g.* a commercial bank working capital facility) and then seek reimbursement when it can draw under the ECA-backed loan.

As far as voting mechanics involving the EIB are concerned, it is submitted that the EIB should generally have no vote to the extent that it is guaranteed by a bank guarantee or standby letter of credit (save to the extent (arguably) that an issuer has ceased to be a Qualifying Institution (see section 8.4) and the EIB has not yet made a demand under that guarantee or standby letter of credit). The clear exception to this general rule is that the EIB should be given a blocking vote for (or some other form of protection against) any decision which might materially alter the nature of the project risk it will take on upon a release of the bank guarantees or standby letters of credit. However, the EIB will also expect to retain certain independent rights in relation to draw-stops, events of default and project covenants which are specific to the EIB even in a transaction which does not include a bank guarantee release mechanism.

Chapter 9

Other Legal Issues

9.1 ENVIRONMENTAL LIABILITY

(a) *Strict liability.* Strict liability — both in criminal and civil law — is an emotive issue. Its champions in the environmental sphere have grown in number as the public becomes more aware of and increasingly concerned about threats and damage to the environment.

If unlimited strict liability for civil law damages is imposed in respect of a particular activity, this has an obvious impact on the underlying economics of that activity. Where a person might be liable in damages irrespective of his own fault, taking out insurance against the potential liability becomes even more imperative. To the extent that insurance is available, the costs will be passed on to the consumer. To the extent that it is not available, anyone carrying on the activity in question is faced with a stark choice: either carry on with the activity and accept the risk of liability (which may be substantial and may lead to bankruptcy) or cease the activity. Any project which involves the risk of substantial damages on the basis of strict liability is unlikely to be bankable on a "stand alone" basis without significant (and probably prohibitively expensive) insurance cover.[1]

Since many activities which involve the risk of environmental pollution are central to modern society, strict liability imposed by governments through legislation tends to be subject to overall monetary limits on liability and not on an open-ended basis.

---

[1] Insurance cover for environmental damage or liability is at present fairly limited. In a power project, for example, insurance would be available for sudden catastrophes (such as damage to the environment caused by the explosion of standby fuel tanks (in a gas-fired project)) but not for gradual pollution (such as the contamination of water supplies through seepage from an unlined ash pit (in a coal-fired project)).

209

Monetary limits obviously mean that society at large or the injured person has to foot the bill for loss, damage or costs (*e.g.* clean-up costs) in excess of the limits. By contrast, judges are unable to afford defendants the benefit of monetary limits to the extent that strict liability arises under common law and, although they may seek to limit a defendant's liability in cases before them by judicious use of concepts such as causation and the remoteness of damage, this can hardly be said to provide any real degree of certainty.

An interesting example of the above principles at work can be seen in the response of the international community and tanker owners to the risk of oil pollution at sea. The main international conventions in this area[2] provide for a system of survey and certification to ensure compliance with various specifications as to structure, systems and fittings, impose strict civil liability on the owners of vessels involved in oil spills subject to monetary limits, require insurance to be carried against such liability[3] and establish a fund (financed by the oil companies and not the tanker owners) to meet claims in excess of the limits applicable to the tanker owners. There is a maximum amount that can be paid out of the fund in relation to any one incident.

(b) *Liability under common law.* There are heads of liability under common law which are capable of applying to environmental damage.

These are:

      (i) trespass;
     (ii) nuisance (public and private);
    (iii) (to the extent it is still a separate head of liability (see below)) the rule in *Rylands v. Fletcher*[4];
    (iv) negligence; and
    (v) breach of statutory duty.

Although not strictly speaking common law, the Occupiers Liability Act 1957 can also be included under this heading in that, quite apart from being based on old common law principles, it is another

---

[2] The International Convention for the Prevention of Pollution from Ships 1973 (as amended) ("MARPOL 73/78"), the International Convention on Civil Liability for Oil Pollution Damage 1992 (referred to as the "CLC") and the International Convention on the Establishment of an International Fund for Compensation for Oil Pollution Damage 1992 (referred to as the "IOPC").

[3] It is the responsibility of the contracting states to ensure that tankers entering or leaving ports in their jurisdiction carry a suitable certificate proving they are insured to the required levels.

[4] (1868) L.R. 3 HL 330, affirming *Fletcher v. Rylands* (1866) L.R. 1 Ex 265.

example of liability under general background law rather than under a piece of legislation dealing specifically with the environment.

Different requirements and defences apply to each head of liability. An action in trespass requires the plaintiff to possess land and the defendant intentionally or negligently to enter on or cause any physical matter to come into contact with such land. Private nuisance is unwarranted interference with the enjoyment of land owned or occupied by another; liability for private nuisance is generally regarded as strict, but is subject to the defence of "reasonable user", the "principle of give and take as between neighbouring occupiers of land".[5] Public nuisance is primarily a crime related to interference with various rights enjoyed by the public (*e.g.* the use of highways) and only gives rise to a civil law claim in damages to the extent that the plaintiff can prove he suffered damage beyond that suffered by the rest of the community. No interest in land is required to sue for public nuisance. In *Rylands v. Fletcher*, the defendants were held liable on the basis that any person who makes a "non-natural" use of land and keeps on that land anything likely to do mischief if it escapes is liable for all the damage "which is the natural consequence of its escape". Successful actions under this head of liability have been relatively rare since the courts have in the past interpreted the phrase "natural use" very widely. The essential requirements for a claim in negligence are well known: the existence of a duty of care in favour of the plaintiff and a breach of the relevant standard of care. The scope for claiming damages for breach of statutory duty has been severely limited by *Lonrho Ltd. v. Shell Petroleum Co. Ltd (No. 2)*[6] which made it clear that the only way an Act can be enforced is generally in the manner in which it states it may be enforced and that, where there are criminal sanctions, the only exceptions to this general rule are when the statutory obligation in question is clearly imposed for the benefit of a particular class of individuals and where the Act creates a public right and an individual suffers damage over and above and different in nature from that suffered by the rest of the public.

The common law remedies are clearly hedged about with various qualifications and do not really represent a sound basis for a coherent and predictable scheme of liability for damage to the environment. None of the common law remedies were held to apply in *Esso Petroleum Co. Ltd v. Southport Corporation*,[7] for example. The

---

[5] *per* Lord Goff in *Cambridge Water Co. Ltd v. Eastern Counties Leather plc* [1994] 1 All E.R. 53 at p.70.
[6] [1981] 2 All E.R. 456. See also *X (Minors) v. Bedfordshire C.C.* [1995] 2 AC 633.
[7] [1955] 3 All E.R. 864.

case involved oil pollution, an area where there is now strict liability under the international conventions referred to in (a) above. A small oil tanker developed a fault in her steering gear in bad weather and ran ashore in an attempt to reach more sheltered waters. The master then jettisoned 400 tons of the vessel's cargo of oil in order to prevent her breaking her back. The oil was washed ashore on land owned by Southport Corporation which sued the shipowners (Esso) for damages in trespass, nuisance and negligence. The only negligence alleged was against the master. The claims in trespass and nuisance failed because the shipowners were able to rely on the defence of necessity (it was necessary to jettison the oil in the interests of the safety of the crew) and the claim in negligence failed because the trial judge held that the master had not been negligent.

The limits on the common law remedies have probably now been fixed for the foreseeable future by the House of Lords in *Cambridge Water Co. Ltd. v. Eastern Counties Leather plc.*[8] Various spillages of perchloroethene had occurred in the course of production over a number of years at a leatherworks run by Eastern Counties Leather ("ECL"). ECL stopped using the chemical in 1976. However, the spillages slowly seeped through the soil and, when they reached an impermeable stratum, travelled along it (at the rate of about eight metres a day) until in 1991 they contaminated a water bore hole owned and operated by Cambridge Water Co. ("CWC"). CWC claimed damages from ECL in nuisance and negligence and under the rule in *Rylands v. Fletcher.* ECL did not seek to defend the nuisance action on the grounds of "reasonable user".

One of the trial judge's findings was that ECL had not been negligent (on the grounds that subsequent contamination of the water bore hole could not have been foreseen in 1976 or before). On this finding, the trial judge dismissed the claims in nuisance and negligence. He then dismissed the action under the rule in *Rylands v. Fletcher* on the basis that ECL's leatherworks constituted a natural user. Despite the fact that CWC only appealed to the Court of Appeal in relation to the rule in *Rylands v. Fletcher*, the Court of Appeal awarded damages to CWC on the basis of its claim in nuisance, stating that previous cases had held that nuisance applied strict liability where the interference complained of was interference with "a natural right incident to ownership". As they had disposed of the case on the basis of the claim in nuisance, the Court of Appeal did not feel it necessary to rule on the claim under the rule in *Rylands v. Fletcher.*

---

[8] [1994] 1 All E.R. 53.

Lord Goff sought to clarify matters in the House of Lords. As far as nuisance was concerned, he stated that the "reasonable foreseeability" test was only relevant to the issue of remoteness of damage and he restated the strict nature of liability in nuisance:

". . . the fact that the defendant has taken all reasonable care will not of itself exonerate him from liability, the relevant control mechanism being found within the principle of reasonable user. But it by no means follows that the defendant should be held liable for damage of a type which he could not reasonably foresee."[9]

Turning to the rule in *Rylands v. Fletcher*, Lord Goff stated that the actual judgement in that case revealed that Blackburn J did not intend to create a liability any more strict than that created by the law of nuisance. As a result, Lord Goff thought it appropriate to hold that foreseeability of damage of the relevant type was a prerequisite of liability in damages under the rule in *Rylands v. Fletcher* as it was in a claim in nuisance. He further stated that it would "lead to a more coherent body of common law principles" if the rule in *Rylands v. Fletcher* were to be regarded as merely an extension of the law of nuisance to cases of isolated escapes from land and be so limited.[10] Given the trial judge's finding on the reasonable forseeability of the contamination that occurred, Lord Goff allowed ECL's appeal. He also stated, *obiter*,[11] that storage of substantial quantities of chemicals on industrial premises was in his view "an almost classic case of non-natural use" for the purposes of the rule in *Rylands v. Fletcher*. This last point may result in an increase in the number of successful actions under this head of liability.

One of the most telling passages in Lord Goff's judgement is the following, however:

". . . I incline to the opinion that, as a general rule, it is more appropriate for strict liability in respect of operations of high risk to be imposed by Parliament, than by the courts. If such liability is imposed by statute, the relevant activities can be identified, and those concerned can know where they stand. Furthermore, statute can where appropriate lay down precise criteria establishing the incidence and scope of such liability."[12]

---

[9] [1994] 1 All E.R. 53, 72.
[10] [1994] 1 All E.R. 53, 76.
[11] [1994] 1 All E.R. 53, 79.
[12] [1994] 1 All E.R. 53, 76.

(c) *Relevant United Kingdom legislation.* The major United Kingdom environmental legislation is the Environmental Protection Act
1990 (the "EPA"), the Water Resources Act 1991 (the "WRA") and
the Environment Act 1995 (the "EA"). The first two Acts are more
concerned with controlling pollution through licensing régimes than
liability for damages (although the EPA does restate the law on
statutory nuisance which allows persons "aggrieved by the existence
of a statutory nuisance" to obtain court orders which require a
defendant to execute any works necessary to abate or prevent a
statutory nuisance[13]). The third Act sets up what it is hoped will
eventually be a unified government agency dealing with environmental matters (the Environment Agency[14]), establishes a new
régime for contaminated land[15] and puts the liability for cleaning up
polluted waters on a similar basis to that régime.[16] The Environment Agency has inherited, *inter alia,* the functions of Her Majesty's
Inspectorate of Pollution in relation to integrated pollution control
("IPC"), the functions of the now-defunct National Rivers Authority
in relation to the control of pollution of water resources and the
management of water resources and the functions of of the old
waste regulation authorities in relation to the control of waste
management.[17] The principal aim of the Environment Agency is to
contribute to "achieving sustainable development"[18] and the Secretary of State is required to give guidance to the Agency with respect
to, *inter alia*, the objectives which the Agency must pursue in the
discharge of its functions.

The most important features of the EPA are its provisions dealing
with IPC, air pollution control and waste management. The IPC
régime governs those industrial and similar processes which are
potentially the most polluting.[19] These processes must be authorised
by the Environment Agency which will set limits and conditions on
their emissions to all environmental media (air, land and water).
The less polluting processes may fall to be governed by local
authority air pollution control, in which case an air pollution

---

[13] s.82 Environmental Protection Act 1990.
[14] See s.1 of the EA. The powers of the Environment Agency do not extend to Scotland which
has its own separate agency, the Scottish Environment Protection Agency, set up under s.20 of
the EA.
[15] By s.57 of the EA, which intoduced new ss.78A–78YC into the EPA.
[16] By s.60, which amends s.161 of the WRA. S.161 itself applies to "controlled waters" within
the meaning of s.104 of the WRA.
[17] *ibid.*, s.2(1).
[18] *ibid.*, s.4(1).
[19] The Council of the European Union adopted a Directive, 96/61/EC ([1996] O.J. L257),
requiring major polluting industrial activities throughout the European Union to obtain
integrated permits covering emissions to air, water and land. The Directive is based on the
U.K. IPC system and Member States have three years to implement its provisions.

214

authorisation is required from the relevant local authority as well as separate consents from the Environment Agency for releases to land or water. The Environment Agency now also issues and enforces waste management licences. Not having a requisite consent or licence or breaching the terms of any such consent or licence is a criminal offence.

The WRA generally provides for a regulatory system (based on consents) for the control of pollution of water resources and for the management of water resources. It lists various pollution offences[20] the principal defences to which are that the discharge in question was in accordance with a consent, *e.g.* a consent to discharge into "controlled waters" obtained from the Environment Agency or an IPC authorisation. In addition, abstraction from "controlled waters" requires the Environment Agency's consent.[21]

The new régime for contaminated land established by the EA has the following principal features:

> (i) Every local authority must periodically inspect its land in order to identify contaminated land and, if it identifies any contaminated land, it must serve a notice to this effect on the owner and any other "appropriate persons".[22] An "appropriate person" is essentially any person who caused or knowingly permitted the presence of the harmful substances to be in the land in question.[23] If, however, no such person can be identified after reasonable enquiry, then the "appropriate person" is the owner or occupier for the time being of the contaminated land.[24] An "owner" of land in England and Wales is defined by the EA to mean "a person *(other than a mortgagee not in possession)*[25] who . . . is entitled to receive the rack rent of the land, or, where the land is not let at a rack rent, would be so entitled if it were so let".[26] So, if the actual polluter cannot be found, the "appropriate person" will be the owner or occupier by default, although a mortgagee who is not in possession will not constitute an owner for these purposes.
>
> But can a mortgagee not in possession be an occupier? It is difficult to see how he can be so long as

---

[20] In ss. 85-87.
[21] ss.24 and 88 of the Water Resources Act 1991.
[22] s.78B EPA.
[23] *ibid.*, s.78F(2).
[24] *ibid.*, s.78F(4) and (5).
[25] Emphasis added.
[26] s.78A(9) EPA.

he is not enforcing his mortgage and, even when he is enforcing his mortgage, whether he is an occupier may depend on the manner of his enforcement. The four types of enforcement of a mortgage possible under English law are (a) sale, (b) receivership, (c) taking possession and (d) foreclosure (which requires a court order). A mortgagee takes possession of a debt (such as an obligation to pay rent) under English law by serving notice on the debtor to pay him rather than the mortgagor. Sale will not constitute a mortgagee an occupier, but taking possession of the mortgaged land will and taking possession (by serving notice) of a rental stream might. (The latter action would render a mortgagee an owner in any event). Foreclosure will make the mortgagee the owner (and possibly the occupier) of the mortgaged land, but appointing a receiver should not constitute a *mortgagee* an occupier because, by legal fiction, a receiver is usually stated in the mortgage documentation to be the agent of the mortgagor. A receiver will probably himself constitute an occupier, however, and section 78X(3) of the EPA provides that a receiver is not personally liable for clean-up costs unless the contamination resulted from anything done or omitted by him which it was unreasonable for a receiver to do or make.

(ii) Where a local authority has identified contaminated land in its area, it *must* serve a notice (a "remediation notice") on each "appropriate person" requiring remediation measures to be taken.[27] The local authority may only require remediation measures which it considers reasonable having regard to the cost which is likely to be involved and the seriousness of the contamination or pollution in question.[28]

(iii) It is a criminal offence to fail, without reasonable excuse, to comply with any of the requirements of a remediation notice.[29] In the case of any such failure, the local authority can carry out the remediation measures itself and recover the reasonable cost incurred in doing so from the appropriate person or persons.[30]

---

[27] s.78E(1) EPA.
[28] *ibid.*, s.78E(4).
[29] *ibid.*, s.78M.
[30] *ibid.*, s.78P(1).

The régime for cleaning up polluted waters will be broadly similar once the EA's amendments are brought into force and will be as follows[31]:

    (a) The Environment Agency may serve a "works notice" on any person who has caused or knowingly permitted any poisonous, noxious or polluting matter to enter controlled waters, requiring him to take preventative or remedial action. Service of a works notice is subject to, *inter alia*, an obligation for the Environment Agency to consult with the person on whom the notice is to be served and rights of appeal.

    (b) Failure to comply with a works notice is a criminal offence and will allow the Environment Agency to carry out the preventative or remedial action itself and to recover the cost of doing so from the person in default.

    (d) *European developments.* A new Title on the environment[32] was added to the E.C. Treaty by the Single European Act of 1986. The Title sets out the objective's of the E.C.'s policy on the environment in very general terms; it states in particular[33]:

> "[Community policy] shall be based on the precautionary principle and on the principles that preventive action should be taken, that environmental damage should as a priority be rectified at source and that the polluter should pay."

E.C. legislation on the environment is to be enacted by the Council of the European Union acting unanimously in certain key areas[34] but otherwise on a qualified majority.[35]

The following European initiatives are of note:

    (i) *Draft Directive on Civil Liability for Damage Caused by Waste.*[36] This draft would impose strict civil liability on producers of waste for damage to persons or property

---

[31] s.161 of the WRA as amended by s.60 of the EA.
[32] Now Title XVI of the EC Treaty.
[33] Art. 130r(2).
[34] Such as "provisions primarily of a fiscal nature".
[35] Art. 130s. This is a change (brought about by the Treaty on European Union of 1992 (the Maastricht Treaty)) to the unanimity requirement originally inserted by the Single European Act.
[36] O.J. No. C192, July 23, 1991, p.6.

caused by waste and for "impairment of the environ-ment". There is no mention of a monetary limit on liability. This draft Directive is likely to be superseded by legislation following on from the Green Paper referred to in (ii) below relating to civil liability for damage to the environment generally and it has for the moment been shelved in any event.

(ii) *The European Commission's Green Paper on Civil Liability for the Repair of Environmental Damage.*[37] This Green Paper (issued some years ago) proposes strict liability for all environmental damage. The issue of monetary limits is to be resolved. The Paper suggests establishing "joint compensation schemes" to cover cases where compen-sation would otherwise not be available; the funds would come from "the economic sectors most closely linked to the type of damage needing restoration" save to the extent that this would impose too great a burden when "the costs of restoring particular damage might be shared more broadly with other sectors or by tax-payers in general". There is a telling reference in the introductory paragraphs to the Paper which states that any action proposed by the Commission would have to be "in accord with the principle of subsidiarity". The Commission received comments from numerous bodies and countries on the Green Paper and it is understood that a draft Directive is in the process of being drafted. A further consultation process may follow.

(iii) *The Council of Europe's Convention on Civil Liability.*[38] The Council of Europe (which is not to be confused with the Council of the European Union)[39] agreed a convention on civil liability for damage to the environment in 1993. The convention provides for operators of "dangerous activities" to be strictly liable for damage resulting from incidents whilst they were in control of the activities and requires such operators to insure against or have other financial security to cover their liability. The parties to the convention have a discretion as to whether or not to provide for a monetary limit on liability. The United Kingdom has announced that it does not at present intend to ratify the convention.

---

[37] Com (93) 47 Final, March 17, 1993.
[38] Convention on Civil Liability for Damage Resulting from Activities Dangerous to the Environment (European Treaty Series No. 150, July 21, 1993, ISBN 928 712 3209).
[39] The Council of Europe was inaugurated in 1949 at Strasbourg and is the body which established the European Convention on Human Rights.

An E.C. Directive[40] also requires an environmental impact assessment to be carried out before development consent is given for specified projects which are likely to have significant effects on the environment. It is the developer's responsibility to submit an environmental statement (a report of the assessment) which must examine the effects which the proposed project will have on the environment and outline how they will be dealt with and mitigated. This, of course, effectively means that a developer is bound by the recommendations he makes in the final environmental impact report since otherwise the development consent will not be forthcoming. At the time of writing, the Council of the European Union had just adopted a Directive amending the original Directive.[41] The amending Directive expands the range of projects for which an environmental impact assessment is compulsory and clarifies the discretion that Member States have when deciding whether an environmental impact assessment is required for a second category of projects.[42]

(e) *Implications for project finance.* The possibility of liability for environmental damage can cause problems with regard to a project's bankability. As noted above,[43] banks involved in project finance do not necessarily object to risk; they object to uncertain and unquantifiable risk against which they may not be able to protect themselves. In the context of the present discussion, banks will therefore be concerned where the carrying out of the project in question could result in unlimited liability (or in liability up to exceptionally high limits) or in any significant unforeseen liability (for example, where the project company will become liable (because of strict liability or retrospective laws) for pollution caused by an event which occurred before it embarked on its project). A typical example of the latter problem is site contamination which occurred during a previous ownership or occupancy of the land.

Whilst insurance obviously has some role to play in mitigating the risk of environmental liability, the types of cover available are very limited. For example, insurance is not available on the London market for damage to the environment caused by gradual seepage (as opposed to a sudden accident) and there will be deductibles and limits for any insurance cover. It may therefore be necessary, in order to make a project bankable, for the risk of significant

---

[40] Directive 85/337/EEC.
[41] Adopted on March 3, 1997.
[42] Note that both the World Bank and the IFC have their own requirements for environmental assessments for projects in which they are involved.
[43] See section 4.1 above.

environmental liability to be borne by a party other than the project company. It would not be unusual for the risk of pre-existing but latent site contamination to be dealt with in this way and for this risk to be borne by the person (sponsor or host government) who owned the site before its transfer to the project company. (This solution will, of course only be acceptable to the banks if that person is a creditworthy entity.) If the banks are asked to accept that the project company should take this risk, they will as a minimum require a detailed environmental consultant's report on the state of the site. Banks may be more willing to accept that the project company should bear the risk of environmental liability caused by the operation of the project in question but they will need to be satisfied (probably again by means of an environmental consultant's report) that adequate measures will be taken during the operating phase to prevent, limit or contain any environmental pollution. The sponsors, project company and banks will need to go through a similar exercise in any event to ensure that the project will operate within the terms and conditions of any pollution consents. As part of the general risk allocation exercise, they will also need to reach agreement on how any additional costs caused by the variation of the terms of any pollution consents are to be met.

Quite apart from being concerned with the project company's potential environmental liability, banks will also be concerned with their own potential environmental liability. A major concern for banks is the risk of becoming liable for environmental damage if they enforce their security or otherwise take over the running of a project. This is a critical issue on which careful advice must be taken.

The position under English law is quite complex but, in general, the categories of person to whom primary environmental liability may attach can be divided into owners, occupiers and persons with operational control or responsibility. A secured lender who enters into possession of a project's assets is likely to be deemed an "owner" for the purposes of environmental legislation but, as has been seen, a mortgagee not in possession will not be an owner for the purposes of the new régime for contaminated land in the United Kingdom.[44] The term "occupier" is generally undefined, although it is clear from case law that occupation may arise from possession and/or control and need not turn on physical occupation of land or premises. A bank is generally only likely to be treated as an occupier in the event of it going into possession of the project and, in particular, the land. A bank which goes into possession could clearly

---

[44] See (c) above.

face potential liability under provisions which attached liability to persons with some form of operational control or responsibility. In addition, if a bank assumes *de facto* control over the project company through day-to-day management of its affairs, there is a risk that the bank may be liable for "knowingly permitting" environmental offences.

The position of lenders and receivers in relation to contaminated land in the United Kingdom has been discussed in (c) above. In general terms, the EA has made it clear that, as far as contaminated land is concerned, a receiver and — through the indemnity they have to give a receiver — the banks will have to reckon with some potential liability if the banks enforce their security by appointing a receiver. The extent to which a receiver is liable for contamination which pre-dates his appointment remains unclear, however. If a receiver does not clean up pre-existing contamination, does the continuing contamination result from something omitted by him?

The position of finance lessors of moveables may be better on the basis that they will not be occupiers of land and are unlikely to assume operational control of a project. The position of a finance lessor of (for example) a pipeline in the North Sea is less clear, however.

Given the above background, the types of provisions one can expect to find in a project credit agreement dealing with the various environmental issues are as follows:

  (i) a condition precedent that all required environmental consents have been obtained;

  (ii) a condition precedent that there is no outstanding environmental liability;

  (iii) a representation and warranty that all required environmental consents have been obtained and that all of the terms and conditions of such consents are being complied with;

  (iv) a representation and warranty that there is no outstanding enviromental liability;

  (v) an undertaking to remedy any environmental damage that occurs;

  (vi) an undertaking to maintain a corporate environmental monitoring and management scheme;

  (vii) an undertaking to inform the banks of any events which may result in an environmental liability;

  (viii) an undertaking to provide the banks with an environmental report in specified circumstances (*e.g.* if the banks suspect that a significant environmental liability has arisen); and

(ix) events of default relating to material branches of environmental laws or the occurrence of events which give rise to material environmental liability.

In addition, the security documentation should include an indemnity from the borrower in relation to all losses and expenses suffered or incurred by the banks or their receiver so that they can at least seek to recoup as a secured claim any damages or other amounts they have to pay out.

9.2 EUROPEAN COMMUNITY ASPECTS

The three areas of European Community law which one is most likely to come across in the context of a project financing are (a) the E.C. Treaty's rules on competition, (b) its rules on state aid and (c) its rules on public procurement.[45] In addition, the completion of the internal market in the energy sector and the European Community's general competition laws and policy should produce project finance opportunities for sponsors.[46]

Before going on to examine briefly the three areas of European Community law referred to above, it is important to look at one major new potential source of project financing opportunities that has recently been produced as part of the drive to complete the internal market and to introduce competition in the energy sector. This is the *Directive concerning common rules for the internal market in electricity*[47] (the "Electricity Directive").

The Electricity Directive was finally adopted by both the European Parliament and the European Council on December 19, 1996

---

[45] The EC may also provide "soft" money for a project under one of its aid programmes (*e.g.* the Regional Development Fund or the Cohesion Fund). In addition, the European Commission published a White Paper on Energy Policy for the European Community (COM (95) 682) in 1995 and announced its intention to instigate a five-year work programme in the energy sector with the threefold aim of competitiveness, security of supply and protection of the environment.

[46] European legislation aimed at achieving a single internal market in the energy sector prior to the Directive on common rules for the internal market in electricity (discussed in detail in this section) includes Directive 90/547/EEC [1990] O.J. L313/30 (Nov. 13) on the transit of electricity through transmission grids, Directive 91/296/EEC [1991] O.J. L147/37 (June 12) on the transit of natural gas through grids and Directive 90/377/EEC [1990] O.J. L185/16 (July 17) on the transparency of gas and electricity prices. See also Directive 94/22/EC [1994] O.J. L164/3 (June 30) on authorisations for the prospection, exploration and production of hydrocarbons. The internal market should have been established in all sectors by January, 1993.

[47] Directive 96/92/EC [1997] O.J. L27/20 (January 30).

after many years of disagreement between the European Commission and certain Member States (notably France) and among the Member States themselves. France's position was largely dictated by a desire to preserve and protect Electricité de France ("EdF"), its vertically integrated electricity monopoly. France believed that EdF's position would be threatened by the European Commission's initial proposals which were, broadly, to force Member States to allow third party electricity producers access to their systems in such a way that they could conclude supply contracts direct with distributors and large consumers. The compromise which finally allowed the Electricity Directive to move forward was to require Member States to permit independent electricity producers in their territory but then to organise access to their systems in one of two ways[48]: they could either give such producers access to the system in such a way that they could conclude direct supply contracts of the sort referred to above[49] or they could require such producers to sell their electricity to a single buyer whilst still allowing large consumers (but not distributors[50]) to conclude supply contracts with such producers.[51]

The other major features of the Electricity Directive are as follows:

(i) There are essentially two ways in which independent producers can obtain the right to construct new capacity[52]: Member States can either provide for an authorisation procedure (setting out the criteria for the grant of authorisations)[53] or implement a tendering procedure.[54] The tendering procedure is more centrally controlled and appears designed to work in parallel with the single buyer system for access to systems. It involves the transmission system operator (or other designated authority) periodically drawing up a list of required generating capacity and tenders being invited for any new capacity that is required. Any Member State adopting the tendering procedure must designate an authority to organise, monitor and control the tendering procedure which is independent of the Member State's generation, transmission and distribution activities.[55] Despite the rather more

---

[48] *ibid.*, Art. 16.
[49] *ibid.*, Art. 17. Access can either be on the basis of negotiations or on the basis of published tariffs (Art. 17(4)).
[50] This may inevitably be the case in a single buyer system, however, since the single buyer is likely to be a monopolistic seller of electricity as well.
[51] Electricity Directive, Art. 18.
[52] *ibid.*, Art. 4.
[53] *ibid.*, Art. 5.
[54] *ibid.*, Art. 6.
[55] *ibid.*, Art. 6(5).

centrally planned system envisaged by the tendering procedure, the Electricity Directive somewhat surprisingly goes
on to provide that a Member State which opts for the
tendering procedure must also allow independent producers
to obtain authorisation on a similar basis to that provided for
in the authorisation procedure.[56] Some of the sting in the
single buyer system (working in conjunction with the tendering procedure) has thus been drawn.

(ii) Member States which designate a vertically integrated electricity undertaking as a single buyer must provide for that
undertaking's single buyer function to be operated separately from its generation and distribution activities.[57]

(iii) Member States are required to open up their electricity
markets so as to ensure that, under either the authorisation
system or the single buyer system, direct supply contracts of
the sort referred to above can be concluded "up to a
significant level".[58] This level is first measured by reference
only to final consumers consuming more than 40 GWh of
power per year, but this is reduced on a sliding scale over six
years to final consumers consuming more than 9 GWh of
power per year.[59] All final consumers consuming more than
100 GWh per year must be able to conclude direct supply
contracts of the sort referred to above.[60]

(iv) The transmission system operator must be independent, at
least in management terms, from any generation and distribution activities.[61] The dispatching of generating installations must be on the basis of published objective criteria
which are applied in a non-discriminatory way and which
ensure the proper functionning of the internal market in
electricity[62] (although priority may be given to generating
installations which use renewable energy sources or waste
and to combined heat and power plants).[63]

(v) Member States may impose public service obligations on
undertakings operating in the electricity sector (relating to,

---

[56] *ibid.*, Art. 6(6).
[57] *ibid.*, Art. 15(1).
[58] *ibid.*, Art. 19(1).
[59] *ibid.*, Art. 19(1) and (2).
[60] *ibid.*, Art. 19(3). This Article also provides, by way of exception, that distribution companies
should at least be able to enter into direct supply contracts for the volume of electricity being
consumed within their distribution system by final consumers who would themselves be able
to enter into such supply contracts.
[61] *ibid.*, Art. 7(6).
[62] *ibid.*, Art. 8(2).
[63] *ibid.*, Art. 8(3).

e.g., security of supply and environmental protection). These obligations must be imposed "in the general economic interest" and must be "non-discriminatory and verifiable".[64]

The Electricity Directive came into force on February 19, 1997.[65] Most Member States have to comply with its requirements by February 19, 1999.[66]

(a) *The E.C.'s competition rules.* The E.C. Treaty's competition rules form a central part of the plan to realise a single internal market within the E.C.: companies should be free to compete on a "level playing field" within the common market and national monopolies should only be tolerated where essential. The main rules are contained in Articles 85–90 of the E.C. Treaty, although there is a degree of secondary legislation and a wealth of case law and European Commission Decisions. Of those Articles, the most important for our purposes are Article 85, which prohibits anti-competitive agreements between undertakings, Article 86, which prohibits the abuse of a dominant position and Article 90, which effectively contains, *inter alia,* a rather obscure exemption[67] from Articles 85 and 86 for undertakings "entrusted with the operation of services of general economic interest" and certain monopolies.

Article 85 provides that the following are *prima facie* void:

> "all agreements . . ., decisions . . . and concerted practices [between undertakings] which may affect trade between Member States and which have as their object or effect the prevention, restriction or distortion of competition within the common market . . ."

It then goes on to give various examples of prohibited conduct, including agreements, decisions and concerted practices which fix prices, control production or share markets or sources of supply.

Article 86 provides that:

> "Any abuse by one or more undertakings of a dominant position within the common market or in a substantial part of it shall be prohibited . . . in so far as it may affect trade between Member States."

---

[64] *ibid.*, Art. 3(2).
[65] *ibid.*, Art. 28.
[66] *ibid.*, Art. 27(1). The exceptions are Belgium, Ireland and Greece who may elect to have an additional year (or, in the case of Greece, two years) within which to comply with the Directive (Art. 27(2)).
[67] In Art. 90(2) of the E.C. Treaty.

It too then goes on to give various examples of prohibited conduct including the imposition of unfair purchase or selling prices and limiting production or markets to the prejudice of consumers.

Article 90(2) provides:

> "Undertakings entrusted with the operation of services of general economic interest or having the character of a revenue-producing monopoly shall be subject to the rules ... on competition ... insofar as the application of such rules does not obstruct the performance, in law or in fact, of the particular task assigned to them. The development of trade must not be affected to such an extent as would be contrary to the interests of the Community."

The European Commission is charged with policing the European Community's competition rules[68] and it has applied them in a variety of sectors. Until recently, however, the Commission was hindered in infrastructure-related areas by arguments as to the scope afforded by Article 90(2) for Member States to create and maintain monopolies to perform a public service duty (such as, for example, the supply of gas and electricity).

The European Court of Justice was finally given the opportunity to pronounce on the applicability of Article 90(2) in the energy sector in *Gemeente Almelo e.a. v. Energiebedrijf Ijsselmij N.V.*[69] in April, 1994. The essence of that case was that Gemeente Almelo and other local electricity distributors in the Netherlands were alleging in proceedings before the Dutch courts that provisions for the exclusive purchase and sale of electricity contained in distribution agreements that they had signed up with N.V. Energiebedrijf Ijsselmij N.V., a regional electricity distributor, were contrary to the European Community's competition rules. The Dutch courts applied to the European Court of Justice for a ruling on the interpretation of various provisions of the E.C. Treaty, including Article 90(2). The European Court of Justice first ruled that Article 85 could apply to the contested provisions on the basis that the required effect on trade between Member States could be found in the cumulative effect of those provisions in a number of similar agreements covering the whole of the territory of a Member State. It then stated that Article 86 was capable of applying if it could be shown that the links between the regional electricity distributors in the Netherlands were so strong that the regional distributors could be said to

---

[68] *ibid.*, Art. 89.
[69] Case C-393/92, judgement of April 27, 1994.

enjoy a collective dominant position (although it was left to the Dutch courts to determine whether or not this was in fact the case). The European Court of Justice then turned to the scope of Article 90(2) and held that the Article could only permit a restriction on competition where this was *necessary* to achieve the performance of a particular service of general economic interest which had been entrusted to the undertaking in question. Whether the exclusive purchase and sale provisions were necessary in this sense in this particular case was left to the national courts, although the European Court of Justice stated that they should consider the economic conditions in which the undertaking in question operated and in particular the costs which it had to bear and the legislation (particularly concerning the environment) to which it was subject.

The Commission's view of the *Almelo* case seems to revolve around the concept of proportionality: is a particular anti-competitive measure no more restrictive than is absolutely *necessary* to achieve a particular public service aim, taking into account *inter alia* the general costs of achieving that aim, or is it disproportionate?[70]

The European Commission can, pursuant to Article 85(3) of the E.C. Treaty, exempt a particular agreement from the *prima facie* prohibition of Article 85 by means of a formal Decision (an "individual exemption") and it can also formally determine that a particular agreement does not in fact fall within that prohibition by giving "negative clearance". The European Commission can also issue simple "no-action" or "comfort" letters as a less formal way of granting an individual exemption or indicating that the prohibition in Article 85 does not apply in a particular case.

An interesting example of the above procedures being applied in a project finance context is the application to the European Commission made by Electricidade de Portugal SA ("EDP") in relation to the Pego power project.[71] EDP was, at the time of the application, the Portuguese state's monopoly electricity generation, transmission and distribution company. As part of the process of privatising the Portuguese electricity industry, EDP ran an international competition for outside parties to acquire and operate the coal-fired power plant it was building at Pego. One of the key aspects of the competition was that EDP would enter into an exclusive 28 year power purchase agreement with the joint venture company formed by the winner of the competition. The 28 year period was intended to give sufficient comfort to the competition winners that they would

---

[70] See the Commission's press release of April 29, 1994 (Ref. IP/94/350).
[71] Details of the application and the Commission's views were published at [1993] O.J. C265/3 September 30, 1993.

see a return on their investment and to their bankers that their loans would be repaid. The European Commission objected to the 28 year period on the basis that it was too long a period during which the joint venture company would be prevented from delivering electricity to consumers other than EDP either in Portugal or in other Member States. The Commission and EDP then entered into discussions and EDP agreed to change the terms of the proposed power purchase agreement so that the power plant's capacity and output would only be provided to EDP on an exclusive basis for the first 15 years and that the joint venture company could thereafter sell to third parties any capacity not required by the Portuguese grid. The Commission then approved the power purchase agreement on the basis of these amendments.[72]

(b) *The E.C.'s state aid rules.* Article 92(1) of the E.C. Treaty states that:

> "Save as otherwise provided in this Treaty, any aid granted by a Member State . . . in any form whatsoever which distorts or threatens to distort competition by favouring certain undertakings or the production of certain goods shall, insofar as it affects trade between Member States, be incompatible with the common market."

Paragraphs 2 and 3 of Article 92 then go on to state that certain forms of state aid are or (if so determined by the European Commission or Council) may be compatible with the common market, for example "aid to promote the economic development of areas where the standard of living is abnormally low or where there is serious underemployment" and "aid to promote the execution of an important project of common European interest." Unlike Articles 85 and 86, Article 92 does not expressly provide that state aids "incompatible with the common market" are automatically void or prohibited; the European Court of Justice has decided that the issue of whether an aid is incompatible with the common market is to be determined by the European Commission, subject to review by the European Court of Justice.[73] Article 93(3) requires a Member State

---

[72] In the second Portuguese IPP brought to its attention, *Tapada do Outeiro* (or *Turbogas*), the Commission recognised that sales by the generator (Turbogas) to third parties after 15 years would effectively have been subsidised by the capacity charges paid by the power purchaser (REN) during that 15 year period. Turbogas was therefore required to compensate REN for the loss of its low cost supply if Turbogas ever exercised its right to sell to third parties.
[73] See, *e.g.*, *Firma Steinike und Weinlig v. Germany*, Case 78/76, [1977] E.C.R. 595.

to inform the European Commission of any plans to grant state aid before the aid is granted. If the Commission considers that the planned state aid is incompatible with the common market, it will require the Member State in question to abolish or alter the aid.[74]

State aid can take many forms but the two forms most often encountered in project financings are the state subsidy and the state guarantee. A state guarantee should only constitute a state aid if it is given on terms on which no commercial guarantor would give a guarantee in the same circumstances. If a project financing is based on a subsidy or guarantee which has been pre-notified to and approved by the European Commission or which falls within a general scheme which has been pre-notified to and approved by the European Commission, there is usually no problem. Problems arise, however, if a state aid is not so pre-notified (or if the aid does not comply with any conditions attaching to the award of aid under a general aid scheme) and the aid is nevertheless granted. The European Court of Justice has held that failure to pre-notify does not in itself render a state aid unlawful[75] but that the Commission has power to suspend the provision of aid pending its decision on whether the aid is incompatible with the common market. If it decides it is incompatible, it will again require the Member State in question to abolish or alter the aid.[76]

Dealing first with subsidies, the European Commission can not only require that future subsidies are not paid, it can also require the Member State in question to seek repayment of any subsidy that has already been paid, notwithstanding any financial hardship this might cause the recipient of the subsidy.[77] In relation to state guarantees, the European Commission has stated[78] that as a condition of its approval it always requires the beneficiary of such a guarantee to exhaust all of its remedies against the borrower before claiming on the guarantee. As regards guarantees which are granted without pre-notification and which are subsequently found to be incompatible with the common market, a Communication in 1991 from the European Commission to Member States appears to give some hope that the position of lending banks will not be prejudiced. It stated[79]:

> "If [an unnotified state] guarantee is deemed incompatible with the common market . . . reimbursement of the

---

[74] Pursuant to Art. 93(2).
[75] *France v. Commission*, Case 301/87, [1990] I–E.C.R. 307.
[76] Pursuant to Art. 93(2).
[77] See *Commission v. Greece*, Case 63/87, [1988] E.C.R. 2875.
[78] See the Twenty-Third Report on Competition Policy (1993), point 386.
[79] [1991] O.J. C273/2 (October 18) para. 38.

value of any aid will be made by the undertaking [concerned] to the government [concerned][80] even if this means a declaration of bankruptcy *but creditors' claims will be honoured*[81]*.*"

(c) *The E.C.'s public procurement rules.* National legislation, policies and practices which allow only companies incorporated in a country to bid for public sector supply, works or services contracts in that country are non-tariff barriers to free trade. Economists believe that, far from protecting and preserving national industries, such barriers may actually damage those industries in the long-term by delaying rationalisation which would otherwise make them competitive in the world markets. National public procurement régimes which discriminate against bidders from other Member States were viewed by the European Commission as incompatible with the E.C. Treaty for a variety of reasons from very early on.[82]

The E.C.'s legislation[83] deals separately with the procurement of supplies, works and services. Whereas the principal targets of early legislation were public bodies with the exclusion of utilities, utilities (whether public or private bodies) have now been brought within the E.C.'s net. "Public utilities" for these purposes are[84] entities (whether or not public bodies) which "operate on the basis of special or exclusive rights granted by a . . . Member State" and public bodies which, in each case, carry on various specified activities in the

---

[80] For example, the undertaking might have to pay to the Member State the fee that a private sector lender would have charged for issuing a similar guarantee.

[81] Emphasis added. See now, however, the Commission Decision of April 30, 1997 [1997] O.J. L186/25 (July 16) in which the Commission ordered Portugal to suspend a state guarantee given to banks lending to a cereal marketing company.

[82] They potentially conflict with Art. 6 (no discrimination on grounds of nationality), Arts. 30-33 (no quantitative restrictions on imports between Member States), Article 52 (no restriction on establishment) and Art. 59 (no restriction on freedom to provide services). It is these Articles, together with Art. 100 (approximation of laws) and Art. 100a (enactments to establish the internal market) which constitute the source of the EC's public procurement rules: there is no express treatment of public procurement in the EC Treaty itself.

[83] The principal E.C. legislation is:
Directive 93/36 (on public supplies), [1993] O.J. L199/1 (Aug. 9);
Directive 93/37 (on public works), *ibid.* page 54;
Directive 92/50 (on public services), [1992] O.J. L209/1 (July 24);
Directive 89/665 (on remedies), [1989] O.J. L395/33 (December 30);
Directive 93/38 (on public utilities), [1993] O.J. L199/84 (August 9) and
Directive 92/13 (on remedies in relation to public utilities), [1992] O.J. L76/14 (March 23).
The U.K. implementing legislation is:
The Public Supply Contracts Regulations 1995 (S.I. 95/201);
The Public Works Contracts Regulations 1991 (S.I. 91/2680); and
The Utilities Contracts Regulations 1996 (S.I. 96/2911).

[84] Art. 2 of Directive 93/38.

230

water, energy, transport or telecommunications sectors.[85] "Special or exclusive rights" are defined as "rights deriving from authorisations granted by a competent authority of . . . [a] Member State . . ., by law, regulation or administrative action, having as their result the reservation for one or more entities of the exploitation of [one of the specified activities]".[86] The legislation does not simply apply to entities which themselves enjoy special or exclusive rights: it will also apply to an entity which supplies drinking water, electricity, gas or heat to a network operated by an entity enjoying special or exclusive rights.[87]

The case for bringing privately owned utilities within the scope of the E.C.'s procurement rules is not readily apparent. One would have thought that, as private companies, the profit motive was sufficient to discourage national favouritism. The recitals to the relevant Directive[88] disclose two ostensible justifications, however. First, the existence of the special or exclusive rights militates against E.C.-wide competition and brings about closed markets. Secondly, national authorities can influence the behaviour of privately owned utilities.

The objectives of the E.C.'s procurement rules are to open up procurement markets for the relevant sectors throughout the E.C. This is intended to be achieved by requiring publicity throughout the Member States for bidding opportunities (through publication in the Official Journal), prescribing non-discriminatory[89] procedures for the award of contracts (above various threshold values) for the provision of supplies, works or services to public bodies or public utilities, requiring decisions to be taken on the basis of specified objective criteria and providing for transparency in the decision-making process so that decisions can be challenged effectively.

---

[85] Not all activities in those sectors are covered. The Utilities Directive lists (in Art. 2(2)) the provision or operation of fixed networks for the production, transportation or distribution for the public of drinking water, electricity, gas or heat; the supply of drinking water, electricity, gas or heat to such networks; the exploitation of a geographical area for the purpose of exploring for or extracting hydrocarbons or providing airports or ports; operating railway, tram or bus networks; and providing or operating public telecommunications networks or services. By Art. 3 of Directive 93/38, Member States can request the Commission to provide that the exploitation of a geographical area for the purpose of exploring for or extracting hydrocarbons is not to be considered a regulated activity provided that certain conditions (designed to ensure non-discriminatory awards) are met. See in this connection the Commission's Decision of July 14, 1993 [1993] O.J. L196/55 (Aug. 5) in relation to the U.K.'s application in respect of its petroleum licensing régime and regulation 9 of The Utilities Contracts Regulations 1996 (S.I. 96/2911).

[86] Directive 93/38, Art. 2(3), first para.

[87] *Ibid.*, Art. 2(3), second para.

[88] *ibid.*, Recitals 11 and 12.

[89] As between nationals of the Member States and the remaining EFTA countries that are party to the European Economic Area Agreement (Norway, Iceland and Liechtenstein).

The scope of the rules is only just beginning to be appreciated in the project finance area. There is no doubt, for example, that the letting of insurances is subject to the rules but utilities have (in the United Kingdom at least) only just begun to consider formally complying with the rules insofar as their insurances are concerned. More problematic is whether lending is covered, although the London market has clearly taken the view that it is not. There is an express exemption for the issue of securities which would cover loan notes but not ordinary lending pursuant to a credit agreement. The European Commission apparently take the view that ordinary lending is caught by the procurement rules, but the United Kingdom government apparently take the contrary view and have implemented the relevant Directives accordingly.

The legislation provides for three different types of procedure:

(i) *The open procedure.* Under this procedure, all persons who wish to submit a bid may do so. There will be no negotiations on price before the relevant contract is awarded.

(ii) *The restricted procedure.* Under this procedure, only those persons invited by the contracting body may submit a bid.[90] There will again be no negotiations on price before the contract is awarded.

(iii) *The negotiated procedure.* Under this procedure, only those persons invited by the contracting body may negotiate a contract with it. By its very nature, this procedure involves discussions with the various bidders (including discussions on price) before the contract is awarded.

For public supplies, works and services outside the utilities area, a contracting body can freely choose either the open or restricted procedure, but the use of the negotiated procedure is confined to specific circumstances. Utilities are free to choose any of the three procedures.

The basis on which contracts are to be awarded is either "the most economically advantageous tender" or "the lowest price only". The "most economically advantageous tender" basis can involve various criteria depending on the contract in question. The Directives include as examples of these criteria completion date, running costs, cost-effectiveness, quality, technical merit, commitments with regard to spare parts, security of supplies and price. The

---

[90] There are, however, certain rules as to the persons the contracting body can invite. Selection must be made on objective criteria, for example: see Art. 31(1) of Directive 93/38.

basis on which the contract is to be awarded must be stated in the "call for competition" published in the Official Journal or in any invitation to tender. Where the basis is "the most economically advantageous tender", the various criteria that will be used must be stated and, if possible, listed in descending order of importance. The remedies for a breach of the E.C.'s public procurement rules are essentially left to national law. The E.C. legislation which deals specifically with remedies[91] merely requires Member States to ensure that awards can be rapidly reviewed at the request of interested parties (including potential tenderers) and that review bodies can take interim measures to correct alleged infringements or prevent further prejudice, can set aside decisions that have been taken unlawfully and can fine and award damages against infringing bodies. Community law does have some part to play in the area of remedies, however, in that any infringement by a Member State can be made the subject of enforcement proceedings by the European Commission under Article 169 of the E.C. Treaty. In addition, the European Court of Justice has held[92] that individuals may rely on unconditional and precise provisions in Directives against an undertaking which has been made responsible by the state for providing a public service under the control of the state and has for that purpose been granted special powers or rights (the rationale for this approach being that such an undertaking can be regarded as an "emanation of the State"). This latter point is important in the context of individuals enforcing (to the extent that they have "direct effect") the public procurement rules set out in the various directives not only against Member States but also against utilities. Of course, if the relevant procurement Directives have been properly implemented into national law, it should not prove necessary to argue a case based on direct effect.

Under English law there are various remedies that can be invoked by an unsuccessful bidder alleging that the contract in question was wrongly awarded. First, the U.K.'s implementing legislation expressly provides for a contractor to be able to bring proceedings before the High Court in relation to a breach of the contract-awarding body's duty to comply with the legislation.[93] Such proceedings must be brought within three months after the grounds for bringing them arose (although the court has power to extend this period if there is

---

[91] *i.e.* Directives 89/665 and 92/13.

[92] *Foster v. British Gas plc*, Case C-188/89, [1990] I–ECR 3313. The *Foster* case was followed in *Griffin v. South West Water Services Limited* [1995] IRLR 15 where Blackburne J. held that the defendant, a wholly-owned subsidiary of a U.K. privatised utility, was a state authority against which persons could rely upon provisions of Directives in national courts.

[93] See, *e.g.*, The Utilities Contracts Regulations 1996, r.32.

"good reason")[94] and the court will only be able to award damages (as opposed to giving an order setting the contract aside) if the contract in question has already been entered into.[95] Subject to this qualification, the court can set aside the award of the contract (including on an interlocutory basis), award damages or do both. Secondly, the contractor may allege not that the awarding body breached its duty to comply with the relevant legislation, but that its actual decision was wrongly arrived at. If the decision was one which could be made subject to judicial review,[96] this would allow the contractor to seek an order for *certiorari*, which would quash the decision. It would seem odd if, by seeking *certiorari*, a plaintiff was able effectively to overturn a concluded contract when he would not be able to do so if he brought proceedings alleging a breach of duty under the legislation. Thirdly, the invitation to bid sent to the contractor may itself have binding contractual effect. A court might well be tempted to find a promise by the awarding body to follow the bid procedure set out in the invitation to bid in consideration for the contractor submitting a bid. This outcome should be capable of being avoided, however, by simply providing in the invitation to bid that it is not itself intended to create a contractual relationship. Finally, although this is not strictly a remedy under English law, a contractor who is disappointed by an award of a contract by a utility can invoke a conciliation procedure involving the European Commission.[97]

The Directive relating to procurement by public utilities[98] (the "Utilities Directive") and domestic legislation implementing the same are the provisions arising out of the E.C.'s public procurement initiative which are most frequently encountered in project financings. Two topical issues in relation to the Utilities Directive are as follows:

(a) *Does the Utilities Directive apply to a project company during the construction phase?* At first sight, this is a startling question. The reason that the question is asked in practice (and it often is) is the failure by the Utilities Directive to make a full transition from the Directives dealing with the public sector (on which it is based) to a Directive which is properly tailored to a privatised

---

[94] *ibid.*, r.32(4)(b), for example.
[95] *ibid.*, r.32(6), for example.
[96] For a discussion on the types of decision subject to judicial review, see Paul Craig, *Administrative Law* (3rd. ed., 1994), pp. 518-9 and Chapter 15.
[97] See Arts. 10 and 11 of Directive 92/13 and r.33 of The Utilities Contracts Regulations 1996.
[98] *i.e.* Directive 93/38.

utility sector. The particular problem is a failure to address the fact that companies in a consortium formed to bid for or to carry out a project are often in the consortium because they wish to enter into one of the major project contracts with the project company themselves. By way of example, a consortium trying to develop a power project may comprise a contractor, a power plant operator and a financial investor. The contractor and the operator will expect to enter into the construction contract and the operation and maintenance agreement respectively. So long as the consortium win the right to build the power plant through a competitive tender, or, if there is no such competition, so long as the consortium are exposed to market forces when the plant generates, why is it necessary for the project company to put its construction contract and operation and maintenance agreement out to tender? The project company is simply a vehicle for the contractor and the power plant operator and the public interest in procuring cheap electricity supplies will either have been secured through the competitive tender which awarded the project company the right to build the power plant or will be achieved by virtue of the market in which the project company will operate.

The legal argument advanced to support the contention that a project company in the utilities sector need not comply with the Utilities Directive during the construction phase is based on what is effectively the definition of a private utility in that Directive. Private utilities are "entitles which . . . have[99] as one of their activities" one of the specified utility activities and which (as has been seen) operate on the basis of special or exclusive rights.[1] The argument is that, during the construction phase, the project company does not *have* as one of its activities one of the specified utility activities (e.g. the supply of electricity to a network); this will only happen after completion.

The argument is attractive in a large part due to the practical consequence it allows. Some element of caution may be justified, however, as the Utilities Directive

---

[99] Emphasis added.
[1] Art. 2(1) of the Utilities Directive. See also the definitions of "utility" and "relevant person" in r.3(1) and (2) respectively of The Utilities Contracts Regulations 1996.

does not make any express reference to different treatment in the construction phase and its recitals are couched in very wide terms. The practical zeal of an English court might be tempered by the requirement that "national courts must construe national law in the light of the wording and purpose of the Directive in order to achieve the requirement of Article 189 of the Treaty of Rome that a Directive is 'binding as to the result to be achieved.' "[2]

(b) *What exemptions does the Utilities Directive contain in relation to intragroup contracts?* The Utilities Directive expressly states[3] that it does not apply to service contracts which a utility awards to an affiliated undertaking provided that "at least 80 per cent of the average turnover of that affiliated undertaking with respect to services arising within the Community for the preceding three years derives from the provision of such services to undertakings with which it is affiliated".[4] This is a very narrow exemption: it only applies to service contracts (so not, for example, to construction contracts) and the three years' track record of supplying services to other members of the relevant group is clearly an anti-avoidance provision.[5] The exemption appears to be aimed at group service companies (such as those providing payroll services). The definition of affiliate is also a relatively standard holding company and subsidiary definition based on a dominant influence test.

Other provisions of the Utilities Directive that are of note are that it does not apply to a power plant's purchase of energy or fuel for the production of energy nor to any acquisition of land or buildings.[6] In addition, the Utilities Directive specifies various instances where a call for competition may be dispensed with, including extreme urgency, a replacement or extension of existing installations where a change of supplier would involve the utility acquiring incompatible equipment, new works consisting of a repetition of existing similar works as part of a general overall scheme and bargain purchases

---

[2] Case 14/83 *Von Colson* [1984] E.C.R. 1891, 1909.
[3] In Art. 13. See also r.8(2) of The Utilities Contracts Regulations 1996.
[4] There is another limited exemption in Art. 13 which applies when the utility is an unincorporated joint venture (which will rarely be the case in a project financing).
[5] It does not appear to have been fully implemented by the U.K.: compare the definition of "relevant affiliated undertaking" in r.8(1)(b) of The Utilities Contracts Regulations 1996.
[6] Arts. 9(1)(b) and 1(4)(c) respectively of the Utilities Directive.

taking advantage of a brief opportunity to procure supplies at a price considerably lower than normal market prices.[7]

Public works concession contracts under the Directive dealing with procurement of public works[8] are also encountered in project finance. Such contracts are public works contracts which include the grant of a right to exploit the works to be carried out under the contract (*i.e.* they are concession agreements).[9] The concessionaire under a public works concession contract must make known his intention to award a works contract to a third party by a notice in the Official Journal.[10] A third party for these purposes does not include "undertakings which have formed a group in order to obtain the concession contract, or undertakings affiliated to them".[11] The definition of affiliate is again a relatively standard holding company and subsidiary definition based on a dominant influence test and the reference to a group seems to refer to an unincorporated joint venture being the concessionaire. There still appears to be no ability for a concessionaire which is owned by various shareholders, none of whom have a dominant influence over it, to award contracts to a shareholder without making a notice in the Official Journal. One should be wary of applying too literal an interpretation to the word "group" in an E.C. Directive, however. In addition, if the concessionaire is a utility, it will also be subject to the Utilities Directive and will have to comply with that Directive which, as we have seen, contains no general exemption in relation to contracts with affiliates.

---

[7] Art. 20(2) of the Utilities Directive. See also r. 16 of The Utilities Contracts Regulations 1996.
[8] *i.e.* Directive 93/37.
[9] Art. 1(d) of Directive 93/37. See also the definition contained in r. 2(1) of The Public Works Contracts Regulations 1991 and, in general, rr.25 and 26 of those Regs.
[10] Art. 11(4) of Directive 93/37. See also r.26(4)(b) of The Public Works Contracts Regulations 1991.
[11] Art. 3(4) of Directive 93/37. See also r.26(3)–(5) of The Public Works Contracts Regulations 1991.

Chapter 10

Some Specific Areas of Project Finance

The purpose of this Chapter is to explain the United Kingdom government's Private Finance Initiative and to give a basic orientation in relation to the legislative, regulatory and contractual background in certain key sectors where there has been or may in the future be significant project financing opportunities.

10.1   THE PRIVATE FINANCE INITIATIVE (THE "PFI")

The origins of the PFI as it is known today are generally traced back to the relaunch of the concept by Kenneth Clarke as Chancellor of the Exchequer in November 1993[1] and the publication by the Treasury at the same time of the booklet *Breaking New Ground*. The subtitle of that booklet was *towards a new partnership between the public and private sectors* and this sums up the objective of the PFI.[2] The United Kingdom government wished to upgrade the nation's infrastructure and improve the quality of its public services but was severely constrained in using public funds and was aware that the public sector could not always provide the most efficient and cost-effective service. In very crude political terms, the PFI seeks to transfer responsibility for financing government[3] projects and the

---

[1] The policy was actually launched in the autumn of 1992 by Norman Lamont when he was Chancellor of the Exchequer.
[2] The PFI is an example of a so-called "public/private partnership".
[3] As this section 10.1 deals with the PFI in general terms, references in the section to government can effectively be read as references to all parts of the public sector, including government departments and agencies, non-departmental public bodies, the National Health Service, local authorities and public corporations. For guidance on the PFI in the local authority arena see *The Private Finance Initiative and Local Authorities — an explanatory note* published by the Department of the Environment and the Welsh Office in October, 1996. Early PFI projects sponsored by National Health Service Trusts and local authorities were dogged by problems with *vires*. Government initiatives to resolve these problems are currently under consideration.

risk of their success or failure away from the government and onto the shoulders of the private sector. Although nothing is really so simple, the PFI enables politicians to regenerate the nation's infrastructure and reinvigorate its public services without having to increase the public sector borrowing requirement or (initially at least) raise taxation. New jobs and new businesses are created on the way almost as a by-product.

The device by which the PFI seeks to achieve its objectives is usually the humble concession, although it is often dressed up in grandiloquent finery: there are DCMF ("design, construct, maintain and finance") prison concessions and DBFO ("design, build, finance and operate") road concessions. In essence, PFI projects are often simply another version (or versions) of the BOT scheme. Much of the general text in this book relating to concessions and BOT schemes and their implementation and financing therefore applies to PFI concessions and, for this reason, this section 10.1 will simply point out various matters which are peculiar to PFI deals.

To illustrate the point behind the PFI further, if the government requires a piece of infrastructure to be built, "old thinking" would have the government entering into a construction contract itself. "New thinking" has the government giving someone in the private sector the right and obligation to construct the relevant piece of infrastructure in return for receiving, once the project is completed, remuneration which is at least partly based on usage of the project. Instead of the government contracting for the construction of a new motorway, it contracts for the provision of a motorway and related services. The theory is that government has become a user, rather than a provider of services. In November, 1994 the Conservative government, in an attempt to anchor the role of the PFI in the heart of the public sector, announced that the Treasury would not approve any capital projects unless private finance options had been explored. Within a week after it was elected in May 1997, the new Labour government abolished this requirement considering it too restrictive and the source of delay.

The Labour government also commissioned an immediate and wide-ranging review of the PFI. The findings of the review were announced on June 23, 1997.[4] It made 29 recommendations aimed at streamlining and improving the PFI. The government accepted all of the recommendations, many of which were designed to improve the PFI process within government itself. The recommendations included the following:

---

[4] The terms of reference can be found in Treasury Press Notice 41/97 and the results of the review in Treasury Press Notice 69/97.

1. The Private Finance Panel should be abolished and the Private Finance Panel Executive disbanded. The Private Finance Panel had been set up under the previous government to promote the PFI and to seek solutions to problems which might otherwise impede the progress of the PFI. Before its abolition, it consisted of 12 leading individuals with relevant experience drawn from both the public and private sectors. It was intended to act as a bridge between both sectors, although criticism had been mounting that it had developed a tendency to take the government's side on issues. The Private Finance Panel Executive was essentially the Private Finance Panel's executive arm.

2. A new Treasury Taskforce should be established in the Treasury "to become the focal point for all PFI activities across Government". It should have a projects arm (with a limited life of two years) and a policy arm. The projects team should comprise a Chief Executive of Projects and up to eight middle-ranking executives from the private sector with direct project management and financial skills and experience. This team's role should be assisting government departments to close PFI projects. The policy arm should comprise a Treasury policy team. It should have "lead responsibility for rules and best practice governing [the] PFI and other public private partnerships".[5]

3. The Treasury Taskforce should agree that any significant project is commercially viable *before* the procurement process is begun by way of publication in the Official Journal.[6]

4. A standard form questionnaire should be used for each discipline in order to obtain information from prospective tenderers and each government department, in consultation with the Treasury Taskforce, should produce model conditions or clauses and then, as soon as they have sufficient experience to be sure they will be bankable, standard or model contracts. (A significant amount of work in this area has already been carried out by the Private Finance Panel and this is addressed in detail below.)

5. Government departments should prioritise their PFI projects in a transparent manner and small PFI projects in

---

[5] One of the main conclusions of the review was that, in the medium term, there should be "highly skilled departmental procurers pursuing their projects without central support and a small Treasury Unit as the guardian of policy principles and promoter of best practice". This explains the limited life of the projects team.

[6] See section 9.2(c) above.

health and education and in local authorities should be grouped together.

6. The appropriate government departments should give appropriate assurance to funders that the money necessary to honour contractual commitments under PFI deals with non-departmental public bodies "represent obligations that will be met for the duration of the contract".

7. The Treasury Taskforce should issue specific guidance on the way in which "public sector comparators" are to be calculated and bids evaluated for value for money. These issues are discussed below. The comment in the summary of the review's findings reads: "The lack of commonality in the way the Public Sector Comparator is calculated, whether one is needed and hesitancy about the most suitable way to make value for money calculations is wasting time and delaying projects".

8. The number of bidders should be reduced to a maximum of four.

9. When a decision is made not to proceed with a project and that decision is not related to the viability of tenders received, tenderers' bidding costs should be refunded.

It is currently difficult to predict how the PFI will move forward under a new government. It is also difficult to predict the extent to which detailed guidance on the implementation of the PFI issued by the Private Finance Panel and the Treasury under the previous government still holds good. The new government has clearly embraced the general philosophy of the PFI[7] and it appears keen to free up what it sees as a log jam of potential projects. Its approach in other areas (such as education) appears to be to refine and improve rather than to change for change's sake. On this basis, and also because more radical change in the implementation of the PFI is probably only likely (if at all) once the new Treasury Taskforce begins work in earnest, this section goes on to discuss the rules that applied to the implementation of the PFI prior to the change in

---

[7] The summary of the review referred to above stated, in paragraph 1: "The . . . PFI provides a mechanism through which the public sector can secure improved value for money in partnership with the private sector. When handled well, the PFI can work to the mutual advantage of users of public services, taxpayers and companies seeking new business opportunities. The Government should take an early opportunity to make a confirmatory announcement of its commitment to [the] PFI as one method of conducting successful Public Private Partnerships".

government. It is anticipated that those rules (or, possibly, some reworked version of them) will continue to apply to PFI projects at least in the short term.

Looked at from the point of view of revenues, there are basically two main types of PFI concession.[8] In one, the concessionaire is entitled to charge the public[9]; in the other, he receives a fee or tariff from the government or a government department in return for providing a service.[10] There are, of course, hybrids: some projects require a certain element of government subsidy but can otherwise be funded from revenues from users.[11] The choice as to which remuneration system is most appropriate for any given project is essentially a political one. It is generally considered to be politically unacceptable to have motorists pay cash tolls for the use of United Kingdom motorways (as opposed to bridges). As a result, the government lets concessions for the private sector to design, build, finance and operate new roads which provide for the government to pay "shadow tolls", so called because, whilst the motorist will not himself pay tolls, the traffic using the completed road is nevertheless measured and the aggregate amount of shadow tolls payable by the government in any given month will depend on usage for that month. Setting the fares of an urban transport system at a level which would repay the private sector's borrowings would be prohibitively expensive and so a combination of subsidy and actual fare receipts might be used. In the competition stage, before the concession is awarded for a PFI project, the bidding consortia from the private sector are required to compete on the level of remuneration (of whatever type the government has chosen) that they require. In fact, there are those who believe that, by requiring the private sector to bid for the amount of government subsidy required in order to run a project, the Conservative administration which introduced the PFI discovered a way of privatising anything, even public enterprises making the most horrendous losses.[12]

Two issues at the heart of the PFI are "value for money" and risk transfer and there is a very direct interrelationship between the two.

---

[8] *Breaking New Ground* identified three types of PFI project from a commercial viewpoint: the financially free-standing project, the joint venture and the sale of services to the public sector.
[9] This is usually the case for bridges.
[10] This is the case in the DBFO roads. Critics claim that this type of PFI project (the most typical) is storing up budgetary trouble in the future. Taxes may not need to be raised now to finance the construction of the projects, but they will have to be in the future to finance payments of the tariffs.
[11] This is usually the case for mass transit projects (*e.g.* the Lewisham extension to the Docklands Light Railway (although the user there is really the operator of the existing system rather than the travelling public) and Croydon Tramlink).
[12] A point which some would say was demonstrated by the privatisation of British Rail.

Value for money is not relevant for "financially free-standing projects" (*i.e.* projects where there is no significant public expenditure (such as tolled bridges)) where the government will instead focus on preventing excessive charging to the public. Nor is it relevant for joint ventures where the public sector's financial contribution will be measured against alternative uses of the same money. Where the value for money test is relevant (*i.e.* essentially in PFI schemes which involve the government paying a fee or tariff for the provision of services), government departments will establish a "public sector comparator" (or *PSC*) before deciding to launch a project as a PFI project. This is an estimate of what the project would cost the government were it to be dealt with on a different basis (normally a direct government let) using only public finance. The public sector comparator will only be applied where a publicly financed solution could be possible on a similar timescale. Since the government borrows at very low rates, it seems curious that any project involving the sale of services to the public sector ever sees the light of day as a PFI project. The answer to this conundrum (apart from the obvious answer about lack of government resources to carry out all projects as direct lets) is to do with risk transfer. The government puts a price on the transfer of risk to the private sector.[13] In fact, not only will the government do so at this stage, but it will also do so when deciding between competing bids. If one consortium is less willing than another to accept the division of risk contained in the model concession agreement presented to all bidders, then, provided that the first consortium's bid is nevertheless eligible,[14] the government may well adjust the value of its bid. Bids are normally reduced to present values and, if the government decides to make such an adjustment, a monetary amount will simply be added to the present value of that consortium's bid.

The government's guiding principle for whether a risk should be borne by the public sector or the private sector is that a risk should be borne by the person best able to manage it.[15] The government has stated, with regard to the public sector's attitude to risk that "with traditional public sector procurement, risk analysis is often

---

[13] In their joint publication early in 1997, *DBFO-Value in Roads*, the Highways Agency and the Private Finance Panel claimed (in para. 1.4) that the first 8 DBFO road projects had delivered an average cost saving (compared with the public sector comparator) of 15 per cent. para. 1.3 of the same publication revealed a National Audit Office report which stated that there was an average 28 per cent increase in price between tender and out-turn price for traditional directly let road-building contracts.

[14] *i.e.* it complies with the essential requirements of the invitation to bid.

[15] See, *e.g.*, the statement in sections 1.9 and 3.6 of the publication issued in November 1995 jointly by the Treasury and the Private Finance Panel entitled *Private Opportunity, Public Benefit — Progressing the Private Finance Initiative*.

weak and risks only become apparent after the event".[16] The government sees little scope for the public sector to retain significant commercial risks in financially free standing projects. In those projects, the government plays an initial enabling role and then stands back from the project (thus making it difficult for it to manage risks).[17]

The government's desire to transfer risks in projects involving the sale of services to the public sector most notably results in the following benefits for the public sector:

(i) A minimisation of the design risk taken by the public sector. The public sector will only produce an *output specification* which sets the parameters of the service the public sector wants. The detailed design and the associated risk are left to the private sector.

(ii) An increase in management incentives. Payment of the fee or tariff by the public sector will usually only commence when a satisfactory service level is achieved. The private sector will therefore be keen to establish this level of service. Under more traditional procurement routes, those who create or procure an asset do not necessarily have direct responsibility for the actual service.

(iii) A limitation on the pass-through of cost overruns to the public sector. The public sector has simply agreed a price for a service. How the private sector organises itself in order to provide such service is its own problem.

The theory that risks should be borne by the party best able to manage them is stretched in the case of changes in law and taxation. The government makes the now familiar distinction between changes in law and regulations of general application and changes which are discriminatory in respect of a particular project. The risk of the former should lie with the private sector, but the risk of the latter may be borne by the public sector to the extent that a discriminatory change of law may in effect constitute a change in the public sector's requirements for a particular project.[18] Similarly, the government believes that the general taxation risk should be borne by the private sector, although value added tax is an exception to this (where the public sector may agree VAT-exclusive prices).[19] The theory is applied more sympathetically in relation to

---

[16] *ibid.*, s.1.9.
[17] *ibid.*, s.3.6.
[18] *ibid.*, s.3.20.
[19] *ibid.*, s.3.21.

the risk that a public inquiry may be required for a particular project. Here the government's view is that the public sector should be prepared to steer a project through a public enquiry if the project departs from the relevant planning authority's existing development plan or if there is likely to be a controversy about whether or not the project is needed.[20]

Some of the most interesting remarks from the government in relation to project finance in the context of the PFI have been made under the guise of a consideration of the "project financing risk" in a project:

> "*Project financing risk* is inherently a risk to be managed by the [private sector] supplier and its financiers. The public sector should, however, consider whether the terms for a conforming response to an invitation to negotiate are such that the supplier may not be able to obtain finance for the project or make it unnecessarily difficult or expensive; and re-examine the terms where appropriate. The public sector purchaser must have an interest in the ability of the supplier and its financiers to fulfil their contracts".[21]

From the very beginning, the government was keen to foster innovation in the bids it received for PFI projects. "Deals not rules" was a catchphrase often repeated in the PFI's early stages. This attitude led in turn to the rejection of the idea of a standard PFI concession agreement. Although espousing similar concepts, the concession agreement for a DBFO road differs from that for a prison and the documentation for the PFI's property transactions is different again (although this is perhaps understandable). Paradoxically, this lack of standardisation, coupled with a readiness on the part of the government to be relatively flexible (no doubt brought about by a political desire to ensure that none of the early PFI projects failed), led to protracted negotiations and a sense of frustration in the early projects. The delay and cost in negotiating PFI projects was for many months the private sector's (and, in particular, the construction industry's) main criticism of the PFI. This criticism was one of the factors which led to the Labour Government's review of the PFI referred to above.

Initially, however, the Private Finance Panel and the Treasury responded to the criticism by publishing two guidance documents, *Basic Contractual Terms*, published in October, 1996, and *Further*

---

[20] *ibid.*, s.3.22.
[21] *ibid.*, s.3.23.

Contractual Issues, published shortly thereafter. The former document provided standard clauses, although their use is not mandatory. The latter document did not provide standard clauses but guidance on some of the more complex issues that will be encountered in a PFI contract.

The clauses contained in *Basic Contractual Terms* are really "boilerplate" clauses. They include clauses such as the entire agreement clause, assignment and sub-letting, confidentiality and value added tax. They also include two rather more controversial clauses, namely *force majeure* and corrupt gifts and payments of commission. The *force majeure* clause is controversial because it is exceptionally narrow, covering only "war, civil war, armed conflict or terrorist attack arising within and affecting the UK" and nuclear, chemical or biological contamination of the [project company's] property arising therefrom. The marginal note states: *"force majeure* events are limited to war and terrorism as defined. No other unusual circumstances should be admitted as being *force majeure* events: instead, these circumstances should be dealt with separately under specific provisions within the [concession agreement]". The key to why this position has been taken lies in the fact that the *force majeure* definition is linked to a clause providing for termination of the agreement with compensation if an event of *force majeure* causes the project company to be "materially unable" to comply with its contractual obligations. The public sector has in practice accepted that a number of other events (such as fire and exceptionally adverse weather conditions) may allow the project company to be relieved from liability for non-performance under the concession agreement. The corrupt gifts clause is controversial because, if a bribe was offered to a servant of the Crown in order to obtain the award of the concession agreement, one of the remedies the awarding body has is to terminate the agreement.[22] This has led to problems with banks who have argued that they have no way of knowing whether or not a clandestine bribe has been offered and that, if the awarding body terminated the agreement, this would cause them undue hardship. The government's response to this is to stipulate that the awarding body's remedy must be proportionate. The relevant part of the clause reads:

"In exercising its rights or remedies under this condition, the Authority shall:

(a) act in a reasonable and proportionate manner having regard to such matters as the gravity of, and the identity of the person performing, the prohibited act;

---

[22] The position may be the same under common law, however.

(b) give all due consideration, where appropriate, to action other than termination of the Contract . . ."

Under paragraph (b), the examples given of alternative action are terminating a sub-contract or an employment contract where the wrongdoing has been perpetrated by a sub-contractor or employee respectively. The clause does not mention the position of innocent third parties (such as banks) who have altered their position in reliance on the agreement in question but it is hoped that the general requirement of reasonableness and proportionality in paragraph (a) will be sufficient to require an awarding body to have due regard to their interests. In any event, there is probably little more that can be done in the contract: the nature of a criminal act such as bribery or fraud is that innocent parties may suffer and the awarding body will argue that it too is an innocent party. Some banks have insisted in the past, however, that if the concession agreement is terminated pursuant to this clause, some compensation should be paid.

Further Contractual Issues is an altogether more interesting publication. It offers guidance on, *inter alia*, the following areas: payment mechanisms, performance incentives, monitoring performance, change of control, termination, step-in rights for both the public sector and lenders, change mechanisms and legislative risk. Each of these areas is considered in detail below.

(a) *Payment Mechanisms.* The publication stresses that the choice of payment mechanism is central to the allocation of risk. For example, delay risk is transferred if the supplier is only paid when the service required under a concession agreement comes on stream. Whilst there can be flexibility as to how the payment is constructed (*e.g.* by reference to availability, performance, usage, capacity or any combination of the same), the publication warns against payments which are fixed irrespective of the quality of the service and states[23]:

> "Such fixed payments are sometimes proposed to protect the private sector's debt service obligations. But they run counter to the principle of payment by results, they negate risk transfer, and consequently throw into question the nature of the project."

Payment in arrears, not in advance, should be the rule[24] and PFI concessionaires should be encouraged to make use of *asset redundancy*,

---

[23] In para. 2.4.
[24] *Further Contractual Issues*, para. 2.10.

i.e. the ability to generate additional third party revenues from an asset which is the subject of a PFI project.[25] An example of asset redundancy could be the ability to run courses for the private sector (outside the hours required by the public sector) in a training centre built primarily for the public sector under the PFI. The public sector is asked to consider whether such third party revenues should be shared and whether the likelihood of such revenues arising is sufficiently high to enable them to be taken into account in the initial invitation to tender.

(b) *Performance Incentives.* The discussion on performance incentives reveals that the government has primarily in mind a system of penalties, not a mixed system of penalties and bonuses (although the possibility of financial incentives for extra performance is not ruled out). Paragraph 3.7 of *Further Contractual Issues* probably sums up the government's attitude:

> "Providing incentives to perform *up to* the contract requirement is essential. Incentives to perform *above* the contract standard can be useful . . . but they are an optional extra."

Penalties should be proportionate, however.[26] One of the examples cited of an effective performance incentive is the Benefits Agency/ Post Office Counters Ltd project (in relation to the computerisation of the United Kingdom's welfare benefits): the project company is paid by reference to completed benefit payment transactions, but an incentive element is added by linking this to ensuring that accurate payments are made and that fraud is minimised.

(c) *Monitoring performance.* As far as monitoring performance is concerned, the publication states that a penalty point system can be used where it is not practicable to reduce the payments to the project company.[27] A penalty point system (which has, for example, the award of a specified cumulative number of penalty points in a specified period leading to the issue of a warning notice and the issue of two warning notices constituting an event of default under the concession agreement) gives the awarding body a remedy other than termination.

(d) *Change of Control.* There is a general presumption that the public sector should not be able to prevent a change of ownership of the project company.[28]

---

[25] *ibid.*, para. 2.13.

[26] *ibid.*, para. 3.3.

[27] *ibid.*, para. 4.9.

[28] *ibid.*, para. 6.1. For a more detailed explanation of the public sector's attitude to this issue see the publication published by the Private Finance Panel and H.M. Treasury entitled *Transferability of Equity*.

(e) *Termination.* Extensive guidance is offered on termination rights.[29] The public sector should not be able to terminate the concession agreement at will. Instead, the public sector should have termination rights for a default by the project company. The language, however, picks up a partnership theme and states that termination should be "very much the last resort" and that termination rights should be for "a catastrophic and long-term failure of the project service" or "chronic and persistently unremedied bad performance".[30] On the thorny issue of whether or not compensation should be paid in the event of a termination for default by the project company,[31] compensation is not ruled out. The principal guidance offered is as follows:

> "compensation to the [*project company*] in the event of *termination* following [its] *default* should be limited. You should ask yourself whether the financial arrangements are equitable. But PFI involves paying for services, and if there is no service being provided, there is no presumption of payment. Clearly the arrangements must provide a keen incentive on the private sector *not* to *default*."

The guidance notes recognise that the case for compensation may be at its strongest when there is an automatic transfer of the project assets on a termination of the concession agreement. In general terms, the public sector is asked to balance various considerations when deciding whether or not compensation should be paid in the event of a termination for default by the project company. These considerations include the effect of a break in the service on the public sector's obligations,[32] the element of value provided in advance of payment by the private sector prior to the default in question and the impact on the financeability of the project.[33] It is accepted that the private sector should be able to terminate for public sector default and that "full compensation" of debt and equity (including anticipated profit) is appropriate.[34] The principle is that the private sector (including banks financing a project) should be no worse off because of the public sector's default than they would have been had the concession agreement run its course.

---

[29] *Further Contractual Issues*, Chap. 9.
[30] *ibid.*, para. 9.5.
[31] As to which see section 3.5.
[32] The person granting the concession may himself be under a statutory duty to provide the service in question.
[33] *Further Contractual Issues*, para. 9.6.
[34] *ibid.*, para. 9.10.

It is also accepted that the private sector may be able to terminate the concession agreement for *force majeure* (but note the discussion above on the narrowness of the definition). The publication acknowledges that termination for *force majeure* "will probably involve some (partial) compensation" for the private sector, but the rather curious justification given is that "some aspect of the service may have been provided already".

(f) *Step-in rights for the public sector.* It is acknowledged that step-in rights for the public sector are not always necessary but that, where they are deemed to be, they should be temporary and relate only to cases of severe failures of service outputs.[35] Step-in rights for the public sector are likely to be necessary where the public sector has a statutory responsibility to ensure the delivery at all times of a high-profile public service.[36] Although the guidance notes state that the reasonable costs of the public sector's step-in should be borne by the project company, nothing is stated as to whether any service fee or tariff continues to be paid by the public sector (although the clear implication is that it is not — no service is being provided).

One point that banks often do not appreciate when discussing the effect of a public sector step-in is that it potentially deprives their carefully negotiated controls on the project of any effect. Their reserved discretions, for example, may no longer have any teeth since the public sector might, whilst they are stepping in, exercise a contractual right in a manner which is inimical to the banks' interests.

(g) *Step-in rights for lenders.* The guidance offered in relation to step-in rights by banks is in the main sound. Few people would really take issue with statements such as "the [direct] agreement should provide that the rights of the [public sector] are unchanged from the main PFI contract".[37] There are, however, two major criticisms of the guidance. First, it fails to acknowledge that the banks may wish to step in because of a problem with their financing — the guidance notes presuppose that the banks wish to step in because the project company is defaulting under the concession agreement. Secondly, the only remedy envisaged for the banks on a bank step-in is substitution of a new concessionaire or project company (usually within a very limited period of time[38]), not the appointment of a receiver to hold office until the banks' debt is

---

[35] *ibid.*, paras. 7.3 and 7.5.
[36] *ibid.*, para. 7.4.
[37] *ibid.*, para. 8.5.
[38] *e.g.* a year.

repaid (the natural remedy in a secured project financing under English law). Much time and energy has been expended in a number of individual PFI projects persuading the public sector to accept both of these points (which it has) and it is submitted that it is time that the guidance notes (if they are to be retained under the Labour administration) are brought up-to-date and into line with practice.

(h) *Change mechanisms.* The public sector is exhorted to try to deal with anticipated changes by requiring the private sector to price options at the time of the bid.[39] It is acknowledged that the public sector may have problems ensuring good value for money for changes where it is locked into a long-term contract with a single supplier. To guard against this risk, the public sector should base remuneration for changes on unit rates, indices and other objective measures, not just on costs which the project company claims. Having agreed a price for the change, payment should usually be made by adjusting the standard payment mechanisms rather than by simply reimbursing the project company (although the adjustment should include an allowance for the project company's expected return or the maintenance of key financial ratios).[40] This has important implications for risk transfer, since it will mean that the project company will have to meet the normal performance standards in order to recoup in full the price that has been agreed for the change. It is not inconceivable that, in the case of a substantial change, a bidder might have negotiated different performance standards had he known of the different scope of work before he entered into the concession agreement.

It is, however, also acknowledged that there may be limits to a project company's ability to deliver changes since a substantial change could require it to raise additional capital.[41] In some limited circumstances, the general approach of merely adjusting the standard payment mechanisms will not be reasonable and a lump sum may have to be paid. No guidance is offered, however, on the critical issue of the nature of the lump sum: is it a grant, a loan (if so, on what terms) or a payment in advance for an enhanced service? Whatever it is, the concession agreement should make it clear.

It is also stated that excessively simple or generous change provisions can impact on a project's value for money and, if they transfer too much risk to the public sector (so that the public sector bears more of the risks and rewards of ownership), even impact on the accounting treatment.

---

[39] *Further Contractual Issues*, para. 10.5.

[40] *ibid.*, para. 10.6.

[41] *ibid.*, para. 10.4.

(i) *Legislative risk.* The guidance accepts that one of the ways in which the private sector reacts to changes in law is to seek to increase its prices to pass on any increased costs. It further concedes that, with the single customer and fixed prices that one often finds in a PFI project, this will be difficult and it explains that this is the reason for the private sector wishing to see legislative change included in the general change mechanism.[42] Nevertheless, the treatment of legislative risk may again affect the accounting treatment and the tenor of the guidance offered is that the private sector should, if possible, take some of the change of law risk. For example, the project company in a PFI project may be able to manage its business effectively to mitigate the impact of a change in law. There are also policy issues at work, as is shown by the following statement[43]:

> ". . . if a future Government decided to impose a tax on the use of a particular material in order to discourage its use, and promote the use of alternatives, it would be perverse if *suppliers* with PFI contracts were entirely protected against the impact of this tax, and so had no incentive to switch away from using the material in question in the services they supplied to Government."

The Private Finance Panel and the Treasury suggested the following risk allocation as "a good starting-point" in a PFI project[44]:

(a) the public sector should accept the risk of specific legislation which targets the project in question, or a class of similar projects or PFI projects in general;

(b) the project company should accept other general legislative risks, including the risk of costs arising from changes of law applying to the whole business sector (including public sector operators); and

(c) a mechanism for sharing risk may be appropriate to cover changes in law which would normally be met by increasing prices to customers.

10.2 THE NORTH SEA

(a) *The underlying legislative and contractual régime.* The central features of the underlying legislative and contractual régime in the

---

[42] *ibid.*, para. 11.3.
[43] *ibid.*, para. 11.5.
[44] *ibid.*, para. 11.7.

United Kingdom sector of the North Sea are the United Kingdom petroleum production licence issued by the Secretary of State for Trade and Industry (the "Secretary of State")[45] and the joint operating agreements entered into by the holders of such a licence between themselves.

(i) *United Kingdom petroleum production licences.* Ownership in petroleum *in situ* in the United Kingdom and on the United Kingdom Continental Shelf is vested in the Crown. Petroleum production licences issued by the Secretary of State permit licensees to extract petroleum and to own it once extracted. A licence can cover more than one petroleum discovery and is nowadays usually granted to more than one person. The terms of the licences are set out in so-called "Model Clauses" which are to be found in various statutes and statutory instruments.[46] The content of the Model Clauses can vary slightly depending on the licensing round in which a particular licence was issued; the promulgation of new Model Clauses to apply for new licensing rounds does not affect the Model Clauses incorporated into licences granted in previous licensing rounds. The Model Clauses applicable to existing licences have occasionally been amended retrospectively by statute.[47]

Certain provisions of the Model Clauses to note are:

(a) The Secretary of State has to approve any programme for the development of a petroleum discovery.[48] Once he has approved a programme, the licensees are obliged to carry it out.[49]

(b) A licence can be revoked on various grounds including the appointment of a receiver over the licensee, a breach or non-observance by the licensee of any of the terms and conditions of the licence and a

---

[45] The licences used to be issued by the Secretary of State for Energy, but this post has been abolished and the Department of Energy subsumed within the Department of Trade and Industry.

[46] *e.g.* The Petroleum and Submarine Pipe-lines Act 1975 and The Petroleum (Production) (Seaward Areas) Regulations 1988 (S.I. 88/1213) (the "1988 Regulations").

[47] By s.17 of the Petroleum and Submarine Pipe-lines Act 1975 (which introduced fairly dramatic changes) and s.19 of the Oil and Gas (Enterprise) Act 1982 and s.17 of the Petroleum Act 1987 (which introduced rather more technical changes).

[48] See, *e.g.*, Clause 17(1) of the Model Clauses contained in Schedule 4 to the 1988 Regulations (the "1988 Model Clauses").

[49] See, *e.g.*, Clause 17(8) of the 1988 Model Clauses.

change in the control of the licensee.[50] A change in control for these purposes probably includes lenders with security over the shares in the licensee exercising their enforcement remedies under that security.

(c) The licensee cannot, except with the consent of the Secretary of State, take any action whereby "any right granted by [the] licence or derived from a right so granted becomes exercisable by or for the benefit of or in accordance with the directions of another person".[51] This is essentially a prohibition on assignments of and the creation of security interests in the licence. Because of this provision, a licensee wishing to give security over his interest in a United Kingdom petroleum production licence requires the Secretary of State's consent. It is not the Secretary of State's practice to give consent where the purpose of the underlying loan is not to finance or refinance costs incurred or to be incurred in "upstream" petroleum activities (including exploration) in the United Kingdom or on the United Kingdom Continental Shelf. The Secretary of State's consent to the creation of a security interest over a licence is given in a formal government consent agreement to which the licensee and the lender(s) are party. This agreement will specifically state that a further consent is required for any enforcement of the security interest. The Department of Trade and Industry also take the view that the Secretary of State's consent is required before a bank can assign its rights under a credit agreement which is secured on a licence. This may not in all cases be a correct interpretation.

(ii) *Joint operating and similar agreements.* Whilst the licence gives the licensees the right as against the Crown to extract petroleum, their rights *inter se* (as "participants") are regulated in a joint operating agreement (or "JOA"). It is really this agreement rather than the licence which gives a licensee an identifiable source of segregated cash flow. JOAs operate on a system of "cash calls" — one of the parties (the "operator")

---

[50] See, *e.g.*, Clause 42 of the 1988 Model Clauses.
[51] See, *e.g.*, Clause 41 of the 1988 Model Clauses.

regularly calls for the other parties to pay to him their respective shares of the expenditure that he has incurred or (more usually) will incur over a specified period. JOAs do not usually contain provisions terminating a particular party's rights on an insolvency or upon a receiver being appointed. Instead, if a party does not meet his share of a cash call, his right to receive petroleum will (after the giving of various notices and the expiry of certain periods) either be forfeited or scaled down. The other participants have to meet their respective shares of the amount of any cash call not paid by a defaulting participant and any failure to meet this additional amount will be a default by them. If they do meet their obligations in relation to the additional amount, however, they have a claim for reimbursement from the defaulting participant. JOAs usually contain restrictions on assignment and, whereas the more modern form of JOAs expressly permit assignments by way of security, older versions do not.

The percentage of each cash call which a participant must contribute is the same as the percentage of petroleum to which he is entitled and the percentage vote which he has on the committee (the "operating committee") which effectively oversees the operator. This percentage is generally referred to as the "participation percentage". All participants are represented on the operating committee.

(b) *Security in the North Sea.* The problem with security over a company's interest in an oil or gas field in the United Kingdom sector of the North Sea is that it is precisely that: it is security over one company's interest alone. It is not security over minerals in the ground and a lease, as in a typical North American mining transaction: it is security over one company's interest in a bundle of contractual rights. The most important rights in the bundle are, of course, the company's rights under the United Kingdom petroleum production licence and the JOA. As with any form of security over contractual rights (as opposed to tangible assets), the worth of the security is heavily dependent on the nature of the contractual rights themselves. Are the rights capable of termination if security is enforced, for example, or if the company giving the security becomes insolvent? Does a bank with security have to continue to meet the borrower's share of cash calls on an enforcement in order to preserve the value of the security?[52]

---

[52] The answer to this question is yes.

As noted above, a licensee wishing to give security over his interest in a licence requires the Secretary of State's consent. The Secretary of State will not give the lenders any comfort in relation to his power to revoke the licence in accordance with the terms of the Model Clauses and lenders are therefore faced with the proposition that the Secretary of State can theoretically revoke the licence if they appoint a receiver. The other participants are similarly concerned to protect their position: security cannot put the lender in a better position as against the other participants and such participants' rights (*e.g.* for reimbursement) on a default by the company giving the security must rank ahead of the lenders' claims. These concerns are usually translated into conditions of any consent the other participants give to security over a participant's interest under a JOA. If their consent is not required (see (a)(ii) above), these conditions are usually included in the assignment clause in the JOA.

Direct agreements[53] are rarely entered into by participants in the North Sea. In other areas (such as electricity projects) the banks are usually financing the whole project and all of the commercial parties involved accept that the project will not proceed if the banks are not happy. The deal history in the North Sea is usually quite different — the JOAs and other agreements are negotiated at a time when the relevant acreage is speculative and no particular development is in mind. Banks at this stage are far from the scene and participants often resent subsequently reopening agreements they thought were done and dusted. The Secretary of State used to give certain assurances (similar in some ways to those found in direct agreements) to banks financing a participant's share of the development costs of a North Sea field but these were done away with in the course of the second Thatcher administration on the basis that the banks should rely instead on the history of the government's involvement in the North Sea.

Bearing in mind the comments in (a)(i)(c) above, the present position with regard to security in the North Sea can probably be summarised as follows:

> (i) The Secretary of State's consent is required for a bank to take a fixed charge over a participant's interest in a United Kingdom licence. (The Department of Trade and Industry takes the view that his consent is not required for a floating charge until it crystallises, but this may not be correct in law.) The bank will receive a bare consent and no assurances or undertakings from

---

[53] See section 6.4.

the Secretary of State whatsoever. A further consent will be needed from the Secretary of State if the bank wishes to enforce its security.

(ii) Whether the other participants' consent is required for a fixed charge over the borrower's rights under the JOA will depend upon the wording of the JOA's assignment clause. If it expressly allows a fixed charge or assignment by way of security, then, subject to the wording of the particular provision, a bank need not go further. If the JOA is silent on the issue of security but requires all of the other participants to consent to an assignment of another participant's interest, then the most that a bank can obtain by way of security without the other participants' consent will probably be a charge on the proceeds of any moneys paid under the JOA to or to the order of the borrower. (As explained in section 4.4, the problem with a charge on proceeds is that it is only of value if proceeds are generated. Banks usually feel a need to control the means of production and not just the production itself!)

(iii) Where the other participants' consent is needed for a charge, the terms of the consent are subject to negotiation between the bank or banks involved and the participants in question. The banks will want to try to get the other participants to give them notice of any default by the borrower under the JOA (so that they can themselves take remedial action if necessary) and will want to try to get the ability to operate the borrower's interest only for so long as they want to. The participants will want to try to lock in the banks on an enforcement as much as possible and to prevent the banks taking the benefits of the borrower's interest without the burden (*e.g.* liabilities in relation to abandonment).

(iv) Whether or not any particular JOA requires the other participants' consent before a fixed charge can be taken, a bank will have to accept that (in the absence of some truly exceptional provisions in a direct agreement or consent) the other participants' pre-emption rights will apply to any purported disposal of the borrower's interest by the banks or their receiver on an enforcement. The Secretary of State's consent will also be required for any such disposal.

Given that security in North Sea transactions is so hedged about with qualifications but is nevertheless frequently taken, it can be

seen as a classic instance of security being taken for defensive
reasons and in order to control the assets the subject of the security
on an enforcement.

A few further issues relating to security in the North Sea merit
consideration:

(a) *Is it possible to take security over a licence only in so far as it
relates to a particular field?* A licence area usually contains
one or more blocks (which may be contiguous but
usually are not) and a block may contain more than one
field. If a licensee cannot offer security over its interest
in different fields to different banks because its interest
in the licence cannot be divided up, it is faced with the
prospect of being restricted to the same bank or banks
for financing its interests in each field in the licence
area or of over-securing its bankers. Both prospects are
equally unappealing.

Nevertheless, when the question was originally raised
in the North Sea, doubts were expressed as to whether
or not the licence was divisible and, if it was, whether
or not those contractual rights which were charged
could be distinguished from those which were not. A
solution was eventually found using a trust: a borrower's interest in a licence would be put into trust and
that part of the beneficial interest which related to the
field to be financed could be charged in favour of the
prospective lender or lenders and the rest of the
beneficial interest could be held on trust back to the
borrower.

There must be some doubt, however, as to whether
or not this rather elaborate mechanism is really necessary. The Secretary of State has in the past given
consent on number of occasions to a charge which has
been expressed to be limited to that part of a licence
which relates to a specific field. If the person who
grants a contractual right (in this case the Secretary of
State) accepts that a right (a licence) is divisible, then
at the very least he should be estopped from denying
that it is divisible. Furthermore, if there are problems
with identifying rights sufficiently insofar as limiting
the scope of a charge is concerned, why do these
problems not apply equally to defining part of a beneficial interest behind a trust? There are admittedly
problems with allowing competing security interests

259

over the same assets and there is legitimate concern with issues such as two different receivers competing for the same computer program and default by the borrower in performing the terms of the licence in relation to field A meaning that the Secretary of State can theoretically revoke the licence in its entirety, even in relation to field B. However, it is submitted that these are problems which go to the practical working out and protection of security, not to the issue of whether or not a charge limited to one field is conceptually possible to begin with.

(b) *Can a borrower charge only part of his interest in a field?* This issue can arise when, for example, a company arranges limited recourse financing to acquire its original interest in a field and then wishes to arrange additional financing, from different banks, to acquire a further interest it is offered by virtue of its pre-emption rights when another participant in the field decides to sell up. It is easier to have sympathy in this sort of case with arguments along the lines that, if it is impossible to say with certainty which part of the borrower's interest is charged to which banks, both security interests may fail. There is, however, probably a greater reason for caution in this type of case in any event: unlike the case in (a) above, there will be one revenue stream and having two sets of lenders with separate but equal ranking security interests could be a recipe for confusion and disaster and a form of mechanism should be put in place to ensure an orderly application of revenues on the enforcement of the security by either or both sets of lenders. So long as this is appreciated, the manner in which security over the interest is taken (*i.e.* whether or not behind a trust) is probably of secondary significance although, in this type of case, a trust is in practice usually used.

(c) *Why does security sometimes have to be taken under Scots law?* On general principles, English law will probably allow a lender to take security over an asset anywhere in the world so long as there is evidence of an intention to create a security interest, the creation of a security interest over that asset is permitted under the laws of the place where it is located (*e.g.* it is not contrary to public policy) and the English rules on perfection (such as registration and other procedures designed to put third parties on notice) are complied with. However, as a matter of obvious prudence, security in order to be secure should be perfected in the place where the relevant asset is located and where any enforcement proceedings may have to be launched and in any place where a serious challenge to its validity might be mounted. Bank security documentation for fields in what can loosely be described as "Scottish waters" usually includes a Scottish assignation of the borrower's rights under the licence and the JOA and the other contractual agreements because, if proceedings were brought by a third party before a Scottish court, the court would not recognise a fixed charge over contractual rights because the concept of a fixed charge does not exist under Scots law.[54]

10.3 ELECTRICITY PROJECTS IN THE UNITED KINGDOM

(a) *The electricity industry.* The enabling legislation for the privatisation of the electricity industry in England and Wales in 1990/91 was the Electricity Act 1989. One of the United Kingdom government's stated objectives in the privatisation was the creation of competition in electricity generation and supply. The generating businesses were transferred to two new generating companies, National Power PLC and PowerGen plc, and the supply businesses and local distribution businesses were transferred to 12 new regional electricity companies ("RECs"). Shares of the generating companies and the RECs were floated on the London Stock Exchange. Whilst the nuclear power plants were originally retained in state ownership, they too were finally floated (under the name British Energy plc) on the London Stock Exchange in 1996.

It was not physically practical to introduce competition into national or local transmission of electricity and these remain monopolies. National transmission is undertaken by The National Grid Company plc ("NGC") which owns the United Kingdom bulk supply network (the "Grid"), while regional distribution is undertaken by the RECs. Transmission charges are regulated, however.

---

[54] Although the practice of taking a Scottish assignation survives, Scots lawyers have doubts as to whether it is really effective under Scots law if the assignee (the bank) does not take immediate possession of the rights the subject of the assignation (which is clearly not practicable and is not done).

NGC was originally owned by the 12 RECs but it has now also been floated.

The most innovative feature of the privatisation was the creation of an electricity "pool". Electricity cannot be stored and the pool is a purely metaphysical concept. The objectives of the pool are to match supply and demand while preserving the ability to dispatch the cheapest energy. The pool and the related payment settlement system are operated by NGC acting as an intermediary and not as a principal. All major generators and distributors are required to become members of the pool. A pool member must sell all of his electricity through the pool and meet a proportionate part of the costs of operating the pool and the payment settlement system. Through a system of half-hourly bidding from generators, NGC establishes prices for electricity by reference to forecast demand from large industrial customers and the RECs. In simple terms, NGC works out a "merit order" of the bids and matches supply with demand starting with the cheapest bid. The highest bid price that must be accepted to meet anticipated demand in each half-hour period (the "System Marginal Price") becomes the basic component of the price (the "pool input price" or "pip") paid to *all* generators for generation in that period. It is also the basis of the price charged to the RECs and other consumers (the "pool output price" or "pop"), although this price also includes an uplift element related to various additional costs borne and payments made by the pool.

(b) *Project financing post-privatisation.* The Electricity Act 1989 not only privatised the then existing state-owned electricity industry but it also permitted new entrants to the market who could apply for generating licences to construct new generating capacity which would compete with National Power and PowerGen. A number of independent power projects have been completed since the early 1990s with the bulk of the funds being provided by limited recourse bank financing. Until very recently, the pool price was considered to be too volatile a mechanism for lenders to rely upon as a secure revenue stream to service the relevant project company's debt and the pool price risk was therefore usually hedged by the project company entering into one or more CfDs to stabilise the electricity price receipts. At its simplest, the counterparty to a CfD will pay the project company the amount by which the pool price falls short of an agreed "strike price", thus guaranteeing the project a minimum revenue stream. In return, the counterparty receives from the project company the amount by which the pool price exceeds the agreed strike price. The strike price is typically a contract charge calculated in the manner described in section 3.11. The counterparties to these CfDs were generally RECs (who used CfDs with generators to hedge their exposure to pool price fluctuations against their obligations to supply customers at fixed prices). As noted in section 3.12, however, the markets have recently seen a move away from project financings based on CfDs for 100 per cent of a project's output.

A number of the limited recourse generating projects which banks have financed in the United Kingdom to date use alternatives to coal or gas as their fuel source. It is generally more expensive to generate electricity using these alternative sources but these non-fossil fuel projects, such as wind or waste, have been facilitated by the statutory obligation that has been placed on the RECs[55] to secure a minimum amount of non-fossil fuel generating capacity and by the fossil fuel levy imposed on the RECs.[56] The pool price risk for a project included in a Non-Fossil Fuel Order[57] issued by the Secretary of State is eliminated for a specified period by the Non-Fossil Purchasing Agency entering into a simple form of CfD at a fixed strike price subsidised by the fossil fuel levy.

10.4 CO-GENERATION PROJECTS

Co-generation projects are power projects where energy is produced in the form of steam for a steam purchaser and in the form of electrical power for a power purchaser. The power plant will contain at least one steam turbine and steam can effectively be bled off at various stages within the steam turbine in order to supply the steam purchaser with high, medium or low pressure steam. The less steam that is bled off, the greater the amount of electrical power that the steam turbine can produce.

The driving force behind a co-generation project is very often the steam purchaser. Co-generation may be a cheaper or more environmentally-friendly way for steam to be produced to satisfy the needs of the steam purchaser's plant (usually a refinery or other large industrial complex). It is important to bear this in mind, because, for the steam purchaser, production of electrical power is often seen as a by-product. If the co-generation project is to be project-financed — as such projects invariably are — this is likely to be the diametrically opposite view of the project finance banks, who will see the production and sale of electrical power as their main

---

[55] By s.32 of the Electricity Act 1989.
[56] See s.33 of the Electricity Act 1989.
[57] Made pursuant to s.32 of the Electricity Act 1989.

source of repayment. When one also considers that the usual arrangement with regard to land is that the power plant is built on land either totally surrounded by the steam purchaser's plant or at least adjacent to it (and that such land is usually only the subject of a lease), the scene is set for some intricate and potentially difficult negotiations.

A steam purchaser's objectives can probably be summed up in the phrase "security of supply". He wants to be sure that, in the normal course, the project company will supply him with the quantities of steam he requires as and when he requires them and that, if it does not, he has a fallback solution to ensure deliveries of steam to his plant. The objectives of the project company are different: it will usually be highly dependent on the steam purchaser for certain key utilities (such as demineralised water) and will be mainly concerned to ensure that these are provided as and when necessary by its steam "host". (The phrases "steam purchaser" and "steam host" are used more or less interchangeably.)

The issues that usually arise for the steam purchaser are as follows:

(a) *What remedies can it have against the project company for failure to supply steam?* The most draconian remedy is to terminate the lease of the land on which the power plant is built, but, as this may mean that the power plant itself becomes the property of the steam purchaser for no consideration, this is unlikely to prove popular with either the project company's shareholders or its banks. A steam purchaser would be lucky to retain such a right without having at least to pay off the banks in full.

A steam purchaser could simply seek to retain its normal rights to sue the project company for damages at large for breach of its obligation to supply steam, but this would run counter to the banks' project financing philosophy which seeks to avoid any project finance borrower being left exposed to open and unquantifiable claims. The banks would have particular problems with any potential claims that the steam purchaser might have for loss of profit or other consequential loss.[58]

For the above reasons, the normal remedy for failure to supply steam is a right to claim liquidated damages which are subject to a cap and which are expressed to be the only remedy that the steam purchaser has for failure to supply steam. The liquidated damages are usually set at a level which is sufficiently high to deter the project company *deliberately* diverting steam away from the steam purchaser in order to generate more electrical revenues.

---

[58] See section 4.1.

(b) *Can the steam purchaser have "step-in" rights?* There is nothing in theory to stop a steam purchaser having "step-in" rights to run the power plant himself in the event of a failure by the project company to supply steam but this is in practice seldom done. There are various reasons for this, including the necessity of coming to a satisfactory agreement with the project company's banks dealing with such a possibility, the possible liabilities that would attach to a steam purchaser who exercised such rights and the fact that steam purchasers are usually not competent to run power plants. A steam purchaser who is genuinely concerned about the ability of the project company to provide his steam requirements in all circumstances is well advised to retain a serious back-up source of steam. Some back-up supply capability will be needed in any event to cope with maintenance of the steam turbine.

(c) *Who should operate the power plant?* It is tempting for a steam purchaser to think that he can be master of his own destiny and forestall any failure on the part of the project company to provide him with steam if he insists that the power plant is operated by his personnel. The power plant is, after all, within or next to his existing plant. This is, however, another siren song since his personnel are unlikely to be trained in the operation of power plants and, even if use of the steam purchaser's personnel were to be accepted by the banks, the banks would insist on the steam purchaser remaining liable for their acts. This could place far more potential recourse at the steam purchaser's door than any notional gain in security of supply could justify.

(d) *What obligations should the steam purchaser accept with regard to the upgrading of common facilities?* Although a steam purchaser's natural inclination would be simply to carry out any upgrading necessary without any particularly detailed contractual arrangements with the project company, the banks providing project finance to the project company are likely to insist that any major works are the subject of a contract which sets out matters such as guaranteed flowrates, a specified time for completion and liquidated damages for failure to achieve completion by the time specified.

(e) *What priority arrangements should exist with regard to the use of common facilities?* This is one of the most delicate areas of negotiation, particularly since it will often be cost effective for the power plant to share the use of certain systems (*e.g.* blow-down flares) which the host refinery already has rather than to build its own. There is no easy answer to this problem in the documentation. Whilst it is easy to say that whichever of the steam purchaser or the project company is experiencing an emergency should have priority

265

over the person who is not, there is no way of resolving in the documentation any conflict which might arise if both are experiencing an emergency. The conflict is therefore probably best resolved through design or engineering solutions.

(f) *Can the steam purchaser's plant be affected by breaches of environmental consents by the project company and vice versa?* The problem here would arise if, for example, the authorities regarded the power plant — although in different ownership (as it almost certainly would be) — as merely an extension of the steam purchaser's refinery for licensing purposes so that the power plant and the refinery shared (for example) one overall umbrella emissions limit. The potential problems of cross-liability in this type of situation would be so great, however, that it is doubtful that such a licensing position would be a bankable proposition without significant mitigating circumstances (*e.g.* a generous emissions limit which provided a certain amount of latitude).

The issues that usually arise for the project company in addition to those set out above are as follows:

(i) *Can it negotiate a satisfactory take-or-pay obligation for the steam?* This is, of course, a purely commercial and financial matter, but, depending on the price being paid for the steam and the project's economics, the project company may not actually want a take-or-pay obligation — it may want the ability simply to use any steam not taken to produce more electricity. Take-or-pay arrangements, with their "make up" quantities, may well limit the project company's flexibility in this respect.

(ii) *Can it prevent the steam purchaser taking such excessive quantities of steam that the revenues from the sale of electricity are severely reduced?* This is, of course, in many ways the converse of the steam purchaser's concern in (a) above that the project company will divert steam to the steam turbine to generate electricity. The engineering and control systems of some projects are set up so that the steam purchaser directly controls his own offtake of steam. In these circumstances, the steam supply agreement needs to have either some financial penalties to prevent excessive steam offtake by the steam purchaser or a compensation mechanism whereby the project company is indemnified against loss of electricity revenues. (There is often an imbalance because the steam purchaser will pay a lower price for the steam than the revenue the steam could produce if it was used to generate electricity.)

266

(iii) *Can it exercise "self-help" remedies if the steam host fails to carry out his obligations (e.g. with regard to the upgrading of facilities)?* "Self-help" remedies are the right to enter onto the steam host's land to carry out the steam host's obligations should the steam host fail to do so. They are an important remedy, although they are likely only to be used as a last resort. Many of the problems that would arise in practice in implementing such a remedy are similar to those referred to in (b) above. Whilst it is tempting to believe that the problems are of a lesser degree for the project company in these circumstances, it is unlikely that its management would relish the prospect of (for example) disconnecting the electricity supply to part of the refinery in order to make an essential connection to the power plant.

(iv) *Is it assured of a continual and reliable supply of utilities from the steam host?* This is, of course, the same concern with continuity of supply that preoccupies a steam purchaser. Similar considerations apply and the project company should primarily seek comfort in extracting a level of liquidated damages from the steam host for failure to supply.

(v) *Does it have all necessary rights of access to the proposed power plant site and all necessary rights of throughput (e.g. for waste water) through the steam host's pipes and culverts?* This, of course, is something the banks will be extremely concerned about. The access rights required are many and varied and may range from the right for the construction contractor to bring his plant over the steam host's land onto the power plant site during the construction phase to the right to bring tankers carrying gas oil over the steam host's land onto the power plant site during the operational phase. The project company will probably also require rights over the steam host's land for the high voltage power lines connecting the power plant to the national grid. The project company should insist upon rights *in rem* (such as easements or servitudes) and not just contractual rights in order to protect itself against the steam host's bankruptcy.

(vi) *Will the steam host indemnify it against any liability it incurs as a result of pre-existing contamination on the site?* The usual (although not invariable) position is that, where the site of the proposed power plant used to be owned by the steam host, the steam host will be responsible for such contamination.

In addition, it may be possible to achieve certain savings on insurance premia if the steam host and the project company take

267

out a combined insurance package. It may also allow them to obtain loss of profits cover in circumstances where, under conventional separate policies, this would not be possible. The key to this last point is that, as noted in Chapter 7, insurers will only write loss of profits cover consequential upon physical damage because their control over the manner of reinstatement allows them to control their losses under the loss of profits head. If the same insurers cover the construction work on the refinery site upgrading facilities and the main construction work on the power plant site, then they may be prepared, for example, to provide loss of profits cover to the project company consequential upon damage during construction to the refinery's facilities which are being upgraded. A combined insurance package does have drawbacks, however. The banks will need persuading that a breach of conditions by the steam host will not invalidate the project company's insurance cover, deductibles will need to be fairly dealt with and the insurers will have to waive subrogation rights against the steam host and the project company. A mutual waiver of claims allows premiums to be saved because neither the steam host nor the project company needs to take out (substantial) third party liability cover to cover claims from the other for damage caused to that other's property. Each party must, in such circumstances, rely on its own (first party) physical damage cover.

Both the steam host and the project company will also have an interest in trying to co-ordinate the maintenance of their respective facilities so that they are shut down at the same time.

10.5 BRIDGES AND ROADS

The PFI has now seen a number of transport infrastructure projects brought to financial close. Before the PFI was conceived, however, Parliament passed The New Roads and Street Works Act 1991. This Act sets out, *inter alia*, a legislative framework for private concerns to be granted concessions to construct and operate new roads in the United Kingdom and to charge tolls. The Act is essentially an enabling measure allowing for the detail of each particular scheme to be addressed in a concession agreement and in statutory instruments. A statutory instrument authorising the charging of tolls by the holder of a concession can only specify maximum tolls if the road in question consists of or includes a major crossing to which there is no reasonably convenient alternative.

268

Although still in force, the Act was not used as the legislative basis of the PFI's DBFO road schemes. The government considered that it had sufficient powers under other more general legislation (including the Deregulation and Contracting Out Act 1994[59]) upon which to base those schemes given that they involved the payment of shadow tolls by the government rather than the payment of actual tolls by users.

10.6 CABLE TELEVISION

The two main licences required to operate a cable television and telephony system in the United Kingdom are licences under the Broadcasting Act 1990[60] and Telecommunications Act 1984. A licence is also required under the Wireless Telegraphy Act 1949 where the system uses radio to distribute its services (*e.g.* by microwave video distribution ("MVDS")).

The licence under the Telecommunications Act (the "telecommunications licence") is issued by the Secretary of State for Trade and Industry and permits the holder to operate a system over which he provides television and telecommunications services. It also authorises the holder to connect his own system to other telecommunications systems. The telecommunications licence is granted in relation to a particular area (the cable franchise) but it is not exclusive so far as the supply of telephony and other telecommunication services are concerned. So far as entertainment services are concerned, under current regulations, apart from video-on-demand services, the telecommunications licence gives the cable operator, in conjunction with the licence issued under the Broadcasting Act, in effect a local monopoly in the provision of broadcast entertainment services by cable or MVDS in his franchise area. Holders of telecommunications licences are regulated by the Director General of Telecommunications (the "Director General") who heads the Office of Telecommunications ("OFTEL"). Telecommunications licences issued in connection with the construction of a cable television network in franchises awarded prior to the Broadcasting Act 1990 include obligations to construct the system to

---

[59] See, in this connection, the Contracting Out (Highway Functions) Order 1995 (S.I. 1995/1986).
[60] A licence under the Broadcasting Act is only required if a cable service (carrying more than just the terrestrial television channels or a sound-only service) is to be provided to more than 1,000 homes: Broadcasting Act 1990, s.72(1)(b) and The Broadcasting (Local Delivery Services) Order 1990 (S.I. 90/2389).

stated specifications in accordance with a timetable and these "build obligations" can be enforced by the Director General. In the case of franchises awarded under the Broadcasting Act 1990, the "build obligations" are included in the local delivery licence issued under that Act rather than in the telecommunications licence. Failure to comply with a build obligation (or other conditions in the licence) can ultimately result in a revocation of the telecommunications or local delivery licence (as the case may be). Telecommunications licences are generally issued so as to run in parallel with the licence issued under the Broadcasting Act and are not transferable.

The licence under the Broadcasting Act (the "local delivery licence") is issued by the Independent Television Commission (the "ITC") and permits a person to provide (in this case) cable television services on an exclusive basis (under current ITC policy) in a particular franchise area.[61] Local delivery licences are only transferable with the prior consent of the ITC. The ITC also regulates the holders of local delivery licences. Local delivery licences under the Broadcasting Act are issued for periods of 15 years with the possibility of a renewal for further periods of 15 years (subject to agreement with the ITC on the amount of the annual fees which are payable under the licences and which comprise both a "cash bid" payment and a percentage of cable television revenue).

One of the main attractions of the cable market in the United Kingdom is the ability of cable operators to provide telephone and other telecommunications services over their networks and not simply television. To do this effectively, cable operators need to be able to connect with the systems operated by the national public telephone operators (BT and Mercury). In general terms, each public telephone operator (which includes cable operators in neighbouring franchise areas) is required[62] to negotiate and agree an interconnection agreement with any other public telephone operator who requests such an agreement and the Director General can intervene and determine the material terms of an interconnection if one party thinks the other is being unreasonable in failing to agree such terms.

---

[61] Most of the existing cable operators, however, have cable television licences (the precursors to local delivery licences) issued under the Cable and Broadcasting Act 1984 which have continued in force under transitional provisions contained in the Broadcasting Act 1990. These differ from new local delivery licences under the Broadcasting Act 1990 in certain respects (*e.g.* they are not "technology neutral" (*i.e.* they do not authorise the use of radio as a means of distribution) and no annual "cash bid" and percentage of cable television revenue payments are required to be made to the ITC by their holders)).

[62] By the conditions of its telecommunications licence.

270

10.7 SATELLITES

A satellite project has various complex stages of authorisation. The main authorisations will be for the launch of the satellite and its positioning in outer space, the transmission of signals to and the reception of signals from the satellite and the use of those signals in any form of broadcasting or telecommunications network. Much of the above is subject to international conventions due to the obvious cross-border implications of satellites.[63] In addition, where a satellite is being manufactured in one country for use by persons in another country, an export licence will usually be required.

There are four main Acts governing the use of satellites in the United Kingdom:

(a) *The Outer Space Act 1986.* This Act applies to bodies incorporated in any part of the United Kingdom and stipulates that such bodies cannot (anywhere in the world) launch or operate a space object or carry out any activity in outer space without a licence from the Secretary of State.

(b) *The Telecommunications Act 1984.* Under this Act, it is a criminal offence to run a telecommunications system in the United Kingdom without a licence granted under the Act and to connect an unlicensed system to a licensed system. A telecommunications system for these purposes includes an orbiting satellite, an earth station and the up-down link between a satellite and an earth station.

(c) *The Wireless Telegraphy Act 1949.* The use of radio frequencies has to be authorised under this Act. (One of the main objectives of the Act when it was passed was to control radio interference.) If a permanent earth station becomes licensed under the Act, international co-ordination procedures provide it with a degree of international protection against interference from competing signals.

(d) *The Broadcasting Act 1990.* This Act governs the provision of television and radio services (as opposed to telecommunications services) by satellite. Providers of satellite television and radio services in the United Kingdom need a licence issued under this Act. A project company owning and operating a satellite which

---

[63] See the Constitution and Convention of the International Telecommunication Union (the "ITU").

merely leased out transponders for others to use for the provision of a satellite television or radio service would not need such a licence, however (on the basis that it was merely the conduit through which others provided such a service).

A licensing system along the lines of the United Kingdom model has been, or is being, adopted by a number of other countries. The United States and Australian models are also popular templates for other countries.

The main contracts required to get a satellite into orbit are a construction (or manufacturing or supply) contract and a launch services contract. The issues arising under the construction contract are essentially the same as those arising under the construction contract for any other type of project (see sections 3.6 and 4.3(d)), although the negotiation over the level of delay liquidated damages is likely to be particularly sensitive since, once the originally designated launch window is missed, there may be considerable delay before another is allocated. If the in-orbit commissioning tests reveal that not all of the transponders are fully operational, there will also be a form of "buy-down" through performance liquidated damages or a form of price rebate. A key concept in a satellite construction contract is "intentional ignition": once intentional ignition occurs, the risk of loss passes from the contractor to the employer (*i.e.* the project company). A launch services contract will also contain liquidated damages clauses and intentional ignition is again a key concept: the launch services contractor usually disclaims responsibility for the operation of the satellite after intentional ignition.

Chapter 11

Current Trends

11.1 THE CAPITAL MARKETS; PROJECT BONDS

In recent years, attention has focused on the possibility of raising finance for projects on the capital markets (as opposed to the bank markets). The attractions of doing so are perceived to be the following:

(a) The capital markets represent a new source of funds for projects. When money is tight in the bank markets, tapping the capital markets might be the only way of financing a project.

(b) Interest rates may be lower or fixed.

(c) Maturities may be longer.

(d) The capital markets generally require fewer representations and warranties, covenants and events of default than banks and those representations and warranties, covenants and events of default that there are tend to be less "hair-trigger" than covenants in typical bank documentation and cover more fundamental issues. This is partly due to the fact that the type of investor in the capital markets does not have the staff that commercial banks have to monitor the progress of projects. It is also due to the fact that the banks' representations and warranties, covenants and events of default are designed to enable them to force borrowers to the negotiating table at an early stage whereas calling bondholder meetings is cumbersome and such meetings should therefore only be convened as and when strictly necessary.

(e) Investors on the capital markets are likely to be more passive than banks if a project encounters difficulties. This

273

belief is based on the logistical difficulties of summoning bondholder meetings and the history of poor attendance at those meetings. The belief may now be a fallacious one with the advent in the late 1980s of the so-called "vulture funds" which deliberately purchase distressed debt with a view to exploiting what they consider to be the bondholders' hidden power: if a debt restructuring requires all of a company's creditors' consent, there may be a price to pay to obtain consent from its bondholders.

The United States has recently led the way in tapping its capital markets for funds for projects and a number of project-related issues have been done under the Securities and Exchange Commission's Rule 144A (a rule, adopted in 1989, which eases the Securities and Exchange Commission's requirements for sales to sophisticated investors). There are signs that the United Kingdom markets are now also mobilising in order to arrange and underwrite project bonds. Recent sterling issues include the bonds financing the Lewisham extension to the Docklands Light Railway in London, those financing, *inter alia*, the A1(M) and M6 DBFO road schemes and those financing Enron's IPP at Sutton Bridge in Lincolnshire.[1] Early United Kingdom examples include the index-linked debenture stock issued for the Second Severn Crossing[2] and, the Debenture Stock issued in connection with the Kilroot power plant in Northern Ireland.[3]

The capital markets are conservative by nature and, until recently, it was considered difficult to get investors in those markets to accept completion risk in a project. Even this attitude appears now to be slowly changing (in both the United States and the United Kingdom[4]). However, where bondholders do not wish to take completion risk, this risk can be taken away from them by banks issuing bank guarantees or standby letters of credit in their favour to cover the construction phase in a manner similar to that found in EIB financings (see section 8.4). As with any multi-source project financing, intercreditor agreements will be required (see section 5.9).

---

[1] The issuers of the bonds in the first three cases were City Greenwich Lewisham Rail Link PLC, Road Management Consolidated PLC and Autolink Concessionaires (M6) plc. The issuer of the bonds for the Sutton Bridge project was an overseas company.
[2] The prospectus for which is dated April 1, 1993
[3] The prospectus for which is dated July 14, 1994.
[4] The Lewisham extension to the Docklands Light Railway and the Sutton Bridge power project are recent examples of bonds issued in the U.K. with the bondholders taking completion risk.

Another issue for project bonds is the issue of credit rating. The higher the credit rating, the greater the number of potential investors. The prize is to obtain an "investment grade" rating (AAA, AA, A or BBB[5]) since this will enable insurance companies and pension funds to purchase the bonds.[6] One way to obtain an investment grade rating for bonds issued by a highly-geared project company in a complex and risky project is to have the bonds "credit enhanced" (or "credit-wrapped") by a so-called monoline insurance company.[7] Such an insurance company effectively lends its own credit rating to the bonds by guaranteeing the payment to the bondholders of all sums due under the bonds. The insurance company will in turn have a counterindemnity from the project company and may also itself have the benefit of guarantees or standby letters of credit issued on behalf of the project company by a bank or banks. Whether such bank guarantees or standby letters of credit need to be issued[8] will depend on the extent to which the insurance company is itself prepared to take project risk. A number of deals have been done where the bank guarantees or standby letters of credit have been released on completion. The involvment of a monoline insurance company will result in a lower interest rate on the bonds but this is offset from the project company's point of view by the need to pay the insurance company a fee.

There are some drawbacks with the use of project bonds. They include the following:

(i) A prepayment fee may be payable. This can lead to a rigid financial structure and limit the scope for refinancing a project with cheaper money (see section 11.2).

(ii) Repayment may have to be on an annuity basis. If so, a repayment profile cannot be "sculpted" to fit the project's anticipated cash flows.

(iii) Any consents or waivers required from the bondholders will take time to organise. This drawback is eliminated, however, when a monoline insurer is involved since, while his guarantee of the bonds is in place, the bondholders should be disenfranchised and the monoline insurer should exercise their votes. (This disadvantage of bonds can sometimes be exaggerated in any event. Eurotunnel cannot always elicit a swift response from its (200 plus) banks.)

---

[5] BB, B, CCC, CC and C ratings are referred to as "speculative grade".
[6] The ratings are issued by private rating agencies such as Moody's and Standard & Poors.
[7] A "monoline" insurer is an insurance company whose sole business is issuing financial guarantees or other forms of credit insurance.
[8] Or completion guarantees issued by the sponsors.

(iv) It may prove difficult to provide for a practical way in which to calculate any cover ratios included in the terms and conditions of the bonds. It is clearly impractical to call a bondholders' meeting every year in order to determine the assumptions to be input into the computer model. The solution to this problem usually involves using published data or indices or information provided by independent third parties.

(v) All of the proceeds of the bonds will usually be made available to the project company on their issue. Whilst the project company will obviously put the funds it does not immediately require on deposit, it will be out-of-pocket to the tune of the difference between the interest rate it pays on the bonds and the interest rate it receives on its deposit. This is referred to as the *negative cost of carry*.

(vi) There are likely to be extensive disclosure requirements.[9] It may be possible to obtain an exemption for particularly sensitive commercial information, however.

11.2 REFINANCINGS

As the project finance market matures, so the number of refinancings of project loans increases. There are usually compelling reasons for refinancing a project, many of which are inherent in the very nature of a project financing. Project financing comes at a cost and that cost is at its highest pre-completion. Even though the banks may have agreed to decrease their margin post-completion depending on the project's performance, the reductions will probably not be as great as those that might be available were the completed project to be taken to the market. Markets move on and banks get used to certain types of risk. This is clearly demonstrated by United Kingdom IPPs which were regarded as cutting-edge (and therefore risky) in the London market in the early 1990s even with contracts for differences. At the end of the 1990s, the London market was getting used to seeing sponsors structure United Kingdom IPPs with much reduced cover from such contracts. Other financing markets might also become available for a project, such as the United Kingdom bond market (opening up the possibility of long-term fixed interest rate money) and the United States institutional markets.

---

[9] See, in the context of the U.K., the Public Offers of Securities Regulations 1995 (in relation to bonds which are not going to be listed on the London Stock Exchange) and Chaps. 6, 23 and 25 of the Stock Exchange's Listing Rules (in relation to bonds which are to be so listed).

Project financings are also restrictive. The pre-completion phase is the period of greatest risk and the banks seek to control that risk by imposing tight conditions. With the passage of time, the project company's management usually wish to become greater masters of their own destiny.

In addition, project financings are generally viewed and analysed as financings of projects, not businesses. The project company carries out a project — that is its *raison d'être*. Its management are not meant to pursue other business opportunities and ventures: it is not their entrepreneurial skills but the project that has been subjected to months of due diligence. The conditions of the credit agreement reflect this approach and will restrict the project company from carrying on any activity other than the project: it cannot borrow or lend money (save for *de minimis* exceptions), it cannot grant any further security interests over its assets and often it cannot even enter into new contracts. For sponsors, this approach is sometimes unfortunate because, after completion, there may be substantial synergies (or tax benefits) to be obtained in combining the project with other projects or businesses. If there is another project or business that the sponsors wish to finance such as another power station on the same site, the only way to avoid impossible complexity at best and being blocked or held to ransom at worst may be to go to the market afresh with a new package.

Yet another, and potentially the most interesting, reason for refinancing is to unlock value for the sponsors. Depending on the initial equity structure of the project company, a refinancing may be capable of providing the funds with which to make a massive one-off payment to the shareholders. A moment's reflection shows how this is possible. Despite claims to the contrary, project financing is in the main very conservative. To take an example, this conservatism usually manifests itself in the average project financing of an oilfield at no less than four separate levels: first, banks will lend against proven and not probable reserves; secondly, they will apply a so-called reserve tail and ignore (say) the last 25 per cent of proven reserves to be recovered; thirdly, they will not necessarily even lend up to the beginning of the reserve tail but may actually want an earlier final maturity date; and fourthly, they will not lend against the full value of the eligible reserves, but will apply a cover ratio and typically lend only 67–75 per cent of such value. In addition, banks will usually adopt conservative views of future oil prices for the purposes of determining cover ratios as the deal progresses.

It is not difficult to see how value can be unlocked in project financings such as this. If nothing else, the further a deal proceeds after completion, the closer one gets to cashflows that were originally considered too remote to lend against. If a project can also point to a couple of years of operation above budget, the scene is set for leveraging up the project company in much more propitious circumstances than those prevailing at financial close. Not only can repayments that have already been made potentially be reborrowed, but it might also prove possible to attack the original debt:equity ratio. A ratio of 80:20 should certainly be vulnerable and, in the circumstances contemplated, so might a ratio of 85:15.

However, a way needs to be found to get the surplus cash out of the project company and into the hands of the shareholders. Paying a super-dividend requires distributable reserves. The same is usually required for redeeming share capital. Borrowing new cash gives a project company liquidity, but it does not give it distributable reserves and, in the first few years after completion, it is unlikely that the project company will have built up much in the way of distributable reserves through simply operating (since these years are the years of peak debt service). So working through a company's share capital will only produce limited opportunities for transferring cash to the shareholders. Other routes include transferring assets to the project company in return for the cash (but the sponsors will probably be reluctant to transfer new assets into what may well be a highly leveraged joint venture) and charging a fee for the provision of services of some kind.

The real solution to the problem of how to transfer surpluses to the sponsors is to plan the original financing with a possible refinancing in mind. The most robust way in which to transfer cash from the project company to the shareholders is to have the shareholders contribute a substantial portion of their equity as subordinated debt and to insist that the refinancing institutions allow a large percentage of that debt to be prepaid out of the proceeds of the refinancing. Planning ahead might also have a significant part to play in the choice of original financing medium. Prepaying banks funding on a floating rate basis should, in this day and age, be without premium or penalty, but (as noted in section 11.1) prepaying a long-dated fixed rate bond issue might involve significant financial cost.[10] The price of opting for a bond financing at financial close might well be to surrender the possibility of paying the sponsors a substantial cash sum within a few years after completion.

The final reason for wishing to refinance a project might be the wish to have a wholesale redetermination of the balance of risk in a project. Banks might be persuaded to accept a greater degree of market or price risk, for example.

---

[10] Because of penalty payments.

However, no refinancing can be successfully implemented if any of the other parties to the project have the right to prevent it. Unfortunately, this can happen in a variety of ways. The most obvious way is where the project company operates under a concession, since the person granting the concession may well have retained some control over the contracts that the project company executes (see section 3.5 above). If the test in a concession agreement is that the original financing documents may be amended only if they do not materially affect the financial ability of the project company, who is to say that reducing the debt:equity ratio from 80:20 to 85:15 will not do this? Furthermore, if the person granting the concession can be required to assume responsibility for or discharge the bank debt in certain circumstances (such as prolonged *force majeure*), the concession agreement usually states that any change in the original financing documents must not increase his liability. But a refinancing almost certainly — if not inevitably — would. There are other, more subtle traps: will any new financing institutions have the benefit of any comfort letters that were originally given or can the persons who originally gave them be compelled or persuaded to issue new comfort letters, this time in favour of the new financiers? Compulsion is rarely provided for and persuasion is usually futile since the comfort letters were usually only given under protest in order for the original deal to complete. The security arrangements can also pose problems: if the security was originally granted to and vested in a bank which will not participate in the refinancing, can the security be transferred to a new security agent and, if so, at what cost in terms of stamp duties, notarial fees and registration costs? This last type of problem is generally more of an issue in civil law jurisdictions than in common law ones.

11.3 SECURITISATION

Securitisation of project receivables is not yet a current trend but the speed with which securitisation has been taken up in other sectors indicates that it might soon be.

(a) *What is securitisation?* The term "securitisation" is very elastic, but for our purposes it means the sale by one person (the "originator") of receiveables to a special purpose vehicle (the "SPV") which pays the purchase price for such sale out of the proceeds of a public note or public bond issue secured on those receiveables. A securitisation therefore provides an originator with immediate cash raised indirectly from the public bond markets. The SPV is usually an "orphan company" — it is not owned or controlled by the originator and will not need to be consolidated with the originator for accounting purposes. The shares in SPVs are in fact often owned by charitable trusts.

There are various reasons for securitising: an industrial company may simply need cash now rather than later; a bank may need to "free up its balance sheet" (by securitising part of its loan portfolio) in order to lend new money in more lucrative areas. An originator who is too highly geared can, of course, use securisation to effectively move part of his borrowings off balance sheet (by using the proceeds of the securitisation to repay some of those borrowings).

(b) *Bankruptcy-remoteness.* Because the SPV's notes are issued into the public bond markets, the SPV and, to a certain extent, the transaction as a whole have to be made "bankruptcy-remote". An important aspect of bankruptcy-remoteness is to ensure remoteness from any risks associated with the *originator's* insolvency. In addition, various types of credit enhancement and other support may have to be offered in order to obtain a rating for the notes from one of the credit rating agencies. Making an SPV bankruptcy-remote might involve, inter alia, arranging for a standby (and subordinated) loan facility to be made available to the SPV to fund any cash shortfalls. Credit enhancement may, in an extreme case, require a bank or financial institution which is rated AAA to guarantee all or part of the notes (as in the case of project bonds (see above)).

(c) *Structural issues and risks.* These can best be explained by looking at a hypothetical example. For our purposes, let us suppose that the originator is an oil company with an interest in a producing gas field in the United Kingdom sector of the North Sea which has sold its share of the gas produced to a United Kingdom power plant under a long-term take-or-pay gas sales agreement. The oil company wishes to securitise its string of receiveables arising under that contract in order to repay the loans it originally borrowed to finance its share of the development costs of the field, to reduce its gearing and to fund further exploration and appraisal expenditure. Some of the more important issues and risks involved in such a proposal are as follows:

(i) *What should be sold to the SPV?* Ideally, the SPV should be sold not only the receiveables, but also the originator's participating interest in the field in order to make the transaction remote from the originator's bankruptcy. The receiveables are contingent future receiveables, dependent on continued production of gas — if the originator retains the participating interest and goes into liquidation, there is a high risk that the SPV's receiveables simply dry up. However, a transfer of the participating interest to the SPV would require the consent of the Department of Trade and Industry who would insist on the SPV having sufficient technical and financial resources to carry out its obligations and who might not grant consent in any event. In addition, a transfer of the participating interest to the SPV would result in the SPV having potentially very onerous long-term liabilities (*e.g.* in relation to the eventual abandonment of the field).

If the participating interest is left with the originator, it may be possible to obtain some protection against the originator's possible liquidation by taking some form of security over the participating interest in question, although it is difficult to see what would be secured. One solution might be to have the originator undertake to the SPV to continue to perform under the gas sales agreement and to secure performance of that undertaking. Security for performance as opposed to payment undertakings is a difficult concept, however, and may only result in providing security for a damages claim.

(ii) *Could the original sale of assets to the SPV be attacked on the originator's insolvency?* This is an important part of the process of making the transaction bankruptcy-remote. The main concern is that the sale could constitute a transaction at an undervalue or a preference under sections 238 and 239 respectively of the Insolvency Act 1986 and so be liable to be set aside on a liquidation or administration of the originator. The only way to avoid this risk is to ensure that the original sale is a true sale for full value.

(iii) *How can the performance risk be mitigated?* The main performance risk is the risk that, for whatever reason, gas is not capable of being produced and delivered to the power plant. Whilst this is to some extent connected with the issue in (i) above, this could also arise for matters unrelated to a possible liquidation of the originator. Even if the participating interest is transferred to the SPV, the SPV may not (and probably will not) be the operator of the field and it may be the operator who causes the problem or the SPV may lose its entitlement to gas by defaulting on a cash call by reason of bad management or lack of funds. It is difficult to see how the risk on the operator could realistically be mitigated and the position is probably that, if there is lack of faith in the operator's ability to perform, a securitisation is not possible. However, the risk of bad management by the SPV could be mitigated by a competent third party agreeing to act as a "standby manager" and the risk of the SPV running out of funds could be mitigated (at least in the short term) by arranging (at a price) for a commercial bank to provide the SPV with a standby subordinated loan facility.

(iv) *How can the originator extract profits?* The originator will not wish to see all of his "upside" transferred to the SPV and, if not all of the income stream is required to service the notes, the originator will wish to benefit from the surplus. Extracting profits from the SPV will often lead to tax inefficiencies and other complications (although tax problems may be avoided by siting the SPV in a suitable tax haven). One technique that is employed to obtain the benefit of surpluses without the need to resort to tax havens is to set up another company which acts as trustee of the receiveables, holding money received on trust for the SPV to the extent necessary to service the SPV's obligations, but otherwise on trust for the originator. The surplus is in this way siphoned off before it reaches the SPV.

(v) *Can capital be repaid by the SPV in a tax efficient way?* If the SPV is subject to tax (*i.e.* it is not in a tax haven), its receipts will constitute taxable income and its interest payments on the notes should be allowable deductions. However, repayment of principal of the notes will not be deductible and will have to be made out of taxed income. There is no simple solution to this problem which remains the single most important reason for siting SPVs in tax havens.

(vi) *Can noteholders be sure that the receiveables will generate sufficient cash to pay interest on and repay the notes?* This risk is mitigated to some extent in the case of the securitisation of receiveables arising under a take-or-pay gas sales agreement because the price is usually a fixed price which is escalated by reference to agreed

282

indices and the take-or-pay nature of the agreement has the effect of guaranteeing base volumes. However, even in such a case, the risk is only mitigated not avoided, since the escalation indices may or may not provide an adequate hedge against continuing opex and, if the interest rate on the notes is a floating rate, against interest rates. There are various ways to mitigate this sort of risk including requiring the SPV to establish and maintain sinking funds or reserve accounts and having the SPV enter into commercial hedging arrangements.

In addition to the above issues, it is critical to get the tax treatment of any securitisation right. One of the most important issues for the originator is the issue of tax on the original sale and it would be prudent to seek the Oil Taxation Office's views on any proposed securitisation involving United Kingdom oil and gas assets.

No securitisation along the lines of the hypothetical example used above has yet been done in relation to North Sea receiveables, although a securitisation done in the past for Pemex, the Mexican oil company, offers useful guidance. In that transaction, the credit rating agency in question satisfied itself that Pemex could continue to make supplies under the relevant sales contracts and so permitted merely the receiveables (and not the underlying assets) to be transferred to the SPV, although it did require letters of credit and other measures to safeguard against short term failures of supply.

Index

290

305